Mission Implausible
Restoring Credibility to the Church

Mission Implausible

Restoring Credibility to the Church

Duncan MacLaren

WIPF & STOCK · Eugene, Oregon

Wipf and Stock Publishers
199 W 8th Ave, Suite 3
Eugene, OR 97401

Mission Implausible
Restoring Credibility to the Church
By MacLaren, Duncan
Copyright©2004 Paternoster
ISBN 13: 978-1-62032-345-8
Publication date 6/1/2012
Previously published by Paternoster, 2004

Contents

Studies in Religion and Culture
Series Preface

Perhaps more than ever before, there is a need for Christians to understand the shifting sands of religion and culture. Unfortunately, it is with some justification that the church has been criticized, by both insiders and outsiders, for failing to understand the deep social, religious, and cultural changes taking place. This major series invites scholars to provide sensitive, empathetic, reliable, and accessible studies that will advance thinking about important subjects such as fundamentalism, mysticism, globalization, postmodernism, secularization, the religious significance of contemporary film, art, music, literature, information technologies, youth culture, religious pluralism, the changes taking place in contemporary world religions, and the emergence of new, influential, and alternative forms of spirituality. Whilst the majority of the contributors will be Christian thinkers writing with the needs of Christian community in mind, the series will be of interest to all those concerned with contemporary religion and culture.

Christopher Partridge

Preface

In the 1960s, sociologists predicted that religion would disappear from the modern world – or at least become much less significant. Modernity, so it was thought, created an environment that was so toxic for religious belief that religion could not be expected to survive. For a while, the prediction held good: a glance at levels of churchgoing, church membership, Christian belief, Christian baptism, Sunday school attendance, numbers of clergy, and so on, seemed to reveal decline right across the board. Then sociologists began to take a closer look. Although many of the major indices of religiosity continued to plummet at an alarming rate, in the past two decades it has become clear that there are other things going on besides decline: Europeans have not abandoned Christian beliefs in the way that was predicted; a huge majority of the British still call themselves Christian; across Europe, confidence in the churches is rising; in cultural terms we are still a Christian continent; religion is increasingly on the public agenda; and, from some unexpected quarters, new forms of Christianity are rising from the ashes of the burnt-out churches of Europe. This leaves us with a paradox that even sociologists find hard to describe: at the same time that the church in Europe is facing a crisis of unprecedented proportions, defiant green shoots of religious revitalization are pushing up through the snow-shroud of moribund religion. Christianity is not about to disappear: the question now is, in what form will it survive?

This book is offered as a contribution to that discussion. It sets out to address the crisis of Christianity in Europe using the tools of sociological analysis. It attempts three tasks in particular. The first is to try to offer an accurate diagnosis of the dramatic shift in the fortunes of Christianity in Europe over the last two or three centuries. In most parts of the world, through most of history, people have been religious: secular Europe is an exception. The current crisis of European Christianity is therefore rather strange, and demands an explanation. The second task is to survey the religious landscape of Europe in search of those forms of religion that appear untouched by the crisis. Where is religion doing well? What can the church learn from these scenarios? The third task begins from the observation that the current crisis is, in part, a crisis of credibility, and therefore sets out to try to understand the dynamics, or inner workings, of credibility. How is it that in modern societies certain beliefs are simply taken for granted, while others – perhaps perfectly reasonable beliefs – are abandoned to the scrap heap of implausibility and deviance? And, knowing how credibility is constructed in the modern world, how might these insights inform our missiological practice?

I should also say what this book is not. It is not intended to be a 'how to' book. Although I have tried to illustrate my arguments with examples, and sometimes even offered proposals (see chapter six), I have not made any attempt to provide a handbook for mission in the light of my conclusions. Instead, the thinking begins a stage further back – providing the theory upon which an informed practice could be based. I have stopped short for two reasons. First, a book that tried to say how my conclusions could be put into practice across the board would have been unfeasibly long. More importantly, however, it is down to those who are working at the coalface of mission – those who know their context intimately – to translate whatever is of use in this book into practical and specific outcomes.

It is also not a book about 'postmodernity'. Curiously, sociologists of religion seem rather reticent about the term, perhaps because the 'postmodern' is more a cultural than a social term. In my own view, there is plenty in our contemporary world that remains firmly modern, and even pre-modern, so that the 'postmodern', if it exists, refers only to one part of social and cultural reality. Put differently, religion is not confined to the clichéd 'postmodern pic 'n' mix global supermarket of faiths', but may be found, say, in the form of modern imperial Catholicism, or premodern Islamic theocracy.

I had various people in mind when writing the book. Most broadly, it is intended for anyone concerned about Christian mission, or interested in the future of religion in Europe; this will include clergy, church leaders, lay preachers, theologians, students of theology and sociology, academics, ordinands, evangelists, missioners and those working in mission agencies. It will also be of interest to students of Religious Studies as there is a good deal of sociological material that does not presuppose a confessional commitment. I have tried to translate what began life as a doctoral thesis into broader terms. The risk here, of course, is that I end up pleasing no one: academics may find some parts too sketchy, while the fabled 'general reader' may wonder whether English is my first language. I hope, however, that there is something here for everyone: a marriage of robust sociological thinking with practical missiological concerns. Particularly in the field of missiology there is a need to bring together the academic and the practical. I hope I have succeeded a little.

Thanks are due to Joe Martin, for intellectual stimulation, humour and friendship over many years; to Alan Storkey, who got me thinking; to Andrew Walker, for liberally exercising his gift of encouragement and successfully steering me through my thesis; to my students in the Sociology of Religion at Oxford, for keeping me on my toes; to countless friends and colleagues with whom I have shared ideas; and to those charitable trusts who generously supported the doctoral research which underlies this book – The Bayne Benefaction, The Crewdson Trust, The Culham Educational Foundation, The King's College London Theological Trust and The Whitefield Institute. Lastly, and not least, to Jane, Alexander, Lindsay and Iona – for being there.

1

1963

For a thousand years, Christianity penetrated deeply into the lives of the people, enduring Reformation, Enlightenment, and industrial revolution by adapting to each new social and cultural context that arose. Then, really quite suddenly in 1963, something very profound ruptured the character of the nation and its people, sending organised Christianity on a downward spiral to the margins of social significance.[1]

What has happened to Christianity in Britain? In just four short decades, the religious landscape has changed almost beyond recognition. Somehow, in the space of a little over a generation, the church in Britain has experienced a trajectory of decline so steep that some have even ventured to date the forthcoming death of entire denominations. The demise of the Church of Scotland through membership loss has been predicted for 2033,[2] while at current rates of decline, the Methodist Church in Britain will effectively disappear by 2031.[3] Some Christian denominations in Britain appear to have little more than a generation to live.

The trajectories on which such predictions are based are equally alarming. Consider how the church in Britain has changed since 1960. First, its membership has plummeted. According to Peter Brierley,[4] in 1960, church membership in the UK was around 9.9 million; in 2000, the figure was around 5.9 million, a drop of 40 per cent. When we compare these figures against a backdrop of wider population growth, we find the figures almost halving: church membership as a percentage of the total population fell from 19 per cent in 1960, to 10 per cent in 2000.[5] Within my own, Anglican,

---

[1] C.G. Brown, *The Death of Christian Britain* (London: Routledge, 2000), 1.

[2] Brown, *Death*, 5.

[3] S. Bruce, 'The Demise of Christianity in Britain' in G. Davie, P. Heelas and L. Woodhead (eds.), *Predicting Religion: Christian, Secular and Alternative Futures* (Aldershot: Ashgate, 2003), 53–63.

[4] P. Brierley, *Religious Trends* (London: Christian Research, 1999).

[5] S. Bruce, *God is Dead: Secularization in the West* (Oxford: Blackwell, 2002), 67.

confession, between 1960 and 2000 church membership halved, from around 3.3 million to 1.7 million.

Secondly, this loss of members has been accompanied by a decline in the number of churches and ministers. In the same period, the number of churches in the UK fell from 54,760 to 48,695, a loss of more than 6,000 churches. Likewise, the number of ministers fell from 41,211 to 33,709, a loss of around 7,500 ministers. The number of full-time stipendiary Church of England clergy dwindled from 13,151 to 8,720, a drop of 34 per cent.

Thirdly, the churches are being used less and less by the population in general. In 1960, virtually half of all marriages took place in the Church of England (168,000). By 2000, less than one fifth did (44,800) registering a drop of 73 per cent. Likewise, the number of baptisms undertaken in the Church of England (as a percentage of all births) fell from 55 per cent to 21 per cent. Similarly, those who attended Sunday school in 1960 represented 24 per cent of the population; in 2000 just 4 per cent attended.

Diagnoses

Why has the unprecedented decline described above taken place? The question is not as obvious as it may sound. If we stop and think for a moment, the contemporary situation seems to be really rather strange. How have we arrived at a situation in which sociologists and historians can speak of the disappearance of whole denominations, indeed, of the 'death of Christian Britain'?[6] What seismic forces in society and culture have conspired to bring about the demise of religion? At one time the Christian church in Britain was the most powerful national institution; people poured money into it in order to build and endow churches and chantries; Christian theology was the 'Queen of the Sciences' and the main source of ethical practice in politics, economics and personal life; universal church attendance was assumed to be the norm, and non-attendance an exception; all the major significant points in the agricultural year and in the life-cycle were set within a meaningful framework of Christian ritual; and the claims of Christianity, although not universally believed, formed a basic consensus of what constituted knowledge about God and the world.[7] Looked at this way, it is not the phenomenon of religion, but the lack of it, that is historically perplexing. Outside contemporary Europe – in the rest of the world, and for most of our history – human beings have been profoundly religious. Contemporary irreligion is a conundrum.

---

[6] Brown, *Death*.
[7] Bruce, *God is Dead*, 62.

1963 and all that

Clearly, 1963 is not really to blame. Callum Brown, whose quotation begins this chapter, sees it as a watershed, and points to the changing role of women as the key to the sudden acceleration of decline: from the early 1960s women ceased to be carriers of a discourse of feminine piety and domesticity – a change which, he argues, ultimately undermined the church. In reality, however, decline had set in long before then. In another way, though, he is right: 1963 is a strangely symbolic year. It is the year in which, according to Philip Larkin, sexual intercourse began; it is the year in which the Beatles – 'more popular than Jesus'[8] – rose to fame; it is the year in which Pope John XXIII died, the architect of the progressive Second Vatican Council; it is the year in which John Robinson's work of popular, radical theology, *Honest to God*, was published and went into nine impressions; and it was the year in which, on 22 November, three major figures died within hours of one another: John F. Kennedy, C.S. Lewis and Aldous Huxley. If Kennedy's assassination represented the death of a kind of mythical optimism among Americans, perhaps the deaths of Lewis and Huxley signified the passing away of a world in which issues of ultimate significance could still be debated in public – whether from a Christian or a Humanist perspective.[9]

Blaming the church

Even so, 1963 is still only of symbolic significance; it does not constitute an explanation for decline. Another set of reasons for the current crisis, that does try to explain the facts of decline, nails the blame firmly to door of the church itself. A range of suspects have been lined up in recent years and subjected to considerable suspicion. From the church's point of view, this approach to explaining church decline has one advantage. If the church has been responsible for her own demise, then in theory it is within her power to make the necessary changes and to reverse the decline. Harder, perhaps, to cope with is the thought that decline would have set in whatever the church tried to do, since this suggests that the church is entirely

---

[8] The fuller quotation from John Lennon, in an interview with Maureen Cleave of the *Evening Standard* on 4 March 1966, said: 'Christianity will go. It will vanish and shrink ... We're more popular than Jesus now; I don't know which will go first – rock 'n' roll or Christianity. Jesus was all right but his disciples were thick and ordinary. It's them twisting it that ruins it for me.' See www.newsoftheodd.com/headlines.html.

[9] For interest see Kreeft, P., *Between Heaven and Hell: A dialog somewhere beyond death with John F. Kennedy, C.S. Lewis, and Aldous Huxley* (Downers Grove: InterVarsity Press, 1982).

at the mercy of forces in society or culture. If decline really is inexorable, then missiologists are out of a job.

No doubt, some of this self-blame is justified. However, there seems to be no agreement as to which of the 'suspects' really are guilty. Indeed, the contradictory nature of several of the charges made suggests that at least some of the blame must be spurious. Which group is correct, if one blames the church's decline on the loss of traditional liturgies and another blames it on the failure to engage with consumer culture? Can the church be simultaneously too conservative and too progressive?

Overhead projectors
Such contradictory claims have been made, in relation to the church's response to culture. For some, the church is simply too trendy. For example, a former Archbishop of Canterbury, Robert Runcie, criticized the 'rave' services of the 1990s, branding them as the 'dangerous' worship of 'candy-floss idols', which 'turn God into a puppet to be manipulated according to people's fantasies and desires'. He went on:

> I am temperamentally against those forms of clappy-and-happy, huggy-and-feely worship which – along with overhead projectors – seem to reduce God to a puppet. I regret that people are not worshipping as they once did ... but turning worship into something fashionable, an ecclesiastical version of a health farm, is a danger.[10]

Such sentiments are not confined to the Anglican Church. A few months after this statement, every Roman Catholic priest and bishop in England and Wales received a plea from a traditionalist group, the Latin Mass Society, claiming that the decline in Mass attendance could be blamed in part on the modern liturgy and the suppression of the traditional Tridentine Rite in Latin, and urged them to recover it.[11]

Poor sales strategy
Others place the blame at the other end of the spectrum: the church is too staid. On this view, the church must learn to become more flexible in responding to contemporary consumer culture. Bob Jackson, for example, a former government economic expert, has pointed to the financial rescue of Marks & Spencer as a model from

[10] J. Petre, 'Runcie lays into trendy clergymen', *Daily Telegraph* (9 February 1997).
[11] V. Combe, 'Catholics plead for Latin Mass', *Daily Telegraph* (22 July 1997).

which the church could learn. 'If certain lines are not working and certain ones are, they will use that information to build the business. That is the sort of thing the Church of England can learn and is beginning to learn.'[12] Likewise, advertising is increasingly being used by churches as a means of mission. Controversial poster campaigns at Christmas and Easter – say, featuring Jesus as Che Guevara – have been launched by the Churches' Advertising Network. During the Easter period of 1997, the Birmingham and Lichfield dioceses produced a television advertisement, which lasted thirty seconds and was broadcast on Central Television, in an attempt to connect with young people and dispel an old-fashioned image of the church.[13] At this end of the spectrum, the accusation appears to be that the church is too traditional, rather than not traditional enough. Both accusations blame what they see as the church's inappropriate response to cultural change.

Arrogant fools
Blame issues in other forms as well. Sometimes the finger is pointed at bishops or the clergy. Early in 2002, the Social Affairs Unit published a study entitled *Called To Account*, which lists twenty-seven criteria suggesting that the collapse of the church is 'across the board.' One of the booklet's editors, the Rev Peter Mullen, said in the preface, 'those bishops and senior lay people in the church's government – that is those who have inflicted their tired liberalism on the church and presided over its continuing decline – should finally take responsibility and resign.'[14] Similarly, David Edwards has expressed the view that, historically, the 'decisive' factor in the secularization of Europe was 'the arrogant folly of the clergy.' Apparently, the clergy are to blame for

> the bitterness of Christianity's internal divisions, for this religion's strange identification with militant nationalism, for its equally strange identification with old science shown to be false, for the Roman Catholic's quarrel with modern democracy and for the alienation of all the churches from the new industrial proletariat.[15]

---

[12] J. Petre, 'Church "needs to read lesson from M & S"', *The Daily Telegraph* (30 October 1997).
[13] V. Combe, 'Church puts its faith in TV advert', *The Daily Telegraph* (20 March 1997).
[14] J. Petre, 'Bishops urged to resign over Church decline', *The Daily Telegraph* (24 February 2003).
[15] D.L. Edwards, *The Futures of Christianity* (London: Hodder & Stoughton, 1987), 297.

For still others, it is those responsible for training the clergy who are to blame. One correspondent wrote to *The Times* that, 'It can come as no surprise to many of us within the Church of England that attendance has decreased…I believe the cause to be largely ill-training for the clergy.' He goes on to bemoan the brevity of training, which issues in, 'interminable prayers, dreary music, ill-prepared homilies and clergy who do not seem to know one end of an altar from the other. The sheer unprofessionalism is quite shocking.'[16] Still more recently, the Rt Rev Nigel McCulloch, Bishop of Manchester, was quoted by *The Times* as saying that the plummeting statistics of church attendance in the Church of England were a consequence of clergy being distracted by divisive issues, and excessive legislation and red tape.[17] The Leader column, for the same day, was of the opinion that, 'Part of the problem is the church's preoccupation with dogma and division, at the expense of its moral message; part is because of its incompetence in managing its finances and organising its workforce.'[18]

Tired liberals
If blame has been pointed at the church's inappropriate response to cultural change, and at the leadership of the churches, one further diagnosis blames the twentieth-century drift towards theological liberalism. We have already noted Mullen's attack on those who have 'inflicted their tired liberalism on the church'. Similarly, in the same article that quoted Lord Runcie's opposition to rave services, the Venerable George Austin, the Archdeacon of York, blamed Runcie's liberalism for alienating many of the Church of England's natural congregation. Austin lamented that, 'We were led for ten years by a man who has admitted that he hadn't much spirituality or faith.'

Examples such as these could be multiplied and, no doubt, there are many more departments of church life at which the finger of blame could be pointed. Perhaps there is truth in some of these criticisms. The problem from a missiological point of view, however, is how to judge where the truth of such criticisms lies. These kinds of criticism are very hard to assess. We have noted, for example, that some contradict others; they cannot all be valid. Furthermore, many of them are of a polemical nature, and hardly come across as balanced judgements. More seriously still, these kinds of blame are

---

[16] G. Elmore, 'Insufficient Training for C of E Clergy', *The Times* (17 January 2004), 31.
[17] R. Gledhill, 'Bishop Warns Church that it May Disappear', *The Times* (20 March 2004), 5.
[18] Leader, 'Raise the Rafters', *The Times* (20 March 2004), 27.

all directed at the churches themselves: what if, however, most of the 'blame' for church decline lies within factors well beyond the churches' control? What if, in the end, the 'death of Christian Britain' is simply an inevitable consequence of social and cultural change?

A Sociological Perspective: Secularization

In this book, I will argue that the decline of the historic churches in Britain has little to do with the kinds of factors outlined above. Self-blame is only a very partial explanation. Instead, I want to suggest that the long-standing tradition of sociological thinking about religious change provides a far more complete account of religious decline than do the kinds of accusations levelled above. The dominant sociological theory by which these religious changes have been understood is the theory of *secularization*. Briefly put, secularization theory states that as societies become more modernized, the scale and influence of religion within them diminishes. Although this theory is now itself contested within the sociology of religion, I think it still remains a valid description of, and explanation for, changes that have taken place within British Christianity over the past, say, century and a half, and accelerating since the 1960s. In the next two chapters, I shall outline how this theory attempts to explain religious decline from a historical and sociological perspective.

Acknowledging that the churches have had little control over their destiny is perhaps a frightening thought. Few of us really enjoy feeling out of control. However, there are two distinct advantages to this view. First, the recognition that decline has been brought about by factors external to the churches relieves (to a large extent) the requirement to point the finger of blame. If church decline would have set in regardless of the faithfulness, creativity, flexibility, or dedication of church leaders and members, pointing fingers can be returned to their pockets, and Christians with very different outlooks can work together with less suspicion.

The other advantage of acknowledging the wider sociological influences that have led to church decline is that we can begin to develop new ways of responding. True, we may have little control over the kinds of social and cultural pressures that bear upon Christian faith and life, but we can still choose how to respond to those pressures. We cannot legislate for what is shown on television each night, but we can find ways to be church in a media-saturated culture. In this way, the missiological task may be reoriented to take account of the sociological factors which explain church decline.

Beyond Secularization: The Dynamics of Credibility

The heart of this book involves an attempt to respond to secularization through an exploration of what I have termed 'the dynamics of credibility'. In late modernity, it is not so much the truth of Christianity that is under threat, as its credibility. By understanding the inner workings – the dynamics – of the ways in which people come to find beliefs and institutions credible, we can begin to develop missiological strategies which address the contemporary crisis of credibility in the British churches.

In what follows, the dynamics of credibility will be explored in three ways: the subjects of chapters four, five and seven. Chapter four will review a variety of tenacious forms of European religion (not necessarily Christianity), which have managed to persist despite the onslaught of modernity. It will seek to locate empirical examples of *religion in modernity*. In the past two decades or so, sociologists have become suspicious of the 'one-way street' theory of secularization, and have begun to discern exceptions and U-turns. An examination of cases which seem to possess a degree of immunity towards modernity may provide a basis for the development of 'vaccines' able to inoculate the churches against a deadly culture.

Chapter five will consider the location of *Christianity in con-sciousness*. What attitudes towards Christianity do people carry around in their heads, and why? Contemporary attitudes to Christianity are socially constructed; they are therefore not immutable. By understanding how people come to ascribe plausibility to some beliefs and not to others, the way is opened for reconstructing the plausibility of Christian faith.

Chapter seven will then seek to locate the *church in society* and culture. Here another set of dynamics are at work. The positioning of church in society helps to determine the credibility of the institution and of the story it proclaims. Once again, understanding these dynamics is a first step towards repositioning the church in ways that support her mission. For example, missiological writers typically observe the end of 'Christendom', and many seem to welcome this development. This means that the institutional church is becoming increasingly disembedded from the historic social and cultural contexts in which it was once the dominant institution. From such an 'establishment' situation, the historic denominations in Britain have been moving towards more intentional, volunta-ristic, sectarian-style churches: churches, in other words, whose members are there by choice, rather than by default. The danger of such a move, however, is that at the same time as the 'bathwater' of

Christendom is thrown out, the 'baby' of the rich, cultural inheritance of Christianity in Europe is also rejected, and a valuable vehicle for mission is overlooked. These two different strategies for positioning the church in relation to society may be characterized, respectively, as a *tension* strategy (the sectarian model), and as a *momentum* strategy (the cultural inheritance model). A third option also exists, which I have termed a *significance* strategy. The meaning of these strategies, and the kinds of successful religious forms that have been identified in each category by sociologists, will be made explicit in chapter seven. Each has the potential to offer missiology fruitful ways forward.

The numerate reader will notice I have skipped over chapter six. This chapter will 'take five'; that is, it interrupts the flow of the argument to consider five practical imperatives that seem to arise from the logic of chapter five. Since the discussion of the dynamics of credibility is loaded with theory – and sociological theory at that – I felt it important to try to root emerging conclusions in practical reality.

Chapter eight will draw together the themes of the book by means of a case study of one form of church that succeeded for around six centuries – the Columban church of the sixth century.

Missio Dei

Some may be sceptical of the value of harnessing sociological insights for the missiological task. It has sometimes been objected that sociology, far from being 'value-neutral' as Max Weber claimed it should be, has been an ideological instrument to bring about secularization. Others have simply argued that theology (of which missiology is a branch) and sociology comprise competing discourses that have no point of contact by which they might enter into dialogue.[19] Still others may object that the task of mission ultimately belongs to God, and that the frantic attempts to harness fallible human thinking, secular or otherwise, is at best audacious and at worst blasphemous.

My own view is that if we are to engage in mission, we have no choice but to think about what we are doing; and if we must think, we can either think hard, or we can opt for a sloppy pragmatism that follows whatever seems to work at the time. If we are willing to do some hard thinking, we then have to make choices about the kind of critical tools we will use. It is possible that sociology could

---

[19] For example, see J. Milbank, *Theology and Social Theory* (Oxford: Blackwell, 1991).

be used (as it has been) as an ideological instrument; however, my experience of secular sociologists of religion is that they are usually scrupulous in editing out their own bias either for or against particular religious truth claims. In this way, their intellectual honesty may lead them to embrace sociological conclusions which conflict with their own ideological position. The charge that secular sociology cannot be trusted does not ring true to me. A more philosophical criticism, that theology and sociology have no common language by which they can speak to one another, seems equally flawed. The church is not only a divine institution, but a human one; it is incarnate in human bodies, practices, symbols, beliefs and institutions. All of these are open to sociological scrutiny. I see no reason why judicial use cannot be made of such research: the counting of heads; the observation of rituals; the surveying of beliefs; the theorizing about institutions; or the use of the sociological imagination to 'see' the location of the church in society. All of these are valuable tools for the missiologist.

The *missio Dei* principle implies, of course, that mission ultimately belongs to God. It is not about human institutions seeking to expand their powerbase, even if, from time to time, church leaders have made this mistake. It concerns God's invitation to the whole of creation to become reconciled to him. In the light of this, missiology must proceed with humility, particularly if the use of sociological tools becomes a temptation to pride and complacency. At the same time, whilst using these tools, mission may be conducted in 'bold humility'[20] as we seek to understand the social and cultural context in which the churches find themselves, and then prayerfully consider how we might respond.

In what follows, I hope to harness some of the insights of contemporary sociological thinking about religion and apply them to the missiological task. The sociology of religion has a long tradition of attempting to describe and explain religious decline. It is an irony that, in the past decade or so, many sociologists of religion have been more optimistic about the future of religion in the West than have the churches themselves. Perhaps the news of religious revitalization currently being discerned by sociologists has yet to reach the ears of church leaders, at least in a form that may be useful to them. I hope that in this book I can offer some of this good news in a meaningful translation.

---

[20] D.J. Bosch, *Transforming Mission: Paradigm Shifts in Theology of Mission* (New York: Orbis, 1991), xiii.

Part 1

The Rise of Incredulity

2

All in the Mind: Enlightenment, Science and Ideology

If the church is not primarily to blame for her decline, then what is? I suggested in the previous chapter that a far larger share of the blame – or, if you like, the explanation – lies with the unprecedented intellectual and social changes that have occurred since the Industrial Revolution. Before we can begin to look at the typical explanations afforded by secularization theory, however, a preliminary question needs to be addressed. What exactly do we mean when we speak of 'decline'? This question is not as simple as it may at first appear.

Explaining What?

So far I have detailed only the *institutional* aspect of the Christian churches: falling membership, fewer clergy, closing churches, fewer marriages and baptisms, and shrinking Sunday school rolls. Many other similar indicators (finance, funerals, adherence, electoral roll figures and so on) could have been cited, with similar trajectories. However, sociologists are interested not only in the institutional aspects of religious life, important as these may be, but also in religious *practices* and religious *thinking*, or beliefs. In other words, religions are typically analysed at three levels: thinking, practices and institutions. Decline may, or may not, take place at any or all of these levels.

One further distinction must be made so that we can be clear about what it is we are trying to describe when we speak of decline. Decline may involve shrinking beliefs, practices and institutions, as we have just described above. In this case, it is religion *itself* that is in decline. Equally, however, it may be the *prominence* of religion in society that is disappearing. One of the best-known definitions of secularization is 'the process whereby religious thinking, practices and institutions lose social significance'.[1] This understanding of secularization is very different from the decline of religion itself. Religions can flourish at the same time as their social impact diminishes. Conversely, the social significance of a religious body, such as the church, can increase even as it suffers declining membership. The Church of England in the latter half of the nineteenth century, for example, seems to have experienced per capita numerical decline at the same time that vigorous debates in parliament (over the rights of the established church versus those of the dissenting congregations) ensured the increasing social prominence of the church.

This means secularization is multifaceted. It can refer to the absolute decline of religious institutions, practices and thinking. It can also refer to the declining social significance of these things. The picture becomes especially complex when some of these factors are increasing, while others are shrinking. According to one survey, across Western Europe in the 1990s belief in God, confidence in the church, and the proportion of those claiming they gain comfort from religion all increased, whereas church attendance, belief in sin and the proportion of those endorsing church involvement in politics all decreased.[2] Is Europe then becoming more secular, or less?

For the missiologist, these distinctions raise important questions. What is it we are really concerned about? Does it matter if the church shrinks to embryonic proportions, provided that it retains, say, a prophetic voice in society? Or, conversely, does it matter if the church loses all social impact and visibility, providing the pews themselves are full to bursting? Can we relax about institutional decline, providing that belief and behaviour remain committed? Or reverse the sequence?

For reasons that I hope will become clear in later chapters, I think that every dimension of secularization matters for the mission of the church, since every aspect is interrelated. However, not every dimension of secularization is equally entrenched; indeed, examples of *de*secularization in British society are not hard to come by. So, while I think it is important to take seriously the evidence of secularization, the recognition that secularization is multifaceted means that there are signs of hope in amongst the harbingers of despair. Secularization and desecularization cohabit in contemporary British society.

---

[1] B.R. Wilson, *Religion in Secular Society* (London: C.A.Watts & Co., 1966), xiv.
[2] L. Halman, *The European Values Study: A Third Wave* (Tilburg: European Values Study, Tilburg University, 2001).

What, then, are we explaining? In using secularization theory to explain religious decline I am attempting to explain the shrinkage of Christian institutions (members, finance, personnel), the flight from Christian norms of behaviour (Sabbath, prayer, church attendance) and the loss of distinctively Christian thinking and beliefs (virgin birth, resurrection, hell, providence). At the same time, I am wishing to explain how these things have also lost *significance* in society as a whole. In other words, we need to explain not only fewer 'bums on pews', but the proposals to reduce the number of bishops in the House of Lords. We need to explain not only the decline of Sabbath observance, but also the change in the Sunday trading laws. And we need to explain not only the doubts in the pew about the virgin birth, but also the loss from society of a basic Christian framework of thinking. These are the areas of decline that secularization describes; these are also what it purports to explain.

Varieties of Explanation

Just as there are varieties of decline, there are also varieties of explanation. Three broad types of explanation for secularization have been advanced. First, there is the *history of ideas*. This approach tries to trace genealogies of thought, in order to demonstrate how the kind of thinking that arose with, say, the Enlightenment, has created a legacy of popular assumptions and ways of seeing the world today, many of which are inimical to Christian thought. Christian thinkers such as Francis Schaeffer[3] and Lesslie Newbigin[4] exemplify this kind of approach. Sociologists tend to give a faint nod of assent to this type explanation, but see it as secondary. Secondly, there is an explanation in terms of *social processes*. On this account, various social processes that arose with, or were intensified by, the Industrial Revolution in Britain are linked with forms of secularization. Thirdly, sociologists are quick to point out that ideas do not exist in a vacuum: the *institutional carriers* of secularizing ideas are as important to the story of secularization as are the ideas themselves.

All three types of explanation have some merit. In this chapter we will consider just the legacy of changing *ideas* for the credibility of Christian faith.

---

[3] E.g. F. Schaeffer, *The God Who is There* (London: Hodder & Stoughton, 1968).
[4] E.g. L. Newbigin, *The Gospel in a Pluralist Society* (London: SPCK, 1989).

A 'History of Ideas' Explanation

Ideas can be revolutionary. Sociologists sometimes miss this, arguing more often that it is the world that changes our ideas, rather than our ideas that change the world. Karl Marx, for example, stressed the priority of social circumstances over ideas. Religious belief is a product of social circumstances ('the sigh of the oppressed creature'), rather than a force for social change in itself. Yet, paradoxically, Marx's power lay not in his political position, but in his intellect. It was precisely his *ideas* that changed the world. We cannot, therefore, entirely dismiss the history of ideas as an explanation for secularization. Ideas transmit, become fashionable, sneak into our minds as unexamined assumptions, pose in the guise of the obvious and oust other ideas, and so on. When the soil is right for certain ideas to gain popular acclaim, they can explode into public consciousness and threaten the stability of established thinking.

There is, then, a place in our explanation for the history of ideas, although it is not always easy to trace the genealogy between the particular emergence of a new idea, and the later eclipse of Christian thinking. However, three streams of thinking can be identified which give reason for the decline in Christian thinking and its social significance: the Enlightenment, the growth of science and the rise of ideology.

The Enlightenment

Missiological diagnoses of the current state of Christianity often lay the blame at the door of the Enlightenment.[5] The Enlightenment refers to a relatively short epoch of intellectual endeavour, concentrated in the latter half of the eighteenth century. Its achievements did not spring out of the ether, but represented the flowering of tendencies that can be traced back to classical Greece. In Renaissance Europe, the dormant seeds of classical thought were brought back to life; they developed through the Reformation and the rise of science in the seventeenth century; and they flourished in the philosophical and political climate of the eighteenth. The Enlightenment is often seen as a pivotal moment in the birth of the modern world. As in human births, however, a considerable period of gestation preceded it.

---

[5] See L. Newbigin, *Foolishness to the Greeks* (London: SPCK, 1986); Bosch, *Transforming*. However, Bosch also qualifies his critique of the Enlightenment, and later extends these qualifications; see D.J. Bosch, *Believing in the Future: Toward a Missiology of Western Culture* (Harrisburg, PA: Trinity Press International, 1995), 6ff.

The philosophical Enlightenment has been characterized by a number of governing preoccupations, which David Bosch helpfully summarizes:

> First, its emphasis on *reason* suggested that the human mind was the indubitable point of departure for all knowing. Second, it divided all of reality into thinking *subjects* and, over against these, *objects* that could be analysed and exploited. Third, it dropped all reference to *purpose* and viewed every process only in terms of cause and effect. Fourth, it put a high premium on *progress*, on expansion, advance, and modernization. Fifth, it proceeded from the assumption that all true knowledge was *factual, value-free*, and *neutral*. Over against *facts* there were *values*, which were not objectively true, the holding of which was, therefore, a matter of taste. Religion was, in the course of time, relegated to this category. Sixth, the Enlightenment proceeded from the assumption that *all problems were in principle solvable*. And last, it regarded people as *emancipated, autonomous individuals*, no longer under the tutelage of 'superiors'.[6]

Clearly, not all of these emphases conflict with Christian thought; yet most of them contain a degree of antagonism towards traditional Christianity, which may have helped to undermine it. Bosch has offered an admirable exposition of their impact on Christian theology.[7] What I wish to attempt here is to relate the characteristics of the Enlightenment to changes, not so much in academic theology, but in popular consciousness, since it is at this level that the greatest impact will have taken place for the churches. This is not to deny that theological innovation can filter down to the pew: clearly there are many churches whose members are theologically literate, and therefore sensitive to academic innovation. Nor is this to deny that, on occasion, theological innovation has penetrated popular consciousness outwith the churches. The best example of this is undoubtedly John Robinson's *Honest to God*,[8] which became a truly popular work of theology in the 1960s. First published in 1963, it was reprinted eight times in that year alone. What I am suggesting, however, is that church decline is far more likely to have been the result of changes in popular thinking within and outside the church, than because of particular changes within the relatively small circles of academic theology. What follows, then, is an attempt to chart the impact of the Enlightenment on popular religious consciousness. Inevitably, some of this will involve guesswork and some will be overly simplified; but hopefully, despite these

---

[6] Bosch, *Believing*, 5.
[7] Bosch, *Transforming*, 269–73.
[8] J.A.T. Robinson, *Honest to God* (London: SCM, 1963).

limitations, some sense of the power of the Enlightenment to shape our thinking will have been conveyed.

From revelation to reason
First, then, the emphasis on reason. The Enlightenment privileged reason as the sole arbiter of knowledge at the expense of traditional sources of theology, such as church tradition, religious experience, and God's revelation in scripture and the natural world. While these traditional sources of knowledge could not actually be disproved, they were marginalized by reason because they were unable to furnish the all-important certainty sought by Descartes and his successors. Only reason could lay claim to indubitable knowledge, whether by exploring apparently self-evident truths ('I think, therefore I am'), or by examining the empirical world of the five senses.[9] Most theological accounts of the world, unable to meet these strict rational or empirical criteria, were simply written off. David Hume typified this attitude when he wrote:

> If we take into our hands any volume ... let us ask: Does it contain any abstract reasoning concerning quantity and number? No. Does it contain any experimental reasoning concerning matters of fact and existence? No. Commit it then to the flames: for it can contain nothing but sophistry and illusion.[10]

One consequence that emerged from this emphasis on rational or empirical criteria for knowledge was the reversal of the traditional order of faith and reason. Augustine (354–430) and Anselm (1033–1109) had both viewed faith as a necessary prerequisite to understanding.[11] Only from the standpoint of belief is the world truly intelligible. The Enlightenment reversed the order so that reason came to be seen as the doorway to faith. Nothing should be believed

---

[9] Colin Gunton distinguishes between 'pure-rationalism' after Descartes, and 'empirical rationalism', descending from Locke. C.E. Gunton, *A Brief Theology of Revelation* (Edinburgh: T&T Clark, 1995), 48.

[10] Quoted in E. Gellner, *Legitimation of Belief* (Cambridge: Cambridge University Press, 1974), 31.

[11] Augustine's formula, '*Credo ut intelligam*' ('I believe in order to understand') and Anslem's '*Fides quaerens intellectum*' ('faith seeking understanding') arguably both express the epistemological priority of faith over reason. Medieval scholastic theologians tended to give reason considerable autonomy as a means to knowledge, but without reason being exercised at the expense of revelation. It is only with the rise of science and the Enlightenment that revelation begins to become eclipsed by autonomous reason.

except on a rational basis – all else is 'sophistry and illusion'. In Lesslie Newbigin's words,

> As the eighteenth century rolls on, we find that the really essential truths are available to us from the book of nature, from reason and conscience; the truths we can only learn from the Bible are of minor importance, adiaphora about which we need not quarrel.[12]

At the level of popular consciousness, this attitude seems to have translated into a change in the status of belief. The Enlightenment insistence that we cannot claim to know something unless we can know it with certainty, and be able to demonstrate it rationally, served to heighten the distinction between knowledge and belief: belief by its very nature implies some degree of uncertainty, even if the belief in question is based on very good evidence. Similarly, some beliefs may not admit of rational demonstration: they may be arrived at intuitively, and their reasons may be 'reasons of the heart'. The unconscious logic of believing does not mean such beliefs are irrational, only that their reasons are not available to consciousness. This (somewhat artificial) split between belief and knowledge has meant that Christian beliefs are no longer taken seriously as knowledge about the world: 'The Church is not generally perceived as concerned with facts, with the realities which finally govern the world and which we shall in the end have to acknowledge whether we like them or not.'[13] Although the majority of people in Britain continue to believe in God, what they think they know of God they do not feel permission to treat as real knowledge. In the modern world, the bus timetable counts as real knowledge: the Beatitudes do not. Christian beliefs constitute a second-rate, privatized form of knowing.

From credulity to criticism
Secondly, the Enlightenment division of the world into thinking subjects, and objects suitable for analysis and exploitation, led 'man' (and they were men, not women) to become the inquisitor and critic of all reality. Where once nature had been our teacher, now it became our laboratory. Under pressure from this critical principle, the biblical view of the cosmos could no longer be taken on trust, but everything became potential fodder for critical evaluation. From the critical principle even 'man' himself was not exempt: he, too, was part of nature. Scientific enquiry, turned back on humans themselves, spawned the disciplines of

---

[12] Newbigin, *Gospel*, 2.
[13] Newbigin, *Gospel*, 7.

anthropology, sociology and psychology. 'Know then thyself, presume not God to scan, The proper study of mankind is man'[14] wrote Alexander Pope (1688–1744), anticipating the human sciences. As these disciplines developed, thinking became increasingly anthropocentric, with the result that man was both the investigator and the object of investigation. Further, just as nature and humanity were placed under the microscope, so too was the Bible subjected to critical historical scholarship, casting doubt on its claim to be inspired. Finally, too, even God himself was treated to the epistemological critique. Gone was the sense of God as prior subject: seeking; wooing; inviting; judging; saving. God came to be viewed as Object. When Napoleon commented on the absence of God from the work of the French astronomer, Pierre Simon Laplace, he received the famous reply, 'I have no need of that hypothesis.' The sacred had been removed from the sphere of personal knowledge to become a mere hypothesis, as if God had nothing better to do than simply to exist.

Kenneth Cragg has observed that, 'In the pagan world of Greek and Roman antiquity, atheism was not an option. Nor, equally, was faith. All was credulity.'[15] A similar claim could be made for popular belief throughout the medieval period: all was credulity. It is precisely such easygoing, popular credulity that the Enlightenment shattered. The Cartesian (i.e. descended from Descartes) method has been characterized as a 'hermeneutic of suspicion': only by doubting everything can we be sure of what is indubitable. Descartes, then, marks a transition from 'all is credible' to 'all is dubious'. Perhaps it is not too big a step to see a connection between the Cartesian method and the cynical, ironic, sceptical, debunking turn of mind which infects contemporary consciousness. We have lost our sense of awe and humility before the mysteries of nature and her creator. We have become like the first-year undergraduate who, in a single, disdainful sentence, dismisses the life-time's work of an eminent professor. When all is dubious, faith is hard to come by; if our minds are open at both ends, no belief can be held for long. Contemporary people have become compulsive doubters left with no criteria according to which they could believe and no evidence that would ever provide sufficient criteria upon which they could base their trust.

---

[14] A. Pope, 'An Essay on Man, Epistle ii (1733), 1.1' in *Oxford Dictionary of Quotations* (Oxford: Oxford University Press, 1979), 379.

[15] K. Cragg, *The Secular Experience of God* (Leominster: Gracewing, 1998), 4.

From meaning to mechanism

The third aspect of the thinking of this period excluded the category of purpose from rational explanation, in favour of causal explanations. A rainbow in the sky was no longer explained in terms of the covenant of God, but as a consequence of the refraction of light. This implied that the universe is a closed system unfolding along predetermined and mechanistic lines. Causal explanations were then treated as fact, whereas explanations in terms of purpose could only be held as private beliefs. Newbigin observes,

> It is certainly not more than a hundred years since children in Scottish schools learned at an early stage the fact that 'Man's chief end is to glorify God and enjoy him forever.' This was as much a fact as the movement of the stars and the Battle of Bannockburn. Today it is not taught as a fact.[16]

One uncomfortable consequence flowed from this: if we no longer know the purpose for which human beings have been created, we have no means of knowing whether or not they are living aright – a mechanistic universe is of necessity an amoral universe. Without a Christian anthropology, Christian ethics appears as an implausible, arbitrary imposition upon human freedom. Furthermore, the loss of explanations in terms of purpose meant that events in history ceased to be viewed within the framework of the coming kingdom of God. Today, to ask how God is at work in some situation (say, in a general election) would most likely be met with incomprehension or ridicule. Yet the story throughout scripture is the story of a God at work in history – on the battlefield, the storm-tossed sea and the marriage bed. If we can no longer talk of the purposes of God in society and history, it is little wonder that contemporary people struggle to believe the biblical narrative. A world rich with sacred significance has given way to a prosaic, mechanistic view of ourselves and our world.

From providence to progress

The fourth preoccupation was the pursuit of progress. History may have come to be viewed without purpose, but this did not stop people inventing one. It has been suggested that Christian eschatology (the doctrine of the 'last things') was simply replaced by secular doctrines of historical progress: in Comte, human thought progresses historically from the theological, through the metaphysical, to the scientific; in Hegel, history is Absolute Spirit coming to self-consciousness; in Marx, society evolves by dramatic leaps through

---

[16] Newbigin, *Gospel*, 15.

class struggles; and so on.[17] Behind the optimism of the nineteenth century was a sense that evolution permeates every sphere of human activity (not just biology); things can only get better.[18] Despite the twentieth century being the bloodiest the world has ever seen, the belief in progress is still with us. The story of the emancipation of women, the black civil-rights struggle in America, and the emergence of the welfare state in Europe, all testify to the reality of progress in the sphere of politics. Even more striking is the progress of science and technology. We have come to expect that 'new' will mean 'new-improved', and 'old' will mean 'obsolete'. Just fifteen years ago we lived in a world without mobile phones, DVDs, personal computers, email, or the internet. In that brief span of time, these technologies have become commonplace, and the speed of the processors that drive them has increased exponentially. Science and technology, even more than politics, embody the ideal of progress in a forceful and convincing way. The sheer instrumental utility of technology is hard to argue with; it confers upon technology a high degree of prestige; technology, like a celebrity at a party, creates an excited buzz, a *frisson*.

Against the gleaming backdrop of cutting-edge technology, Christian faith looks a little tired. Its homely doctrine of providence – God is working his purpose out as year succeeds year – cannot compete with the adrenaline-rush injected by scientific and technological progress. Nor can its story compete with technology's underlying evolutionary narrative.[19] More than that, whereas progress exalts the idea of the 'new', Christianity trades on the value of the 'old', the traditional, and the authoritative. In a world bewitched by progress, Christianity suffers cognitive dissonance; it

---

[17] David Martin, for example, has argued that certain versions of history are really displacements of sectarian Christian utopianism. See, D.A. Martin, *The Religious and the Secular: Studies in Secularization* (London: Routledge and Kegan Paul, 1969). See also, Newbigin, *Gospel*, 90.

[18] Interestingly, this phrase was the mantra of the British Labour Party at their landslide victory in the general election of 1997.

[19] Newbigin claims, for example, 'In our contemporary culture, as exemplified in the curriculum of teaching in the public schools, two quite different stories are told. One is the story of evolution, of the development of species through the survival of the strong, and the story of the rise of civilization, our type of civilization, and its success in giving humankind mastery of nature. The other story is the one embodied in the Bible, the story of creation and fall, of God's election of a people to be the bearers of his purpose for humankind, and of the coming of the one in whom that purpose is to be fulfilled. These are two different and incompatible stories.' Newbigin, *Gospel*, 15–16.

tries to tell the old, old story, but people think they have heard it before. Who wants to hear the obsolete, obsolete story? In the modern world, then, while science, 'is a culturally successful – or rather, perhaps better, confident – form of practice, in the West the church is not'.[20]

From public to private

Fifthly, the Enlightenment created a separation between facts, which could be proven with certainty, and beliefs and values, which could not. Facts belong in the public sphere, the sphere of common concern, whereas beliefs, since they cannot be proven with certainty, were gradually consigned to the private dimension of people's lives, along with values, preferences and opinions. Beliefs that were once taken for granted as immutable truths about the world – the reality of creation, sin, judgement and redemption – were relegated to the private sphere of personal interest and whim. Today, to 'talk theology' in public is to commit a social *faux pas*. There is a widely held taboo towards conversation on religious themes. Try talking about God as a public reality and you will quickly find yourself surrounded by wry, embarrassed, pitying smiles. Kate Hunt has noticed this response among non-churchgoers she interviewed: they often spoke of the penalties they fear of speaking of their religious beliefs.[21] There seems to be a widespread, unwritten rule that serious conversation about religion should only be practised by consenting adults in private. If the objects of faith are continually treated as not being real in any objective sense, it becomes difficult even for Christians to maintain the sense that their beliefs refer to something – or someone – real, out there. The privatization of belief is therefore more than simply a cognitive curfew; it involves the forced adoption of a split personality; it is a tacit invitation to self-deception – to maintain in private a set of beliefs as if they were objectively true, while at the same time living a 'public' life that requires the denial or suppression of these beliefs. No wonder faith is hard to sustain when it is stripped of its sense of reality and denied a public voice.

From resignation to responsibility

The sixth emphasis was upon the responsibility of humans to find their own solutions to problems. The human condition was no longer to be accepted as inevitable, nor the world to be regarded as a

---

[20] Gunton, *Theology of Revelation*, 92, n. 11.
[21] K. Hunt, 'Understanding The Spirituality of People Who Don't Go to Church' in G. Davie et al. (eds.), *Predicting Religion*.

vale of tears to be endured with fortitude and resignation while we await salvation. Instead, the feeling arose that it was incumbent upon humanity to make full use of human ingenuity to change adverse circumstances, and that all problems were, in principle, solvable. Crane Brinton calls this,

> the basic idea and striking novelty of the Enlightenment ... the belief that all human beings can attain here on this earth a state of perfection hitherto in the West thought to be possible only for Christians in a state of grace, and for them, only after death.[22]

In part, this attitude was shared by Christians; it can be seen in the immense energy of the Victorian Christian philanthropists and activists, who worked tirelessly to tackle a formidable array of social needs: education, leisure, health, welfare, housing, social reform and so on.

The problem-solving approach has been termed the 'melioristic attitude'. Meliorism expresses confidence that the world is manipulable, controllable, and able to be turned to the service of humanity. Meliorism means that humans sought to ameliorate the suffering of the human condition through technical and political means – improved agriculture, industrial technology, medical research, welfare provision – rather than practising prayer, incantation, or spell. This attitude has not made prayer entirely obsolete: there are still crises beyond the reach of modern medicine for which prayer is the only resort. Yet, typically, in the face of practical problems prayer is a last resort, or at best a mere accompaniment to proven technical procedures. The overwhelming practical success of modern technology and the modern welfare state has thrown Christian faith into a crisis of relevance.[23]

From authority to autonomy
Finally, the Enlightenment rejected the idea of truth as the preserve of an authoritative elite. If reason is the sure route to knowledge, it follows that, in principle, every person has equal access to the truth, and need not depend upon the pronouncements of a prophet or priest. Tom Paine (1737–1809), one of the most significant popularizers of Enlightenment and Republican thinking at the end of the eighteenth century, exemplified the shift from authority to autonomy when he wrote in *The Age of*

---

[22] C. Brinton, *The Shaping of the Modern Mind* (New York, NY: Mentor Books, 1953), 113.
[23] A.D. Gilbert, *The Making of Post-Christian Britain: A History of the Secularization of Modern Society* (London: Longman, 1980), 32.

Reason (1796): 'I do not believe in the creed professed by the Jewish Church, by the Roman Church, by the Greek Church, by the Turkish Church, by the Protestant Church, not by any Church that I know of. My mind is my own Church.'[24] So-called 'free-thinking' came to be contrasted with thinking that was 'bound' within the confines of a religious tradition claiming an authority higher than human reason. (The rhetoric of this position failed to notice that in fact all thinking takes place in a tradition of one sort or another, so that the individual 'free thinker', unfettered by any constraints, is a myth. People think socially.) In reality, the key thinkers of the Enlightenment were themselves authorities: indeed, it may be truer to describe this shift not from authority to autonomy, but from the authority of the church to the authority of the academy. Nevertheless, the legacy of this contrast can still be encountered today in the widespread assumption that to be religiously committed involves a 'leap of faith' – an irrational step into the arms of some or other authority which claims privileged access to the truth. The possibility that submission to an authoritative religious tradition may be a rational step to take is less easily acknowledged.

How, then, has the Enlightenment contributed to the secularization of consciousness? From the widespread consensus prior to the eighteenth century that Christianity (despite its internal divisions) is a true account of the world, how have our minds changed? Summarizing the above, a range of consequences emerge. Christian beliefs are treated as a second-rate form of knowledge, or fail to count as knowledge at all. God is reduced to a plausible hypothesis – one mere object in a crowded world of objects that we can doubt and ultimately ignore. We no longer seek any pattern or meaning in the accidental events of history or in our lives: success and suffering alike have no meaning. At the same time, we believe things are getting better all the time and that human ingenuity has replaced the need for God. Religious conversation is taboo, resulting in wide ignorance of Christian content and vocabulary. Christianity is perceived to be largely irrelevant to everyday problems. And, if someone is going to be religious, they will be more inclined to mix and match a creed for themselves than to submit to the authority of historic Christianity.

Consequences such as these are deeply entrenched in contemporary consciousness, so much so that most of the time we probably hardly even notice them. This makes it all the more painful and confusing for the Christian self when it collides with this

---

[24] T. Paine, *The Age of Reason* (London: The Pioneer Press, 1937), 1–2.

internalized worldview. The Christian (or any religious person) has to endure what Peter Berger has termed the 'pluralization of consciousness',[25] the feeling that he or she is carrying two discrepant realities in his head simultaneously, and that he or she owes loyalty to both. Most of the time we can avoid this confusion, by shifting in and out of gear depending on whether we are in church on Sunday, or in our secular work place on Monday. But when we try to bring these worlds together, say, in the task of mission or evangelism, the gears tend to grind painfully. No wonder, then, that Christians find mission implausible. The attempt to share their faith with their peers replicates a conflict which they already experience internally. We want to communicate the reality of faith as we experience it on Sunday (or wherever we experience it), but we also have a Monday worldview within us that we have imbibed from the secular world that we inhabit. We are unable to do justice to both worlds. On Sundays we reconnect with and celebrate the reality of our faith; on Mondays we devise subtle means of disguising it. If we fail to disguise it, or openly try to share it, we often experience embarrassment; this is not because we are ashamed of the gospel, but because we are breaking society's unwritten rules. We are committing a *faux pas*. These rules are our inheritance from the Enlightenment. They run deep and affect us all.

It should be stressed that not everyone, of course, has inherited the rationalism of the Enlightenment. Other streams of thought have combined with it to colour and complicate the pattern. Nineteenth-century reactions to rationalism, for example, have bequeathed a rather different ideational inheritance. There was a good deal of subterranean spirituality circulating in the Victorian era, which re-emerged in the sects, cults and new religious movements of the 1960s and 1970s. This means that contemporary people are not all equally alienated from the faith of their ancestors. It should also be said that we owe much to the Enlightenment, for all its arrogant presumption. As Newbigin puts it, 'The "light" in the Enlightenment was real light.'[26]

The Enlightenment, then, is one explanation for the secularization of consciousness. A second factor may be suggested in addition: the impact of the rise of science, from the seventeenth through to the nineteenth century.

---

[25] P.L. Berger, *The Heretical Imperative: Contemporary Possibilities of Religious Affirmation* (Garden City, NY: Anchor Press, 1979), 26.
[26] Newbigin, *Foolishness*, 43.

The rise of science

A common explanation for the loss of Christian meanings from popular consciousness, and the growth of doubt within the pew, is found in the rise of science. For Alan Gilbert, the story begins with the emergence of critical methods of enquiry in the humanism of the Renaissance, coupled with the recovery of secular, classical perspectives. The subsequent scientific revolution, 'gave impetus to secularization not because it was anti-religious, but because it redrew the distinction between "religious" and "secular" knowledge which the twin influences of Platonic and Christian thought had obscured'[27] – biased, as they were, against the material world. It did this, according to Gilbert, in at least two ways. First, science cultivated a field of human awareness in which religious consciousness was epistemologically irrelevant. Secondly, science formulated hypotheses to explain aspects of human experience hitherto only explicable in supernaturalistic terms. 'The scientific revolution, in short, gradually reduced religion's *instrumental* and *cognitive* utility in the present world.' Rodney Stark and William Bainbridge illustrate this displacement of religious explanations by scientific ones with the case of the lightning conductor, a technical device which put paid to the notion that churches struck by lightning were under the judgement of God. They conclude that 'science engenders skepticism toward religion'.[28] Likewise, Hugh McLeod attributes the growth of doubt in the nineteenth century to three factors in particular. The first of these concerned new discoveries: Darwin's theory of the origin of species; fresh geological dating; and the 'scientific' higher criticism of the Tübingen school, all of which called into question the reliability of the Bible. Secondly, doubt arose on account of scientific suspicion towards Christian epistemology and the miraculous. The third factor concerned protest over the morality of some Christian doctrines, such as hell. The first two of these factors are explicitly scientific. The third may rest in part on emerging psychological theories which recognized the limits of human responsibility and consequently, too, the seeming injustice of eternal punishment. Nineteenth-century science seems strongly implicated in the growth of doubt.

Other observers have noted the more *indirect* impact of science on popular consciousness. Perhaps the real impact of science is not to do with the dissemination of scientific method into popular thinking – after all, how many of us formulate careful hypotheses

---

[27] Gilbert, *Post-Christian Britain*.

[28] R. Stark and W.S. Bainbridge, 'Secularization, Revival, and Cult Formation' in L. Dawson (ed.), *Cults in Context: A Reader in the Study of New Religious Movements* (Toronto: Canadian Scholars' Press, 1996), 122.

about the world which we then rigorously test? Rather, as Bryan Wilson points out, scientific accounts of the world are privileged because science enjoys considerable prestige. Cosmetics are still sold in department stores by assistants wearing white lab-coats; the message implied by this is that the cosmetic products will work because they have been formulated *scientifically*. (By contrast, imagine the response if the cosmetics counter were staffed by assistants dressed as nuns!) Science has gained this status both because it has provided some very powerful explanations (the structure of matter; the origin of species) and also because of its practical fruits (penicillin, electricity, carbon dating).[29] Steve Bruce similarly points to the indirect role played by science in the secularization of consciousness. 'The clash of ideas between science and religion is far less significant than the more subtle impact of naturalistic ways of thinking about the world.'[30] What matters is the 'cognitive style' engendered by scientific thinking.[31] In other words, it is the impact of scient*ism* on popular consciousness which has had the greater effect, rather than formal scientific thinking, or even the debates between science and religion.[32] Christian faith once enjoyed the prestige now conferred upon science; it no longer does. It once provided the lens through which people made sense of their world; it now represents a deviant cognitive style. We expect our doctor to apply her medical knowledge to our ailments in an attempt to heal them – we do not expect to benefit from her theological wisdom. Theology has precious few footholds in the modern world.

Ideology

One further kind of explanation for the secularization of modern consciousness involves the impact of various ideologies on Christian thought. Scientism and Darwinism have already been mentioned as ideologies which competed with the Christian story, but whose ideas probably did not have much of an impact at the popular level in the nineteenth century.[33] Marxism, on the other hand, may have carried more influence. 'Marxism was the most powerful philosophy of secularization in the nineteenth century,'

---

[29] Wilson, *Secular Society*, 47.

[30] S. Bruce, *Religion in the Modern World* (Oxford: Oxford University Press, 1996), 48f.

[31] S. Bruce, *Religion in Modern Britain* (Oxford: Oxford University Press, 1995), 132f.

[32] See also S. Budd, *Sociologists and Religion* (London: Collier-Macmillan, 1973), 143; and A.D. Gilbert, *Post-Christian Britain*, 56.

[33] O. Chadwick, *The Secularization of the European Mind in the Nineteenth Century* (Cambridge: Cambridge University Press, 1974), 106.

argues Owen Chadwick. 'Its power was intrinsic: the systematic and original exposition of a theory of secular society, based partly upon philosophical axioms and partly upon theories of contemporary economics.'[34] As John Milbank and others have argued, a secular society did not simply emerge as a blank space left by a retreating church: the secular sphere had to be imagined every bit as much as the sacred cosmos that preceded it, and ideological systems functioned to conceive of that sphere, and to bar the door to the church's re-entry.[35]

Another ideological movement of the nineteenth century was the secularist movement. 'Secularism' was the name given by George Jacob Holyoake (1817–1906) to an ethical system founded on the idea of natural, as opposed to revealed, morality. Secular societies emerged in the towns in the mid 1850s, with the movement peaking around 1885. In many ways, these groups resembled small religious sects and it is generally agreed that their influence was never very great.[36] Paradoxically, indeed, secularist and humanist movements struggled to retain their relevance in a society that was not especially anti-religious, but rather just indifferent to the kinds of debates that Christians and secularists might have had. Once again, it is the cognitive style of secular humanism – its indifference to religion – rather than its specific contents, which presented the real and pervasive threat to Christianity. The same style of thought persists today. As Steve Bruce suggests, people today do not reject Christianity as such – they are merely indifferent to it.[37] And, as Edmund Burke cautioned in the eighteenth century, 'Nothing is so fatal to religion as indifference.'[38]

Other ideological streams of the nineteenth and twentieth centuries may also have played their part in dismantling the hegemony of Christian thinking, including nihilism, existentialism, and romanticism. Perhaps, however, it is true that the British are far less ideologically committed than their neighbours on the continent – that we tend to be more interested in practical, empirical concerns than in weighty matters of principle. As a result, we are far less likely to revolt over God than we are, simply and politely, to ignore him.

---

[34] Chadwick, *Secularization*, 66.
[35] Milbank, *Theology*.
[36] Chadwick, *Secularization*, 90; B.R. Wilson, *Religion in Sociological Perspective* (Oxford: Oxford University Press, 1982), 149.
[37] Bruce, *God is Dead*, 240.
[38] E. Burke, 'Letter to William Smith, 29th Jan. 1795', *Oxford Dictionary of Quotations* (Oxford: Oxford University Press, 1979), 111.

Conclusion

In the past a 'sacred canopy' of religious meaning overarched European societies, providing their inhabitants with a coherent view of the world, and supplying their leaders with religious legitimation for the power structures of the day. The sacred canopy has now collapsed.[39] An explanation for its collapse may be found, in part, in the history of ideas. Viewed in this way, three particular engines of change can be identified: the Enlightenment, the rise of science, and the role of ideology. Together these form a powerful explanation for changes in the popularity and social impact of Christian beliefs in Britain in the past three centuries.

They are, however, only part of the story of secularization – they detail the impact of one set of *ideas* upon another. However, the story of secularization is also concerned with the impact of two further factors, *social processes* and *social institutions*. In the next chapter we will consider how these social factors have impacted upon Christian thinking, practices and institutions.

---

[39] P.L. Berger, *The Sacred Canopy: Elements of a Sociological Theory of Religion* (Garden City, NY: Doubleday, 1967).

3

Modernity: Catalysts and Carriers

This chapter continues to tell the story of secularization, but from the point of view of the impact of changing social processes and social institutions on Christianity in Britain. If the Enlightenment and associated changes in *ideas* form one part of the explanation for religious decline, another equally important explanation is rooted in changes in *society*. The catch-all term to describe the advent of these changes is *modernity*. Modernity is one of the chief suspects in the demise of Christianity in Britain.

Modernity 'refers to modes of social life or organization which emerged in Europe from about the seventeenth century onwards and which subsequently became more or less worldwide in their influence'.[1] It is characterized by a number of features:

> Among the most important are institutional differentiation and bureaucratic augmentation. This process results in a structural bifurcation – a split between public and private spheres of life; intense cultural pluralism which follows from urbanization and the proliferation of the media of mass communications; and social mobility and geographic mobility, among other things.[2]

Two different aspects of modernity have contributed to secularization: modern *processes* and modern *institutions*.

In the previous chapter we explored the impact of changing *ideas* upon Christian faith: yet ideas do not float freely in the ether. As Berger points out, 'no "history of ideas" takes place in isolation from the blood and sweat of general history.'[3] It is too simple to imagine that a grand philosopher of the Enlightenment thinks a new thought, and that this new thought is somehow gossiped down through the ranks until it settles as an unexamined assumption in

---

[1] A. Giddens, *The Consequences of Modernity* (Cambridge: Polity, 1990), 1.
[2] J.D. Hunter, *The New Religions: Demodernization and the Protest Against Modernity* (New York NY: Edwin Mellen, 1981), 106.
[3] P.L. Berger and T. Luckmann, *The Social Construction of Reality* (Harmondsworth: Penguin, 1966), 145.

the consciousness of the plough-boy. Ideas do not simply float down through the intellectual strata like flakes of snow. Instead, ideas are carried, and ideas are driven. They are embodied in brains and books and social structures, and these in turn are influenced by flows of capital, power, or personnel. In other words, ideas must be carried within social institutions of one sort or another, and they are subject to the forces at work within those institutions. A sociological explanation for religious decline will therefore have to go beyond the history of ideas, to consider both the processes – or *catalysts* – of change in modernity, and the *institutional carriers* of change.

The Processes of Modernity

Before embarking on this explanation, it is worthwhile recalling the question we are seeking to answer: how is it that in just a few centuries the church in Britain has suffered the decline of its power, wealth, intellectual prestige, moral authority, membership, and cultural hegemony? And how is it that this decline has become precipitous in just the last four decades? Some seismic changes must have occurred to wrest a deep-rooted Christian faith from the soil of these islands where it has grown and flourished for more than a thousand years.

Sociologists identify a range of modern processes which seem to explain how Christianity came to be uprooted. The crucial event in this story is the Industrial Revolution. Apart from the obvious process of the *industrialization* of production, and the development of technology, the Industrial Revolution brought with it a range of associated processes. Industrialization required labour to be concentrated in one place, and so required the growth of cities. In other words, *urbanization* went hand in hand with it. The city, in turn, facilitated the specialization of roles and institutions. There is no point in everyone baking their own bread when a single baker can supply the local community more cheaply and efficiently. Roles and institutions therefore became *differentiated* from one another: in place of the rural home as a centre of production, products and services came to be increasingly supplied by a growing number of specialized agencies: the butcher, the baker, the candlestick maker, and so forth. Differentiation along class lines also took place. These different spheres of work encouraged the proliferation of different subcultures, which in turn fostered a growing variety of lifestyles and beliefs. The process by which institutions and lifestyles proliferated has been termed *pluralization*. Furthermore, as roles and institutions became increasingly differentiated, society became more complex, more interdependent, and more in need of some form of overarching organization. Two additional processes flowed out of this need for overall co-ordination: one is the process of *societalization* in which life became increasingly organized not at the level of the local community, but of a whole society, and chiefly of the nation state;[4] the other was the process of *bureaucratization* in which local, face-to-face relationships were replaced by structured encounters within a bureaucratic framework. In such encounters, people meet within prescribed roles (doctor/patient, consultant/client, waitress/diner) and typically observe set rules of engagement. The expansion of a rationalized, bureaucratic sphere of relations threw into stark relief the kind of local, personal relationships that belonged between friends and relatives. One is personal and private, the other impersonal and public. (Sociologists call them 'mechanical' and 'organic' solidarity, respectively.) In this way, modernity brings with it one further process: *privatization*. Human friendships, domestic life, feelings, leisure, marriage, children and religious faith belong in the private sphere. Impersonal roles, work and a range of public institutions, including those of politics, economics, health, welfare, education and law belong in the public sphere.

These, then, are the kinds of processes involved in the emergence of the modern world. So far, though, nothing has been said about their impact upon Christian faith. How did these processes impact upon Christianity in Britain? Here we must turn to the classical sociological account of secularization for an answer, as we revisit each of these processes in turn.

Industrialization

Industrialization and urbanization have been labelled the 'twin cumbersome nouns'[5] of the secularization narrative. Certainly, the vocabulary typically used by sociologists deserves no prizes for elegance. For all that, the notions of industrialization and urbanization form an important opening chapter in the narrative of secularization.

At the outset, a correlation can be found which suggests that those who are the least exposed to the forces of urbanization and

---

[4] Wilson, *Sociological Perspective*, 154. Societalization is Bryan Wilson's term for a process by which, 'human life is increasingly enmeshed and organized, not locally, but societally (that society being most evidently, but not uniquely, the nation state).'

[5] Chadwick, *Secularization*, 100.

industrialization are the most religious. Steve Bruce, for example, observes:

> The basic pattern can be shown by identifying the three main social groups with the strongest commitment to organized religion in Britain (and most other industrial societies): women, country dwellers, and the petite bourgeoisie. In their different ways, each of these three groups is removed from the urban industrial world. Women more often than men do not work outside the home. People in rural areas tend to be more remote from cosmopolitan culture and values. And small shop-keepers and 'lesser' professionals are also isolated from the secularizing influences of industrial culture.[6]

It follows, therefore, that those with greater exposure to the urban industrial world have less than the strongest commitment to orga-nized religion. We cannot prove that these two factors have any causal relationship, but it seems likely that they are linked. If this is the case, how might we explain the connection?

Consider first industrialization: a strong case can be made for saying that industrialization has a profound *rationalizing* effect. (The notion of 'rationalization' is another unfortunate creature of the swamps of sociological jargon: briefly put, it denotes a system-atic, practical, formulaic and technical approach to organizing social life – often at the expense of the personal, emotional, and spiritual dimensions of being human.) The effects of rationalization are evident in a number of contexts and it is not hard to see their impact upon religious life.

One such area is the rationalization of consciousness. Industrializa-tion goes hand in hand with the growth of technology. Berger and others have argued that the increasing intrusion of technology into everyday life promotes 'technological consciousness',[7] a way of seeing the world that is conditioned by the promise and limitations of tech-nology. Industry and technology proceed on the basis that the material world can be manipulated and controlled in order to achieve some desired goal: to make a car; to develop a new drug; to send a message. It promotes a way of thinking about the world that is *instrumental* – a way of thinking oriented towards getting things done in a way that is the most pragmatic, efficient, and planned as possible. Technological consciousness represents a shift away from pre-modern conscious-ness. Bryan Wilson has described it in terms of:

---

[6] S. Bruce, *God Save Ulster: The Religion and Politics of Paisleyism* (Oxford: Clarendon Press, 1986), 59.

[7] See P.L. Berger, B. Berger and H. Kellner, *The Homeless Mind: Modern-ization and Consciousness* (Harmondsworth: Penguin, 1974).

The shift from primary preoccupation with the superempirical to the empirical; from transcendent entities to naturalism; from other-worldly goals to this-worldly possibilities; from an orientation to the past as a determining power in life to increasing preoccupation with a planned and determined future; from speculative and 'revealed' knowledge to practical concerns, and from dogmas to falsifiable propositions; from the acceptance of the incidental, spasmodic, random, and charismatic manifestations of the divine to the systematic, structured, planned, and routinized management of the human ...[8]

The rationalization of consciousness helped to foster an attitude of indifference towards Christian faith. Why ask God to do something that he may or may not do (such as heal a sick person) when the technology has been developed that will do it for certain? In the face of expanding technology, Christian claims about God became increasingly limited to the sphere of unseen, moral transactions (repentance, faith, forgiveness) and withdrew from making instrumental claims about, say, healing, crop production, or the weather. The world ceased to be 'charged with the grandeur of God'[9] and instead suffered 'disenchantment'.

A world led by science, technology and industry has a tendency to spread the principle of rationalization to many other spheres of life – work, time, friendships, education and even to the churches themselves. On this last point, the rationalization of religion may be seen in the expansion of denominalization, ecumenism, organizational centralization, increased bureaucracy, the professionalization of religious personnel, and in changing financial practices.[10] Over time, the church ceased to function with awe-inspiring authority as the keeper of the keys to death and hell, and instead took up a more prosaic role as merely one bureaucratic institution among many. In sum, industrial society seems to have contributed to 'the disenchantment of the world',[11] and encouraged the church to adopt the style and outlook of rationalized, bureaucratic institution, with a much reduced role in society.

---

[8] B.R. Wilson, 'Secularization: The inherited model' in P. Hammond (ed.), *The Sacred in a Secular Age* (Berkeley: University of California Press, 1985), 14.

[9] G.M. Hopkins, 'God's Grandeur' in *Poems and Prose* (Harmondsworth: Penguin, 1985), 27.

[10] Wilson, *Secular Society*, 22; B.R. Wilson, *Contemporary Transformations of Religion* (Oxford: Oxford University Press, 1976), 86.

[11] M. Weber, 'Science as a Vocation' in H.H. Gerth and C. Wright Mills (eds.), *From Max Weber: Essays in Sociology* (London: Routledge, 1991), 155; see also 51. Weber popularised the term, but the phrase itself seems to have been coined by Friedrich Schiller.

Before moving on from this picture, it is worth observing that the corrosive effects of industrialization on religion are not necessarily being reproduced in other parts of the world. We have to be careful about extrapolating from the European situation to the contexts of the developing world and elsewhere. There is plenty of evidence that religion is able to co-exist with expanding technologies, as in Latin America,[12] India, Japan or Egypt.[13] Similarly, evangelicals in the United States have shown their ability to make use of satellite technology in order to spread their message.[14] Technology and religion are not necessarily enemies, then, even if the Industrial Revolution in Britain does seem to have had far reaching effects on religious life.

Urbanization

The second of the 'twin cumbersome nouns' associated with secularization is urbanization. Urbanization describes the process by which an increasing proportion of the population live and work in towns and cities. Industrialization and urbanization go hand in hand, not only because the former necessitates the latter, but also because many of the consequences for religion that they create are similar.

Many commentators have linked the growth of cities with the decline of religion.[15] The French sociologist Gabriel Le Bras wrote that, 'out of a hundred villagers who settle in Paris, roughly ninety will cease to be churchgoers by the time they step out of the *Gare Montparnasse*.'[16] Similarly, Martin Robinson observes, 'It is a fact

---

[12] D.A. Martin, 'Religion, Secularization, and Postmodernity: Lessons from the Latin American Case' in P. Repstadt (ed.), *Religion and Modernity: Models of Co-existence* (Oslo: Scandinavian University Press, 1996), 35–43.

[13] D. Herbert, *Religion and Civil Society* (Aldershot: Ashgate, 2003), 41, 112.

[14] S. Bruce, *The Rise and Fall of the New Christian Right* (Oxford: Clarendon, 1988).

[15] See, for example, A. MacIntyre, *Secularization and Moral Change* (Oxford: Oxford University Press, 1967), 11; Budd, *Sociologists*, 131; W.C. Roof, 'Traditional Religion in Contemporary Society: A theory of local-cosmopolitan plausibility', *American Sociological Review* 41 (1976), 195–228; S.S. Acquaviva, *The Decline of the Sacred in Industrial Society* (Oxford: Blackwell, 1979), 50, 133f.; Gilbert, *Post-Christian Britain*, 84.

[16] Quoted in D. Hervieu-Léger, *Religion as a Chain of Memory* (Cambridge: Polity, 2000), 135.

that even in Africa many of those who have been church attenders in rural areas migrate to the cities and never connect with a church.'[17]

Why should this be so? What is it about cities that make them less hospitable to Christian faith? Or, perhaps we should ask, what is lost in the move away from a traditional, pastoral setting?

Alasdair MacIntyre suggests that urbanization, and the associated migration it implies, disrupted older forms of community to which religion had given symbolic expression. Feudal society and the religious world supported one another in a relationship of mutual legitimation. With the collapse of traditional hierarchies, the established church lost much of its value to society as a source of legitimation for the temporal powers. At the same time, it was ill-placed to respond to the rapid redistribution of population associated with expanding urbanization. Dissenting congregations, however, were far less affected by these changes, given their more flexible nature, and the fact that they had far less of a stake in the wider society. It is interesting to see that, by and large, these congregations did rather better in the urban context.[18]

Another reason why urbanization may have had a secularizing impact is that religious meanings require particular social structures in order to survive. David Martin has argued that urbanization and industrialization upset the kind of structures that were conducive to the retention of Christian meanings – 'the small home, the medium-sized school, the bounded town, the family firm' – and replaced them with, 'the structures of large scale bureaucratic rationality'.[19] Torn from the soil of the traditional rural community, Christianity lost the natural hold upon its constituents once provided by these constraining structures.

Furthermore, urbanization redrew the boundaries of social control. In the context of the pre-modern rural community, prohibitions and expected behaviour were enforced by localized means that included family honour, social opprobrium, community punishments (such as the stocks or the ducking stool), excommunication, or even the witch hunt. The urban environment, by contrast, offered anonymity. As a result, the urban migrant found himself in a situation of relative freedom with regard to his behaviour, including whether or not he chose to attend church. At the same time, the urban environment exposed the migrant to a plethora of lifestyle

---

[17] M. Robinson, *To Win the West* (Crowborough: Monarch, 1996), 237.

[18] Gilbert, *Post-Christian Britain*, 80.

[19] D.A., Martin, *A General Theory of Secularization* (Aldershot: Gregg Revivals, 1993), 91–2.

options. Suddenly he was faced with choice. The novel experience
of anonymity, freedom and choice made the urban environment
particularly unconducive for religious monopolies hoping to retain
their members in the new context.

To balance this, however, it is also the case that too much
freedom and choice leads to bewilderment – or, in the sociological jargon, to *anomie* or 'normlessness'. Anonymity implies
'namelessness' and *anomie* implies 'lawlessness'; without a
'name', or sense of identity, and without a 'law', or sense of how
to live in the urban context, the stranger may quickly have felt
overwhelmed. Churchgoing, paradoxically, could then have
become an attractive option for some, because it restored a sense
of belonging and of social boundaries for behaviour. It is no accident that the religion of migrants in many societies is often the
most vibrant. So urbanization may have disrupted religious
belonging, particularly for the established churches; yet it may
also have promoted religious choice, enabling new sects and
dissenting congregations to flourish.

One more consequence of urbanization deserves mention: as
well as upsetting traditional structures, urbanization is a process
that takes place on the level of *consciousness*.[20] Urban people learn
to think 'urbanely', in the sense of thinking in more sophisticated
and less 'credulous' ways, whether this manifests itself as being
'streetwise' or 'cultured' – what Wade Clark Roof terms 'cosmopol-
itanism'.[21] Urban consciousness has been characterized as 'rational,
intellectual, and shaped by mechanical and artificial imperatives;
blasé, cynical and essentially withdrawn from personal contact
with all but a small, inner core of friends and family'.[22] In addition,
the urbanization of consciousness is a process which affects all of
society, as the mores and thought-styles of the urban centre are disseminated via various media (initially through the expansion of
school education) to the rural areas.[23]

Urbanization, then, may form part of the explanation for secularization. It seems to have disrupted local Christian communities,
fostered alternatives, and disseminated a cognitive style that is
antagonistic to traditional believing. At the same time, however, we
have to be careful about making a blanket assertion. It may also be
the case that urbanization favoured the dissenting churches,

---

[20] Berger et al., *Homeless*, 64.
[21] Roof, 'Traditional Religion', 198.
[22] Gilbert, *Post-Christian Britain*, 83.
[23] Acquaviva, *Decline*, 135; T. Luckmann, *The Invisible Religion: The
Problem of Religion in Modern Society* (New York, NY: Macmillan,
1967), 29.

increased per capita church provision,[24] enabled the proliferation of Christian agencies and, in turn, increased the social significance of Christian institutions.[25]

Perhaps the secularizing power of urbanization lies not so much in the intrinsic features of the urban context, as in the alliance between urbanization and various other processes – industrialization, pluralization, societalization and differentiation – which seem to have had a stronger independent effect. What the urban environment contributed was an incubator in which the consequences of the other processes could rapidly multiply and disseminate. At the very least, then, urbanization has been a catalyst for secularization.

Differentiation

Industrialization and urbanization are concrete processes which can be witnessed in the proliferation of industry and the growth of cities. Less visible, but no less significant in the narrative of secularization, is the process of differentiation.

Differentiation refers to the parcelling out of various roles or functions once integrated within the community, church and family, to specialist agencies and experts who exercise those roles within the formal context of work. These roles or functions include the exercise of social control, the legitimation of power, the production of goods, the provision of welfare, education, health care, and leisure facilities, and influence over the economy, the judiciary and the legislature. The dissemination of these roles and functions in society led inevitably to the multiplication of institutions which served these functions. It also signalled the separation of home and work, work and leisure, and public and private. Thus, the processes of pluralization and privatization (which will be examined in more detail below) are the direct descendants of differentiation. Differentiation may also be understood in terms of the emergence of different classes, whose members had hitherto been unified within the

---

[24] Robin Gill has made a persuasive case, however, that excessive church building actually contributed to secularization: it led to church closures; it created a debt burden; it spread the clergy too thinly; it shrank congregations making it more difficult for fringe members to attend; and closed churches helped to confirm the rumours of secularization, even when those rumours were false. See, R. Gill, *The 'Empty' Church Revisited* (Aldershot: Ashgate, 2003).

[25] R. Gill, *The Myth of the Empty Church* (London: SPCK, 1993); C.G. Brown, 'A Revisionist Approach to Social Change' in S. Bruce (ed.), *Religion and Modernization: Sociologists and Historians Debate the Secularization Thesis* (Oxford: Clarendon, 1992).

feudal hierarchy, or in terms of the proliferation of religious groups in the wake of the Reformation.[26]

Differentiation had a number of serious consequences for the churches. Perhaps one of the most serious is the loss of social significance resulting from the churches being stripped of their traditional roles and functions. At the turn of the nineteenth century, for example, a clergyman might have functioned as teacher, social worker, doctor, magistrate, academic and counsellor in addition to his liturgical responsibilities. Today, many, if not all, of these tasks have been wrested from him (or her) and placed in the hands of specialised professionals. The clergyman who attempts to perform these roles in addition to his liturgical duties will be expected to gain secular qualifications for them; his ministerial training is no longer thought to be adequate. (Contrast this with the situation of the clergyman at the turn of the nineteenth century who did not even receive a formal ministerial training!) Differentiation has therefore pared down the role of the clergyperson to the narrow functions of a liturgical specialist. As a result, the clergy, and their churches, have become marginalized in society, only able to offer a narrow range of specifically 'religious' products to a shrinking market. For the contemporary person, uninterested in such products, the churches are largely irrelevant.

The loss of social status of the clergy is a good index of the loss of social significance suffered by the churches as a result of differentiation. Gilbert observes that, 'A century-and-a-half ago the Anglican ministry was still the most prestigious of all professions in British society, and for many aspirants probably the most lucrative and secure.'[27] From this high point the loss of social status of the clergy can be traced. Towards the end of the nineteenth century, concerns were being expressed about the loss of gentlemen candidates for the ministry. By 1900, the incomes of the clergy had dropped by about a third, compared to real increases in other professions. The proportion of Anglican bishops drawn from the Peerage dropped steeply and the number of clergy acting as magistrates had fallen to an insignificant level from the peak of the 1830s. Today, a plumber in London is likely to earn more than an archbishop; clergy are drawn from a range of social and education backgrounds; and the prestige of the clerical profession (judging by paedophile scandals and the image of clergy projected in television drama) is fairly low.

Differentiation along *class* lines has also contributed to decline. The emergence of class consciousness in the nineteenth century

---

[26] Bruce, *Modern World*, 38f.
[27] Gilbert, *Post-Christian Britain*, 113.

forced many working-class people to make a choice between loyalty
to class or to church. Winnington-Ingram, head of an Anglo-
Catholic mission to East London and later Bishop of London, commented in his lectures on pastoral theology in the Divinity School at
Cambridge in 1895, 'mixed up with this class feeling – there is the
feeling against the church ... the church is largely looked on still as
the Church of the higher class, and as being always conservative.'[28]
Equally, the feeling of not having respectable clothing and not being
overly concerned with abstract questions of truth, may have kept
the working man away. When he did come, it has been suggested, he
came not for worship or education but for entertainment.[29] Further,
the specialization of roles in the work place increased the depend-
ency of workers on the system. Instead of their meaning being
derived from their place in the social order, their identity and useful-
ness became bound up with processes of production. Consequently,
it paid to think along rational lines. In this way, the differentiation
of economic roles may have contributed to the rationalization of
consciousness.[30]

Societalization

Societalization is Bryan Wilson's term for a process by which,
'human life is increasingly enmeshed and organized, not locally, but
societally (that society being most evidently, but not uniquely, the
nation state)'.[31] Moreover:

> All this we may contrast with the life of the community of the past.
> Work was then undertaken with kinsmen and neighbours – well-
> known persons with whom the individual had life-long relationships
> and with whom he shared common assumptions about nature and
> society. The supernatural appeared to enter intimately into work rela-
> tionships, into the very stuff – the products directly of nature – on
> which work was undertaken.[32]

Societalization disrupted such localized relationships, as society
came to be organized over ever increasing spans of time and space.
Anthony Giddens has paid particular attention to the way in which
this took place. Time and space, he suggests, became divorced from
one another, with the dissemination of the mechanical clock at the

---

[28] Quoted in W. Shenk, *Write the Vision: The Church Renewed*
(Leominster: Gracewing, 1995), 18.
[29] Chadwick, *Secularization*, 102.
[30] Wilson, 'Secularization', 12; Gilbert, *Post-Christian Britain*, 65.
[31] Wilson, *Sociological Perspective*, 154.
[32] Wilson, *Transformations*, 7.

end of the eighteenth century. Increasing communications and improved methods of storage and retrieval of information meant that the necessary link between people, places and times – in human scale, face-to-face encounters – was broken. Time and space became 'emptied out', with *kairos* (significant moment, opportunity) giving way to mere *chronos* (sequential time) and place giving way to space. For example, suppose I want to give my wife some flowers. In the pre-modern world, I must wait until we are together, then I will pick a bunch of flowers for her from the meadow. Today, by contrast, I can order her flowers online and have them delivered to her on a different continent. At the time she receives them, I may be thousands of miles away and fast asleep. This separation of time and space enabled social relations to be 'lifted out' of local contexts of interaction and restructured across indefinite spans of space-time. Increasing geographical mobility also contributed to this restructuring. With social relations 'disembedded' from local contexts, the basis for trust shifted towards expertise, and the symbolic tokens of money. Giddens terms this shift the 'transformation of intimacy'.[33]

What were the consequences for religion? Urbanization, industrialization and differentiation all formed aspects of the shift from local to societal organization that Wilson terms societalization. The overarching consequence of this process for religion is that it upset the local organization of human life and, in so doing, disrupted the soil in which religion most readily flourished. As Wilson writes:

> a concomitant of that process of societalization, I suggest, is the process of secularization. Put it in another way, religion may be said to have its source in, and draw its strength from, the community, the local, persisting relationships of the relatively stable group.[34]

When that community is dispersed, religious meanings struggle to take root elsewhere. The anonymity of mass society is far less amenable to Christian faith, Wilson suggests, than are the more traditional face-to-face contacts.

In short, the intimacy of local relationships within a shared universe of meaning provided a settled soil for Christian faith to flourish. The shift in the organization of social life from the local community to the mass society tore up this soil and, in Britain at least, no equivalent universe of meaning was re-established at the national level. This does not mean that societalization is always corrosive of religion: American civil religion or Iranian theocracy

---

[33] Giddens, *Consequences*, 21.
[34] Wilson, *Sociological Perspective*, 154.

represent ways in which a religious universe of meaning may be established at a national level. In England, however, it did not happen; at most, an increasingly marginal established church clings precariously to the coat-tails of a largely secular nation state.

Pluralization

The modern world confronts us with diversity. In a pre-modern context, beliefs, values, behaviour and identity were simply *given* by the circumstances of birth. Likewise the range of goods, services, locations and relationships open to people were extremely limited. The modern world, by contrast, presents us with an array of options, forcing us to choose between a bewildering spread of belief-systems, lifestyles, products, cultures and so on. The process by which the number of such options in society has multiplied has been termed 'pluralization'.

The impact of increasing pluralism on Christianity (or any religion) is not a simple question; indeed, there is a complex and unresolved sociological debate surrounding this issue.[35] Nevertheless, a good place to start in trying to understand the impact of cultural pluralism on religious consciousness is the work of sociologist Peter Berger. A key notion in Berger's understanding of the relationship between society and belief is the 'plausibility structure'. Berger contends that in order for beliefs in a society to remain subjectively real, they require a social base to buttress the reality of those beliefs and the 'world' they represent. This social base is the plausibility structure.[36] Examples include the social structures of family, church, school, workplace, or community. Only from within the plausibility structure can the plausibility of the 'world-taken-for-granted' be maintained.

The recognition that all 'knowledge' requires a social base helps us to understand the impact of pluralism upon religious beliefs and values. Increasing pluralism has profound implications for plausibility structures and therefore for the buoyancy of religious beliefs. One of the most obvious consequences of increasing pluralism is the pluralization of plausibility structures themselves.[37]

---

[35] I outline some of the positions in chapter seven.

[36] For example, 'Subjective reality is thus always dependent upon specific plausibility structures, that is, the social base and social processes required for its maintenance.' Berger and Luckmann, *Construction*, 174. The term is frequently, but mistakenly, used to mean a structure of *ideas*, akin to a 'worldview' or 'mindset'. In Berger and Luckmann's thinking, by contrast, it always refers to a *social* structure.

[37] Berger, *Heretical Imperative*, 17.

What happens when plausibility structures begin to multiply in close proximity? First, it becomes more difficult to maintain the boundaries of the group, and seal off external influences. If adjacent structures hold competing visions of the world, both groups are likely to experience conflict at their mutual frontier. In one street in Oxford, a Buddhist Centre sits right next door to an Evangelical Free Church. I don't know how much conversation takes place over the garden fence, but I imagine that if serious dialogue took place, the plausibility of the world of both groups might start to waver. In practice, however, such diverse groups can usually ignore one another.

Far more serious for the maintenance of religious plausibility is the fact that where there are many competing plausibility structures, it becomes very difficult not to migrate between several of them, even in the course of a day. Imagine a teenager from a Christian family trying to make sense of the world. At breakfast her mother prays for the day ahead. At school, in her RE class, she learns about Hinduism. At lunch, she discusses the class with her peer group, and there is a wide consensus that there may be 'something out there,' but we can never know quite what. In the afternoon, she is engaged on a work experience placement in a small business, and observes an almost religious commitment to efficiency and profitability. In the evening, watching television, she gets the impression that she is finally seeing into the 'real' world out there, and although she does not consciously think it, she comes away with a sense that the faith of her parents is all but irrelevant. Then the youth worker from her church knocks at the door ...

Like this teenage girl, modern people habitually migrate between plausibility structures. The experience of multiple plausibility structures makes it very difficult to take the claims of any one structure at face value. Two consequences follow. One is that the pluralization of plausibility structures comes to be mirrored in the way we think – what Berger has termed the 'pluralization of consciousness'. In effect, we carry around with us a series of competing definitions of the world. We do not necessarily try to resolve them; we simply switch to whichever view of the world makes sense of the group we are with. The other consequence is that we begin to suspect that all truth claims are in fact relative. Either truth does not exist, or if it does, we cannot ever be certain of what is true. There is, therefore, a direct connection between pluralism and relativism.

Berger contends that where plausibility structures multiply, overlap in our experience, or dissolve at their boundaries, it becomes far harder to maintain the reality of the 'world' of any one of those structures. He maintains that it is still possible to hold on to the content of beliefs, but no longer with any certainty. Religious certainty, in particular, is a casualty of pluralization. It is easy to believe in the resurrection when it is taken-for-granted as axiomatic for a whole society. It is much harder to be certain when most inhabitants of a multi-faith society (including an Anglican bishop or two!), deny it. Ultimately, pluralization leads to what Berger has diagnosed as a condition of 'cognitive homelessness'.

A further consequence of the pluralization of plausibility structures is that the reality definitions of some structures gain power over others. Not all structures are equal. For example, the tendency for pluralism to foster relativism creates a kind of meta-structure composed of people who think that truth is inaccessible. This becomes the new reality. Similarly, the split between public and private privileges the reality definitions of the public sphere over those of the private. Prestigious institutions in the public sphere – say, of finance, media, industry, or politics – have a far greater power in society to define what is real and what is significant than do groups in the voluntary or private sectors. In the voluntary sector, environmental pressure groups can speak up for the 'reality' of impending ecological doom; Pentecostal groups can proclaim God's prophetic message to society; young activists can protest against the evils of global capitalism. Yet all of these groups represent cognitive minorities. Over against the monolithic reality definitions of the public sphere, these groups have little power to convey the reality of their own worlds. Typically, of course, the churches themselves come into this category. Their members are cognitive deviants from the point of view of the dominant, secular plausibility structure composed of institutions in the public sphere. In short, the pluralization of plausibility structures has meant a significant loss of reality-defining power for the churches.

This means that 'deviant' groups, such as churches, now have to work much harder to maintain the reality of their worlds. This in itself may explain much of the drift from the churches. Unless churches can maintain a cultural niche, or can successfully compete in the competition for significance, their only recourse is to create a strong boundary around their plausibility structure in order to insulate them from the corrosive 'acids of modernity'. This is hard work. Many of the more conservative churches are good at doing this, and this is reflected in the relative strength of conservative over liberal churches and denominations. They are also better at performing the various maintenance tasks within the structure which Berger and Luckmann say are vital to its health. These include the successful socialization of each new generation, the opportunity to maintain the reality of their world through 'rehearsing' it in ongoing 'conversation' (preaching, Bible study, conferences) and the development of sophisticated 'legitimations' (such as Christian apologetics) that demonstrate the coherence of a Christian worldview and the inferiority of competing views.

In the end, no plausibility structure is entirely watertight: even the Amish have a website. Most evangelicals (in Britain at least) leave church on Sunday and on Monday enter secular schools or workplaces. They read the newspapers, turn on the television and chat to their friends. The pluralization of plausibility structures makes it more appropriate, in my view, to speak of 'plausibility shelters' rather than 'structures'. A structure suggests something robust; by contrast, a shelter implies something less permanent, like a bus shelter, or an air-raid shelter. A bus shelter lacks walls, proper seating and a solid roof. It is not comfortable and the weather can get in. In a similar way, contemporary plausibility shelters offer a modicum of protection for beliefs and values; yet they do not offer cosy belief, still less a guarantee of immunity from a hostile climate of belief. It is shelters such as these that we typically move between, as we struggle to retain the sense of the reality of our beliefs in the contemporary world.

At the beginning of this section I hinted that not everyone shares this view. In particular, one group of American sociologists[38] have suggested almost the opposite: that pluralism increases religious vitality because it increases choice. There is 'something for everyone'. Certainly, neither the cultural nor the religious pluralism of the USA seems to have done much harm to religion there. Sociologists differ as to how to explain this coexistence of pluralism and religious vitality. I will not rehearse these arguments here,[39] except to say that Britain and the USA differ considerably in history, geography, culture and politics, which may explain why pluralization has had different consequences in each place.

Despite so-called 'American exceptionalism', Berger's notion that pluralism has relativized religious absolutes and undermined plausibility structures seems to be sound. It seems fairly safe to say that modernity greatly increases the options available to modern people, and that the psychological impact of this increase is to undermine the plausibility of religious beliefs and, in particular, their absolute, overarching claims. In a postmodern context, the shift from toleration to celebration of difference may challenge

---

[38] See, for example, R. Stark and W.S. Bainbridge, *A Theory of Religion* (New York, NY: Peter Lang, 1987).

[39] A good way in to the debate is Bruce, *God is Dead*. See also my brief outline of the positions in chapter seven.

Berger's assumption that differing perspectives will necessarily be in competition with one another. Yet even the celebration of difference represents a radical departure from the pre-modern hegemony of Christian beliefs. Pluralization and secularization, at least through the period of modernity, seem to have gone hand in hand. In short, 'pluralization has a secularizing effect'.[40]

Privatization

The final process in this narrative of secularization is privatization. Privatization represents the evacuation of religion from the public sphere – from politics, the economy, law, education, welfare and health provision – to the private sphere of leisure and family life. In England, the privatization of Christian institutions has never been complete, with the churches retaining some influence in the public sphere, including the establishment of the Church of England, the restriction on Sunday trading, the blasphemy laws, the prevalence of church schools, and state-church partnerships in some forms of health and welfare provision. In Scotland, the national Presbyterian Church has performed similar roles. Nevertheless, the declining social significance of Christian institutions can be seen in the ways in which these involvements in the public sphere have been increasingly circumscribed from the pre-modern situation.[41]

The evacuation of religion from the public sphere has not signalled the total disappearance of religion because people still require answers which make sense of suffering and death, and to give overall meaning to their lives. Indeed, religions can flourish in the private sphere, providing that they are sufficiently inoculated against competing definitions of reality in the public sphere. The expansion of so-called New Religious Movements (NRMs) since the 1960s is evidence of the possibility of religious vitality in the private sphere; although this must be balanced with the recognition that such groups represent only a tiny proportion of the population.

Yet, even if some forms of religion have survived privatization, the overall impact of this process seems to have been corrosive of Christianity. Privatization meant that Christian practice ceased to be the shared way of life for the majority of people, and was demoted to the status of a private preference or interest for those who like that sort of thing. It shifted the basis for behaviour from the collective to the individual. In the pre-modern situation, for

---

[40] Berger et al., *Homeless*, 76.
[41] Wilson, 'Secularization', 19.

example, one's choice of how to spend Sunday would largely have been determined by local community, or even societal, norms. Privatization reduced this basis down to the slim constraints of the family, or even left it up to individual choice to decide behaviour. There is, therefore, a direct connection between the loss of collective norms, increasing individualism, and the expansion of personal choice. At its extreme, rampant individual choice is expressed in a consumer mentality. In short, then, privatization discouraged behaviour based on collective norms (and a sense of duty towards them) and fostered an environment of individual consumer choice. Applied to Christian faith, this attitude means that many people only go to church for what it can give them, and no longer out of a sense of duty or respectability.

Perhaps an even more serious consequence of privatization has taken place at the level of consciousness. When Christianity is driven from the public sphere, it loses social significance. This might not be problematic were it not for the fact that the plausibility of Christian faith depends to some degree on its representation in the public sphere, as a worldview that is making public truth claims. A faith that has public relevance, whose vocabulary is widely understood and which is able to engage in public debate commands far greater plausibility than one which appears cognitively deviant. Consider, for example, the British government's decision to go to war against Iraq in 2003. Imagine that Parliament had delayed the decision until full account had been taken of the biblical texts relating to war, until the whole tradition of Just War thinking had been carefully debated, and until a week of prayer and fasting had been completed for the whole nation. Then, after all this, the final decision to go to war was delegated to the Archbishop of Canterbury, as the person best placed to discern the will of God. In this situation, the plausibility of Christian faith would have been strongly buttressed by the seriousness with which it had been taken at the public level. Contrast this with the plausibility of, say, a UFO cult, whose claims have no representation in the public sphere. In sum, then, the more privatized the religion, the less it is able to gain the plausibility conferred by the public sphere: as Christianity has progressively lost its hold in public life, fewer and fewer people have felt the need to take it seriously.

This concludes the review of the *processes* of modernity that have been credited with causing the decline of Christianity in Britain. The final chapter of this 'narrative' of secularization concerns the *institutional carriers* of modernity

The Institutional Carriers of Modernity

James Hunter understands modernity to have been ushered in, or 'carried', by three main 'institutional carriers'. He identifies these as 'industrial capitalism,' 'the nation state' and 'the knowledge sector'. The latter he understands to include all those institutions which produce and disseminate 'knowledge' in society, including the academy and the mass media.[42] Hunter's institutional carriers can readily be applied to the question of secularization because it is the same modern processes carried by them which contribute to the symptoms of secularization. We can ask, therefore, what impact has there been from the carriers of modernity on Christian faith?

Industrial capitalism

Industrial capitalism refers to the particular marriage of technology and capital which characterizes the economies of modern, industrialized nations. Prior to the modern era, various other forms of capitalism existed; but it is only with the advent of modernity that industrial capitalism emerged as a forceful engine of change. We have already seen the power of technology in fostering a rationalized consciousness, leading in turn to the rationalization of work, time, relationships and even religion. The marriage of technology and capital has provided perhaps the most powerful catalyst for change the world has ever seen. It would be surprising if there had been no consequences for Christianity during the twentieth century; this, after all, has been an epoch that deserves to be identified with technology in the same way that the sixteenth century spells Reformation, or the eighteenth, Enlightenment. The kinds of processes explored above were set in motion by this great catalyst, and to that extent it carries the seeds of secularization. I will not labour the possible connections between technology and religious consciousness; Berger and others have explored this area in some detail.[43] The significant point here is that industrial capitalism is a force for change the like of which the world has never seen before: religious ideas and institutions have not been exempt from its power.

The nation state

The modern nation state differs from the pre-modern in a number of important ways with respect to religion, and therefore it, too,

---

[42] J.D. Hunter, 'What is Modernity?' in P. Sampson, V. Samuel and C. Sugden (eds.), *Faith and Modernity* (Oxford: Regnum/Lynx, 1996), 12–28.
[43] Berger et al., *Homeless*.

acts as a carrier of secularization. The modern state no longer acts
to enforce the reigning religion, but becomes a mere guardian of fair
competition between religions. Any attempt to enforce the claims of
one religion would pose a threat to the economic order since this
would constitute an attack on the highly rationalized and specialized nature of this order. Moreover, the religious legitimations once
maintained by the state are abandoned, or kept as mere rhetoric.
Berger contrasts this situation with pre-modern political power
which looked to religion to provide sanction for its activities: 'As
the drums roll before battle there is always a moment of silence in
which the impending carnage is commended to the supernatural
powers ...'[44] Over time, Berger suggests, the economic and political
spheres develop an affinity of structure and ethos which is exclusive
of religion.[45]

Bryan Wilson has also argued that the modern nation state is
responsible for secularization because it has shifted the basis on
which it can claim legitimacy. In particular,

> the secularization model has been taken as referring to the shift in the
> location of decision making in human groups from elites claiming
> special access to supernatural ordinances to elites legitimating their
> authority by reference to other bases of power.[46]

It seems, then, that the rise of the nation state was accompanied by a
loss in the political significance of religion, and to some extent it
may be credited with assisting the process of secularization.
However, if we take a more textured, historical look at secularization in Europe, it is clear that church and state have interacted in a
variety of different ways specific to particular countries, with a
range of consequences for the churches. David Martin has developed a 'general theory' of secularization along these lines.

The 'crucial event' he suggests, which determined the patterns
which followed was the success or failure of the Reformation in any
given country of Europe. Countries in which the Reformation
failed, retained a Catholic, state-sponsored monopoly. Countries in
which it succeeded, developed state-sponsored Protestant churches
(Anglican, Lutheran, Calvinist), and allowed a degree of religious
dissent. A third option obtained, which Martin characterizes as the
'universalization of dissent', where pluralism became the norm (e.g.
in the USA). Subsequent conflicts with political conservatism which

---

[44] P.L. Berger, *The Precarious Vision: A Sociologist Looks at Social Fictions and Christian Faith* (Garden City, NY: Doubleday, 1961), 109.
[45] Berger, *Sacred Canopy*, 128f.
[46] Wilson, 'Secularization', 12.

emerged (generally as a consequence of the Enlightenment) in each country then provided the catalyst for a reaction to whatever condition emerged from the Reformation. Those countries with a Catholic religious monopoly (such as France) could not avoid the revolutionary forces reacting simultaneously against both church and state. This could only be ameliorated if the threat was external. In those 'mixed' Protestant countries admitting religious dissent (such as Britain), however, the state church could become the focus of revolutionary anger without Christianity itself being seen as the problem, since its dissenting churches were capable of supporting the mood of revolution. Countries (such as the USA) which strictly separated church and state were able to experience political revolution without the churches being implicated at all. Consequently, France, with a virtual religious monopoly, is one of the most secular countries in Western Europe; England, with both state and nonconformist churches, suffers a degree of resentment against Christianity, but churchgoing is higher than in France; and America, with complete separation of church and state, has higher indices of religiosity than any country of Western Europe.[47] What this means is that the nation state has been a force for secularization to the degree to which the church has been identified with it.

The knowledge sector

The final institutional carrier of modernity is the 'knowledge sector,' which includes any institution that disseminates 'knowledge,' such as the schools or universities. Since the idea of a 'knowledge sector' is rather abstract, I will explore its impact through possibly the most powerful institution of the knowledge sector, the mass media. Of course, the 'mass media' refers to no single institution, but is rather a convenient term to describe a range of communications media as diverse as billboard advertising, film, newspapers, magazines, radio and television. Most probably, it was coined by advertisers wishing to impress the idea upon their clients that their services could reach a mass of people. This has led some commentators to question the validity of the term, particularly the idea that there is a 'mass' of people 'out there' who are uniformly on the receiving end of these media.[48] Nevertheless, the term is a useful catch-all to describe these media.

How has the development of the mass media impacted upon Christian faith? By their very nature, the mass media tend to emanate from single, productive centres. Martin suggests that these

---

[47] Martin, *Secularization*.
[48] P. Sorlin, *The Mass Media* (London: Routledge, 1994).

centres, 'will be the most cosmopolitan, rootless and urbanized sector[s] of society', and that the effect of their norms being disseminated from centre to periphery is increasing homogeneity across both urban and rural communities. For example, teenagers from Inverness to St Ives may dress identically to teenagers in Islington. In the same way, norms of Christian practice may have become homogenized. Except for some extreme peripheries of the British Isles, for example, it is significant that Sunday trading is widely acceptable to Christians and non-Christians alike. The values of, say, a London media elite come to be taken for granted by those who consume its output on a regular basis. Martin also makes a connection between the mass media and increasing 'communal passivity': people less and less frequently engage in communal activities, which includes churchgoing.[49]

In addition to the increasing homogeneity and passivity promoted by the media, a possible further consequence lies in the relativizing effects of the media. Berger's argument that pluralism leads to relativism has already been considered. Pluralism only has this power, however, if people are made aware that there is a plurality of options available. The mass media are the primary means by which alternative options for lifestyle, purchases, beliefs, and so on, are disseminated, and it is arguably through the mass media that the relativizing of beliefs and norms most effectively takes place.

The mass media are also responsible for commanding much of our time and attention, streamlining our perceptions of the world, and providing powerful competition to the churches' attempts to focus our eyes on the eternal. The capture of human attention by the media in the twentieth century is breathtaking. For example, undoubtedly the most influential mass media to date are radio and television. Alan Gilbert notes that within three years of the first radio broadcast in November 1922, 1,140,000 licences were issued. A new focus for news and entertainment entered the home, and threatened more communal forms of entertainment. This trend for private listening was checked in the 1930s and 1940s by the boom in cinema-going, which peaked in 1946 with 30 million attendances per week. However, after World War II, television took over. Although BBC television came on air officially in 1936, it was not until the post-war years that the steep growth in licence holdings occurred. From 11,000 in 1938, the number of licences issued grew to 6.4 million in 1957. This number doubled by 1964, and virtually trebled by 1976, by which time the average weekly hours spent watching television amounted to between 15 and 20 per cent

---

[49] Martin, *Secularization*, 86.

of the total waking hours of those over five years old.[50] Given these statistics it is little wonder that the kind of voluntary associations (religious or not) which proliferated in the nineteenth century have suffered from the competition from television (and other new technologies) for the time and attention of their members. More recent statistics (for America) show a similar picture. Every day the average household has the television switched on for over seven hours, and individual family members watch it for about three hours.[51] Those who wish to find recreation outside the home are forced, in Robert Putnam's evocative phrase, to go 'bowling alone'; that is, to do something in a solitary way that once was done socially.[52] Putnam is describing the decline of American associations, including the decline of church membership and attendance. This decline he blames on the loss of 1950s values, the increase of women in paid employment, urban and commuter sprawl, and significantly, television. In addition, then, to the consequences already outlined above, the mass media have acted as an agent of secularization due to the massive competition they represent for the time and attention of their audiences. Churches, which thrive on community life and association, and which seek to maintain for their members a sacred reality, have simply been unable to compete.

In sum, the narrative of secularization would be incomplete without taking into account the impact of three institutional carriers of modernity. Industrial capitalism has acted as a powerful catalyst, able to generate powerful processes that have been corrosive of religious life in Britain. The nation state has jettisoned its former alliance with religious forms of legitimation, and looked elsewhere for justification. And the knowledge sector – pre-eminently the mass media – have disseminated secular, urban norms, discouraged communal activity (including churchgoing), and streamlined attention away from eternal realities to the mundane. These three have carried the processes identified at the start of this chapter, ensuring that the flow of secularizing ideas has not progressed merely in books and brains and speeches, but also through being embodied in the very structures of social life. No wonder the churches have felt the impact.

---

[50] Gilbert, *Post-Christian Britain*, 97f.
[51] G. Weimann, *Communicating Unreality: Modern Media and the Reconstruction of Reality* (London: Sage, 2000), 4.
[52] R. Putnam, *Bowling Alone* (New York, NY: Simon and Schuster, 2000).

Part 2

The Dynamics of Credibility

4

The Desert Shall Bloom: Religion in Modernity

Since the 1960s, the secularization story has been told over and over so that today it has attained the status of a modern myth. This is not to say that its claims are untrue – sociologists remain divided over this – but rather to draw attention to the fact that it has become a narrative by which we make sense of our progress as a society. Once we were all religious; now few of us are. The world has changed irrevocably.

The myth of secularization has been celebrated by secular humanists and Christian theologians alike. For secular humanists it served to confirm their ideology of progress – slowly and surely humanity is being emancipated from the dark dungeons of religious dogma to be enlightened by the daytime of reason. Paradoxically, in the 1960s, some Christian theologians also celebrated the 'death of God'. The decline of institutional Christianity was to be welcomed, they argued, since it heralded 'man come of age'. Their view was of a God who wants us to grow up and relinquish our fawning dependence upon him; instead, we must pursue a 'religionless Christianity'. One consequence of this embrace of secularization by these radical theologians was a degree of confusion in the sociological fraternity. Surely secularization was supposed to be bad news for religion? This confusion exposed an unwritten sociological assumption that decline equals decay. It pointed to the difficulty of distinguishing between an observable downward trend in the raw data, and a myth about the vanquishing of religion by modernity.

For the vast majority of Christians, however, news of shrinking membership, closing churches and financial crises was indeed bad news. Secularization understood as simple decline was evident wherever you looked. The overall picture was depressing, not least for church leaders with an eye on the figures. The myth of secularization seemed to be borne out by experience. It was, in C.S. Lewis' phrase, a 'true myth'.[1] Leaders could be forgiven for turning away from the harsh light of its statistics and trajectories, and focussing instead on the small encouragements around them.

Yet the story painted above in the previous two chapters is not the whole story. As I indicated in chapter one, in the past two decades there has been an increasing swell of opinion among sociologists of religion that secularization is not a simple, one-way process that will always accompany modernization. Rather, they point to evidence of *de*secularization in Europe. (They also point to the virtual absence of secularization in many countries around the world that are well down the path to modernization.) In other words, even in secular Europe, there is evidence of religious persistence and even religious resurgence. The report of God's death may yet turn out to be an exaggeration.

What is this evidence? In this chapter, I will lay out some of the scenarios envisaged by sociologists in which religion, far from disappearing, is holding its ground or even expanding. Some of these scenarios are to do with the success of Christianity as such; others concern religion more widely. Either way, we may be able to learn important missiological lessons from them. If sociologists of religion can see light on the horizon for the beleaguered faiths of Europe, it is incumbent on Christian missiology to sit up and take notice. It would be an irony indeed if the 'secular' discipline of sociology were to prophesy the coming of the Lord, while our Christian theologians were to miss it – and thereby fail to fill and trim their lamps in anticipation. If there is light on the horizon, it is surely time to greet the dawn.

Scenarios of *Desecularization*

In what follows, I will present a series of scenarios, each of which suggests the ongoing viability of religious life in Europe. Some of these suggest a reversal of secularization: what was once a trajectory of decline is now on the up. Others chart the persistence of religion where we have been led to expect its disappearance. Still others represent novel ways of being religious in the modern world; these

---

[1] Lewis expressed the tentative belief that, 'Myth in general is not merely misunderstood history (as Euhemerus thought) nor diabolical illusion (as some of the Fathers thought) nor priestly lying (as the philosophers of the Enlightenment thought) but, at its best, a real though unfocused gleam of divine truth falling on human imagination.' C.S. Lewis, *Miracles* (Fount, 1947), 138, n. 1.

represent outbreaks of unexpected religiosity which are unantici-
pated and surprising. I will review eleven such scenarios of
desecularization, instances of the ongoing strength of religion in
modernity.

Sectarian religion

One of the success stories of contemporary religion is what may be
termed 'sectarian' religion. The term is not intended to convey
approval or disapproval, but is intended to be purely descriptive.
Ernst Troeltsch was largely responsible for developing the category
of 'sect'. It developed in contrast to the notion of 'church' (and to
that extent caution must be taken when applying it to religions
other than Christianity.) In Troeltsch's conception, sects

> are comparatively small groups; they aspire after personal inward per-
> fection, and they aim at a direct personal fellowship between the
> members of each group. From the very beginning, therefore, they are
> forced to organize themselves in very small groups, and to renounce the
> idea of dominating the world. Their attitude towards the world, the
> State, and Society may be indifferent, tolerant, or hostile, since they
> have no desire to control and incorporate these forms of social life; on
> the contrary they tend to avoid them; their aim is usually either to toler-
> ate their presence alongside of their own body, or even to replace these
> social institutions by their own society.[2]

Sociologically, then, the sect is a sub-society within a wider host
society. It does not seek to serve society as a whole (as an established
church might do), but is largely self-serving. In order to maintain its
distinctiveness, it will tend to erect strong boundaries between itself
and its host culture. It will also seek to intensify its life within, both
through deepening internal relationships ('direct personal fellowship between the members'), and typically by adhering to a more
conservative theology, which acts as a point of common agreement
between the members. Internal threats (say, from apostasy or
heresy) and external threats (say, from competing worldviews) will
tend be dealt with severely, in order to preserve the group.

It may appear counter-intuitive that sects remain successful in
the modern world, since sect members must shoulder the higher
costs of membership, which may include the stigma of social deviance, the renouncing of 'worldly' pleasures and friendships, the
tightening of moral strictures, increased financial commitment, less
leisure time, and so on. The fact is, however, that sectarian or

---

[2] E. Troeltsch, *The Social Teaching of the Christian Churches* (London:
Allen and Unwin, 1931), 331.

conservative forms of religion seem far more resilient in the face of modernity than do more diffuse, 'established', or liberal forms of Christianity. Nigel Scotland, who has conducted a study of sectarianism in Britain, has suggested why this may be so. Against the continual threat of *anomie* the sect offers several advantages: cognitive certainty; clear moral boundaries; a sense of identity; a community in which to belong; the immediacy of spiritual experience; the safety of an authority-figure; and a sense of mission.[3]

Sectarian forms of religion, then, seem to work. From a global perspective, Peter Berger notes that, 'on the international religious scene, it is conservative, or orthodox, or traditionalist movements that are on the rise almost everywhere'.[4] The chief success stories are the Islamic and evangelical (including Pentecostal) movements. In Latin America, for example, it is not the more open, reflective and liturgical base communities of the Catholic Church that are enjoying exponential growth, but the theologically conservative and sociologically sectarian Pentecostal movements.[5] In the USA, conservative or charismatic evangelicalism is the religion of perhaps 50 million people, whereas the liberal denominations (e.g. the Episcopalians) are in eclipse. In Great Britain, too, while the more liberal Anglican, Methodist and United Reformed churches have experienced steep decline in membership over the past three decades, the more evangelical (and typically sectarian) parts of the church – particularly the Baptists, the New Churches and evangelical Anglicanism – have maintained their numbers or grown.[6]

Against the spectre of ongoing secularization, then, conservative, sectarian forms of religion seem to be holding their ground. Champions of theological liberalism and more 'open' and 'inclusive' churches may not much like this conclusion. Indeed, they may feel torn between what they perceive to be 'successful' religion and 'honest and open' religion; they find theological justification for the latter in the themes of weakness and vulnerability in the gospel, and in a rejection of theologies of power and success. Equally, they may dislike the tendency for such groups to desert the public sphere. No doubt, these are important

---

[3] N. Scotland, *Sectarian Religion in Contemporary Britain* (Carlisle: Paternoster, 2000).

[4] P.L. Berger, 'The Desecularization of the World: A Global Overview' in P.L. Berger (ed.), *The Desecularization of the World: Resurgent Religion and World Politics* (Grand Rapids, MI: Eerdmans, 1999), 6.

[5] D.A. Martin, *Pentecostalism: The World Their Parish* (Oxford: Blackwell, 2002).

[6] Bruce, *Modern Britain*.

theological debates to be worked out within the church: however, the simple sociological point I am making is that sectarian forms of religion seem capable of resisting the corrosive influences of modernity. Whether we like them or not, Western missiology may need to learn something from them. We will examine the reasons for their success more closely in chapter five, and consider what might be their missiological significance.

Transitional religion

Another context in which Europe seems to be becoming more religious, not less, is with the phenomenon of 'transitional' religion. Steve Bruce and Roy Wallis qualify their predictions of the demise of religion in Europe by arguing that religion persists where it, 'finds or retains work to do other than relating individuals to the supernatural'.[7] The kind of 'work' they have in mind includes those times when religion helps people to negotiate cultural transitions, as in the case of immigration, for example. These transitions occur as people migrate from one culture to another, bringing with them their religious beliefs and traditions, and clinging to them as a way of preserving their identity and binding themselves to one another in a new, strange and potentially hostile environment. For example, a larger proportion of the Afro Caribbean population in Britain go to church than do the Anglo-Saxon population. Immigrants to Britain from Islamic backgrounds are clearly more religious than the population at large. And if we look further afield, a country such as the USA, which is virtually a nation of immigrants, has far higher rates of religious identification and participation than any country of Europe.[8]

Other kinds of transition may also result in greater religiosity. This may occur, for example, in contexts where the culture, rather than the population, is in transition. In such circumstances, religion may be clung to as a bulwark against social and cultural change. The strong resistance to doctrinal, liturgical or architectural change in relation to the village church in many rural parishes in England among older, more conservative people is one such example of this. Another example, from further afield, is Bryan Wilson's contention that, in the absence of stable communities, religion retains

---

[7] R. Wallis and S. Bruce, 'Secularization: The Orthodox Model' in S. Bruce (ed.), *Religion and Modernization: Sociologists and Historians Debate the Secularization Thesis* (Oxford: Clarendon, 1992), 17.

[8] An interesting discussion of the significance of immigration for religiosity can be found in R. Gill, *Changing Worlds: Can the Church Respond?* (Edinburgh: T&T Clark, 2002), 105f.

relevance, 'in serving as a surrogate for genuine community in such highly mobile societies as the United States'.[9]

Migration within one's own society is a weaker factor in supporting religiosity; it seems to have both positive and negative effects on churchgoing. Leslie Francis and Philip Richter conducted research into the precipitating reasons for church leaving and found that there were three main explanations offered by their respondents: unfulfilled expectations; the 'changes and chances' of life; and loss of faith. The second category, 'changes and chances', included various developmental changes (puberty, leaving home, marriage, retirement, etc.), as well as crises of one sort or another. The change to which they give most attention, however, is the impact of moving home on churchgoing. They suggest that moving house can be disruptive of patterns of churchgoing and provides new freedom to dispense with church. Geographical mobility provides the opportunity, or excuse, not to go any longer. This can also work the other way, though, in that such transitions can jolt people into a decision to *start* going to church, and to this extent their research supports the notion of transitional religion.[10]

What are the missiological implications of transitional religion? Clearly, migration and mobility have an impact on religiosity, but quite how the church should respond to people in transition can only be answered at a local level.

For example, the opportunity for the churches to respond to refugees in their communities is clearly a missiological opportunity. Likewise, the ways in which rural churches seek to foster community for urban-rural migrants also presents a missiological challenge. Similarly, the church may provide a haven for those at sea in an increasingly breathless, complex, technological society.

The churches are uniquely poised to serve those who have experienced dislocation, whether refugees, urban-rural migrants, or those at sea in modernity. This is because the church embodies a great deal of what sociologists like to term 'social capital'. Social capital is a way of describing the degree to which communities are interconnected in a web of supportive relationships. It is not necessarily related to the wealth of a community: a dormitory commuter suburb of London, where few people live during the day and few community associations exist as a result, may offer very little social capital. The jobless single mother in such a community could find

---

[9] B.R. Wilson, 'New Images of Christian Community' in J. McManners (ed.), *The Oxford History of Christianity* (Oxford: Oxford University Press, 1993), 588.

[10] P. Richter and L.J. Francis, *Gone but not Forgotten: Church Leaving and Returning* (London: Darton, Longman & Todd, 1998), 65f.

herself very isolated. By contrast, a northern mining town where families and friends meet regularly and support one another personally and through a wide range of voluntary groups may provide high levels of social capital. Churches, as human communities, typically form ready-made supportive communities. Not only so, but their members also tend to give more to the wider community as citizens. Robin Gill, for example, has found significant correlations between churchgoing and other activities which strengthen social capital: 'Regular churchgoers are two or three times more likely than non-churchgoers to be involved in secular voluntary service in the community, they are more charitable, more concerned about the poor overseas ... [and] less racist.'[11] The churches have the resources to capitalize on the inherent forces of transitional religion.

Defensive religion

Another context in which religion 'finds or retains work to do' which ensures its ongoing relevance is in situations where it offers a rallying point in order to defend ethnic or cultural identities – 'defensive religion'. Steve Bruce points to the role the Catholic Church played in defending national identity in Poland and Eire against hostile alien powers.[12] With the collapse of Communism, the churches of Eastern Europe were stripped of an important culture-defending role, and consequently suffered a crisis of relevance. However, the collapse of Communism did not mean the end of defensive religion. In many parts of Europe, religion is still tied closely to ethnicity or nationality (or both) in ways that ensure it remains a crucial marker and defender of identity – in Northern Ireland, Sweden, Iceland, Italy, the Balkans, Romania and Greece. In all of these places, some or all of the typical indicators of religiosity remain exceptionally high.[13]

Defensive religion in the contemporary world looks set to stay. The marriage of religion and nationalism is convenient for both

---

[11] Gill, *Changing Worlds*, 10. See also R. Gill, *Churchgoing and Christian Ethics* (Cambridge: Cambridge University Press, 1999).

[12] Steve Bruce argues this in a number of places, for example, S. Bruce, 'Fundamentalism, Ethnicity and Enclave' in M. Marty (ed.), *Fundamentalisms and the State - Remaking Polities, Economies, and Militance* (Chicago: University of Chicago Press, 1993), 50; S. Bruce, *The Edge of the Union: The Ulster Loyalist Political Vision* (Oxford: Oxford University Press, 1994), iv; Bruce, *Modern World*. See also David Martin, for example, D.A. Martin, *The Religious and the Secular: Studies in Secularization* (London: Routledge and Kegan Paul, 1969), 115; Martin, 'Secularizationn Issue', 469.

[13] Halman, *European Values*.

partners in many different contexts, whether in support of Balkan
nationalisms, Iranian theocracy, or American civil religion. On this
score, defensive religion is undoubtedly strong. There are problems,
however, in harnessing its energies in support of Christian mission.
Perhaps the biggest problem here is that defensive forms of religion
tend to be pathological; they are exclusive, or destructive, or they
lend legitimacy to the crimes of the state. The Orange Order may be
certain of what they believe, but their religious certainty comes at a
high price. The lecture halls of Qom may preserve the finer points of
Islamic theology, but Iran is not an easy place for a woman to
pursue her career in journalism. The Western or Wailing Wall in
Jerusalem may inspire fervent prayer, but peace seems to be a long
time in coming. Likewise, religion co-opted to serve the state may
sometimes find itself reduced to a mere tool for defending nation or
culture and denied its own voice.

Is there anything, then, that the Christian missiologist may
learn from the immense energies of defensive religion, or is 'de-
fensiveness' simply opposed to the values of the gospel? Certainly, the Jewish faith in Israel in the first century enjoyed
renewed commitment in reaction to Roman occupation, most
vividly illustrated by the Zealots. Our English word 'zeal' is
derived from the energies of defensive religion. Jesus, however,
did not seem to encourage zeal fomented on defensive grounds.
Instead, he encouraged a subversive compliance: 'If anyone [a
Roman soldier] forces you to go one mile, go also the second
mile.'[14] His own most visible act of defensive zeal, the cleansing
of the Temple, was not in defence of national or cultural pride,
but was in furious defence of God's house as a place of prayer for
all nations. At the same time, however, we also see signs of a filial
love of place, as in the episode where Jesus approaches Jerusalem
and, seeing the great city spread out before him, weeps for its
unwillingness to accept God's embrace.[15]

Perhaps, then, a love of place, family, culture or nation is the
acceptable side of defensive religion. If so, there may be forms of
religion that can legitimately benefit from these impulses. One
example of a more benign form of defensive religion may be the
way in which rural Anglican churches in England, and to some
extent chapels in Wales, are often supported by the local community, even by those who do not attend. These churches and
chapels are important markers of local identity. In England, the
rural parish church stands for a particular way of life, against the

---

[14] Matthew 5:41, NRSV.
[15] Luke 19:41f.

incursions of the urban, industrialized world. In Wales, the chapel stands for resistance to historic forms of English imperialism. In Scotland, the Presbyterian Church enjoys lower levels of antagonism among Scots than does the Anglican Church in England, perhaps on account of its historic role in resisting cultural incursions from England in the form of liturgy, episcopacy and other forms of patronage.

No doubt there are many ways in which these impulses could be channelled in the service of mission. Many rural churches, for example, attract enormous loyalty from local people who, nevertheless, only ever set foot inside the church at major festivals. They are staunch members of the 'Friends of ...', say, St Egbert's Church in Piddling-on-the-Marsh. Often this group of people feel strongly that their parish church must be preserved, even when they do not attend. What motivates such people? What relationship do they see between the church as a cultural artefact and the message and community it embodies? And crucially, what might build a bridge between the two? If a way could be found for those who love their church to belong to that church and to support it from within, then the defensive impulse could be turned into a viable missiological opportunity.

Latent religion

Another scenario of desecularization is the phenomenon of latent religion, sometimes called 'folk', 'ambient', or 'immanent' religion. Latent religion describes the range of religious impulses latent in a population which are only manifested in response to some kind of event or crisis which is beyond the normal routine of life. These religious responses are latent within a large section of the population who do not attend church and have no regular means of expressing these religious impulses; yet they are there and they are witnessed at times of national crisis or celebration, at focal community events, or at significant moments in individuals' biographies.

This subterranean spirituality has been witnessed and studied by sociologists in a range of contexts. Tony Walter and others have studied, for example, the growing trend for World War II widows to visit the war graves of their dead husbands. Walter is particularly interested in the many parallels between these visits and conventional religious pilgrimage. He notes, for example, that both have a specific personal goal – the goal is single and does not involve touring around; in both cases the goal is the 'centre out there'; both are usually folk events, initiated from low in the social hierarchy; both come to pay homage to the dead, either saints or war heroes;

and both perform a therapeutic function.[16] Pilgrimage is enjoying a
resurgence in popularity.

A second example of latent religion becoming manifest in
response to bereavement was the range of responses to the
'Hillsborough Disaster' in 1989. Hillsborough stadium is the home
of Sheffield United Football Club. On the 15 April that year, it
hosted two other clubs competing in the FA Cup semi-final, Liverpool and Nottingham Forest. Shortly after the match began it was
abandoned as a crowd surge among the Liverpool supporters
claimed the lives of ninety-five people who were crushed against a
barrier. What interested sociologists of religion was the unprecedented response which followed. Within hours of the disaster,
Liverpudlians were massing at Anfield, the home of the Liverpool
team, to pay their respects to the dead. Around a million people
made the pilgrimage to Anfield, to lay scarves and flowers, while the
twin Cathedrals in Liverpool also became foci of mourning. Grace
Davie suggests that through all this the boundaries between football
and religious symbols collapsed entirely: concrete terraces turned
into altars, and Cathedral altars were draped with Liverpool
banners.[17] A latent religiosity was being poured out through
mourning and through the language and symbols that made sense
to football supporters. This, too, Davie interprets as a kind of
pilgrimage.

A third example of the outpouring of latent religiosity came in
the aftermath of the death of Diana, Princess of Wales, in a car crash
in a Paris underpass on 31 August 1997. After her death, there was a
spontaneous outpouring of grief, much of which was set within a
'religious' framework. Shrines, candles, vigils, flowers, prayers, pil-
grimages, and sacrifices of time and money were offered in her
memory. She was beatified and venerated. Like at Anfield, this
display of folk religion was spontaneous, diffuse and lacking in
theological coherence. It revealed the latent religion of the very
large numbers of people who made the 'pilgrimage' to Kensington
Palace.

Latent religion need not be in response to bereavement. There is
considerable evidence, for example, that a high proportion of the
population have had what may be termed a religious experience.
Alister Hardy, David Hay and others have found, for instance, that

---

[16] T. Walter, 'War Graves Pilgrimage' in I. Reader and T. Walter (eds.), *Pilgrimage in Popular Culture* (London: Macmillan, 1993), 63–91.
[17] G. Davie, '"You'll Never Walk Alone": the Anfield Pilgrimage' in I.
Reader and T. Walter (eds.), *Pilgrimage in Popular Culture* (London:
Macmillan, 1993), 201–19.

when asked, 'Have you ever been aware of or influenced by a presence or a power, whether you call it God or not, which is different from your everyday self?' over 60 per cent of people will say that they have.[18] More recent studies suggest that this proportion has increased in recent years. If religious experience itself has not become more prevalent, this suggests that people are increasingly inclined to admit to religious experiences, or at least to interpret their experiences in religious terms.

These examples could be multiplied, but the basic point they are intended to illustrate is that there exists a widespread subterranean spirituality which has no regular visible or institutional expression, and which pops up in response to events, or questions from interviewers. Latent religion presents an important reminder not to assume that the majority of people, because they do not practise any religion, are therefore not religious. In the 2001 UK Census, only 15.5 per cent identified themselves as having 'no religion', and presumably an even smaller proportion would positively identify themselves as 'atheist'. Most people in Britain hold religious beliefs, have religious experiences and may, from time to time, try to express their spirituality through a range of religious practices. This is latent religion, and it holds missiological promise if we remain alert to it.

What kind of missiological opportunities does latent religion afford? At the very least, it challenges our assumptions about the faith of those outside the church, and about what God may be doing in the lives of those with little knowledge of Christianity. If we are going to assume that those outside the church (other faiths excepted) are basically liberal secular humanists who have yet to encounter God, we will tend to adopt missiological strategies that reflect these preconceptions. Many courses in basic Christianity begin from such assumptions. They tend to assume that most people lack religious beliefs and experiences. Consequently, they ask a set of questions intended to introduce people to Christianity (Who is Jesus? Why and how do I pray?) and sometimes provide contexts in which they can experience God for themselves. These are perfectly valid activities, but the prevalence of latent religion suggests that they fail to do justice to the actual beliefs and experiences of the majority of people in society. As Mark Ireland observes of two of the most popular courses introducing Christianity, 'Both

---

[18] D. Hay, 'Religious Experience Amongst a Group of Post-graduate Students: A Qualitative Study', *Journal for the Scientific Study of Religion* 18 (1979), 164–82; D. Hay and A. Morisy, 'Secular Society, Religious Meanings: A Contemporary Paradox', *Review of Religious Research* 26 (1985), 213–27.

Alpha and Emmaus have a strong didactic content that starts with the Church's agenda rather than the agenda of those who are beginning to ask big questions about the meaning of life.'[19]

Instead of beginning by presenting the gospel as a package for the outsider to handle and weigh, then accept or discard, latent religion suggests that we could begin from the experiences and beliefs of those we encounter, and ask a different set of questions. What do *you* make of Jesus? How do *you* pray? What is the story of God's dealings in your life? How – and what – do you worship? Such an approach would aim to make latent religion manifest. At this stage in a group, there is likely to emerge a plurality of beliefs and experiences, some of which will reinforce one another and others of which will conflict. This may appear to be a chaotic way to proceed, but in fact this chaos of conflicting beliefs and experiences exists within any such group, whether we choose to keep the lid on it or not. In my experience, courses in basic Christianity sometimes try to tidy up the chaos of people's beliefs and experiences in order to bring them into line with the topic of the day. If, instead, we let loose the chaos, we give course members a valuable opportunity to articulate what they do believe and experience, and perhaps to reflect upon it further. This may be the first chance they have ever had to think these things aloud and explore them openly. Christian faith can then be discussed, not as a package to swallow whole, but as a framework for making sense of their experience of God and for providing their latent beliefs with a theological home.

Vicarious religion

A variant of latent religion is the phenomenon of vicarious religion. According to Grace Davie, vicarious religion is, 'the willingness of the population to delegate the religious sphere to the professional ministries of the state churches ... recognizing that these churches perform, vicariously, a number of tasks on behalf of the population as a whole'.[20] This works in two ways. First, the 'passive' majority of northern Europeans expect the 'active' minority of the church to be *guardians* of the Christian tradition for them. They do not attend churches themselves, but they are glad that they are there and they do not much want them to change. Secondly, they expect the churches to perform various tasks on their behalf, such as baptisms, weddings and funerals. They do not think of themselves as 'religious', but they feel the need for the churches to articulate their

---

[19] M. Booker and M. Ireland, *Evangelism – Which Way Now?* (London: Church House Publishing, 2003), 39.
[20] G. Davie, *Religion in Modern Europe: A Memory Mutates* (Oxford: Oxford University Press, 2000), 59.

religious impulses for them. The church is not only guardian, therefore, but *servant*.

Not every country in Northern Europe is equally supportive of this thesis; but nor can Davie's insights be lightly dismissed. The country that best illustrates vicarious support for the state church is Sweden. According to data from the 1999 European Values Survey, 72 per cent of Swedes claim to belong to a religious or church organization, and a massive 24 per cent do unpaid voluntary work for it.[21] This figure is the highest in Europe, and substantially higher (more than double) than any of the other thirty-one European countries surveyed. Clearly, there is a high level of support for the Lutheran Church, which suggests that people are grateful for it, rather than being resentful. This opens the way for the population to entrust various tasks to the church. By contrast, when we consider active religious participation and levels of belief in God, we find that in Sweden they are the *lowest* in Europe! The Swedes seem proud of their national church, and want it to continue to function on their behalf, even if only 9 per cent of the population actually attend religious services more than once a month.

Is vicarious religion good news for the churches' mission, or bad? For some, this kind of detached, parasitic form of religion is nothing more than 'nominal' Christianity and deserves be exposed as an anaemic substitute for the real thing. I once heard an Australian evangelist tell of the time he was walking down the street wearing his 'dog collar', when a tramp on the pavement called out to him, saying, 'Say a prayer for me, Father.' The evangelist retorted, 'Say a prayer for yourself, you lazy beggar!' This response exemplifies the rejection of vicarious religiosity. At the other extreme are those churches whose priest conducts mass on behalf of the whole parish, regardless of whether or not its residents attend the church or are even aware that something is being done for them. Different church traditions adopt a range of attitudes towards the vicarious religion of the wider population: some adopt strict baptismal or remarriage policies while others welcome all comers without asking questions. Some clergy take seriously the aesthetic concerns of the 'cultured despisers' of the faith, and take a responsible attitude towards preserving the liturgy, architecture and tradition of their church – curates are curators. Others do not see why they should fulfil this role, accepting no responsibility to guard a tradition merely for the sake of some interested outsiders.

I think it is a mistake to discount vicarious religion as mere 'nominal Christianity'. Clearly, for those with a sectarian cast of mind, vicarious religion is to be condemned as a false idol, 'holding to the

---

[21] Halman, *European Values*.

outward form of godliness but denying its power'.[22] Those who peddle such wares are castigated as mere chaplains to culture. In practice, however, the church down the ages has always functioned vicariously in some sense. In the medieval church of the thirteenth century, for example, worship was largely done for you: masses were conducted in Latin by a priest with his back to the congregation; the congregation were left to mill around the church (pews were a fourteenth-century innovation), together with animals and children. Most of these people had not volunteered to be there; they were not taking notes on the sermon; they had no pew Bibles to follow; they were not singing heartfelt hymns. They were simply there. Steve Bruce comments, 'We might find such behaviour disrespectful and see it as proof of slight commitment, but we would miss the important point that people still felt obliged, by God as much by social pressure, to be there even when there was so little for them to do.'[23] Being there constituted their religious duty. The reason there was little for them to do was that something was being done for them, on their behalf, by the priest at the altar. They were worshipping vicariously.

Today, even the appointment of a religious professional – a pastor, minister, priest – implies that someone is giving their lives to prayer and scripture *on behalf of* those people in the pews whose week is filled with more mundane responsibilities. Moreover, churches themselves inevitably attract both 'core' committed members, and a 'fringe' of people who are less involved. The core members anchor the church on behalf of the fringe; a church comprised solely of a lukewarm fringe would quickly dissipate. Still further from the 'centre' are those who perhaps live in the vicinity and have a sense of ownership of their local church, but attend infrequently. They applaud those who do attend, and (it never ceases to surprise me) make frequent apologies for their own absence.

Vicarious religion, then, is practically inescapable and a realistic missiology will reckon with the necessity of it. In *The Idea of a Christian Society*, T.S. Eliot observed that if the whole of society is ever to be 'Christian', practical allowance will have to be made for the majority of people who lack the theological vocabulary or the temperament to be deeply religious. He writes,

> For the great majority of the people ... religion must be primarily a matter of behaviour and habit, must be integrated with its social life, with its business and its pleasures; and the specifically religious

---

[22] 2 Timothy 3:5, NRSV.
[23] Bruce, *God is Dead*, 51.

emotions must be a kind of extension and sanctification of the domestic and social emotions ... The mass of the population, in a Christian society, should not be exposed to a way of life in which there is too sharp and frequent a conflict between what is easy for them or what their circumstances dictate and what is Christian. The compulsion to live in such a way that Christian behaviour is only possible in a restricted number of situations, is a very powerful force against Christianity; for behaviour is as potent to affect belief, as belief to affect behaviour.[24]

A realistic missiology will relinquish the expectation that the ultimate goal of mission is to reproduce in every British citizen the ethos of the Plymouth Brethren, or some such 'strict' sectarian group. It will acknowledge that many people are Christian vicariously, and seek to build bridges of inclusion, rather than to shut them out. Already this happens through the sensitive pastoral practice of many churches. Baptisms, weddings and funerals provide important opportunities for some churches to minister wisely among vicarious worshippers. Many churches offer follow-up options, whereby married couples are later invited to reaffirm their vows, or attend a marriage enrichment course, or in which bereaved families are given ongoing support from a team of trained visitors. In addition to these obvious points of contact at which churches will 'hatch, match and despatch', many churches make creative use of Harvest, Christmas and Easter, as well as patronal festivals to include the wider community. In the midst of the recent British farming crises, for example, some rural churches were also able successfully to revive services based on the agricultural year, such as Plough Sunday, which helped farmers re-establish their ancient relationship with the church. Whether or not these points of contact lead to greater Christian commitment, they are important because they provide a realistic mode of belonging for the majority – for the great mass of people who, in Eliot's view, 'should not be exposed to a way of life in which there is too sharp and frequent a conflict between what is easy for them or what their circumstances dictate and what is Christian'.[25]

Civic religion

Another context in which religion seems to persist in modernity is the phenomenon of 'civic religion'. Sophie Gilliat-Ray defines civic religion as

---

[24] T.S. Eliot, *The Idea of a Christian Society* (London: Faber and Faber, 1939), 30.
[25] Eliot, *Idea*, 30.

occasions in which members of the public participate in activities intended to place the life of villages, towns and cities in a religious setting. It includes such things as annual services for the local emergency services and judiciary, the recital of prayers before council meetings, the decoration of public places at times of religious festival, as well as Annual Civic services and services such as Remembrance Sunday.[26]

Events such as these tend to be localized and low profile; they are therefore easily overlooked. But civic religion is widespread. My local shopping centre in Oxford hosts parade services for the Scouts and Guides, carols are sung there every Christmas, and all year round in a prominent position stands a neat plinth with a posting slot, inviting people to write down their prayer requests and submit them to local churches. As I write, in a nearby shopping street a huge illuminated banner has been erected across the street proclaiming 'Happy Eid', surrounded by a moon and stars motif festooning each lamp post.

Such expressions of civic religion frequently jar with people's expectations because they do not fit the widespread assumption that we live in a secular society. They remind us that there is more religion being practised by people 'on the ground' than is typically reflected in the national media. The national press can get away with limiting their religious output to stories of scandal and absurdity; the local press, by contrast, is nearer to the real lives of people and therefore tends to cover the humdrum events of civic religion with some sympathy. Since the rumour of secular society tends towards self-fulfilment, intransigent eruptions of localized religion are an important counter to this myth. If the invisibility of Christianity is one of the factors contributing to its loss of plausibility (as I shall argue in the next chapter), civic religion provides the context and opportunity to put religion back on the map.

Gilliat-Ray points to the pressures placed on traditional forms of civic religion by increasing religious pluralism. In a society with many religious groups, whose version of the sacred is to be articulated? She cites the example of mayors or council leaders in multi-faith areas who themselves are from a minority faith tradition. When the need for a civic religious ceremony arises, some have appointed a chaplain from their own faith tradition, others have avoided a religious element in the ceremony altogether, and still others have sought to integrate various traditions in one service. Gilliat-Ray observes that, 'In each of these cases, however, the specifically Christian element has been superseded and the role of the

---

[26] S. Gilliat-Ray, 'Civic religion in England: Traditions and transformations', *Journal of Contemporary Religion* 14 (2) (1999), 233.

Church and its clergy as focal points for the wider community has had far less influence.'[27]

Clearly, the church cannot hope to cling on to her historic privilege of hosting every civic service in a multi-faith society. Yet religious pluralism also offers the chance to strengthen civic religion, rather than lose it. Religious pluralism forces on civic authorities (many of whom are people of faith) the need for more expressions of religious celebration and commendation, rather than fewer. Multi-faith society challenges the assumptions of secular society. In a secular society, the religious symbols are eradicated, so that the illuminated banner across the street says something innocuous like 'Happy Holidays', and the lamp posts are adorned with snow-flakes. In a multi-faith society, the banner says 'Happy Eid' at Eid, 'Happy Hanukah' at Hanukah, and 'Happy Christmas' at Christmas. Making space for Muslim and Jewish celebrations means that space is made for the festivals of every faith, including Christianity. In this way, different faith communities may co-operate with one another to dispel the rumour of a secular society. Paradoxically, in a multi-faith society the Christian churches have a responsibility not to abandon their civic profile.

Stable religion

Another form of religious persistence which has escaped the corrosion of modernity is 'stable religion'. Stable religion asserts quite simply that, across a number of typical indicators, religion has not declined.

This case is easier to make out for America than it is for Europe. In Will Herberg's *Protestant, Catholic, Jew*, for example, the author concluded from religious statistics from the early 1950s, that 'virtually the entire body of the American people, in every part of the country and in every section of society, regard themselves as belonging to some religious community', and that this represents, 'an all time high in religious identification'.[28] Similarly, since the 1970s, Roman Catholic sociologist Andrew Greeley has argued that, 'There is no major decline in American religious faith and devotion.'[29] This is true across the indicators of belief, denominational affiliation, and church attendance. Other studies have lent weight to this position.[30]

---

[27] Gilliat-Ray, 'Civic religion', 237.

[28] W. Herberg, *Protestant, Catholic, Jew* (Garden City, NY: Doubleday, 1960), 46.

[29] A.M. Greeley, *Religious Change in America* (Cambridge: Harvard University Press, 1989), 11.

[30] See, for example, W.C. Roof and W. McKinney, *American Mainline Religion* (New Brunswick, NJ: Rutgers University Press, 1987), 230f., and

What about Europe? It is far harder to claim that church attendance in Europe has remained stable, when, quite clearly, it has
plummeted in many countries. Nevertheless, some other indicators
can lay claim to stability, or even growth. Three indicators in particular have held up: religious belief, religious identity and confidence
in the church.

A decade ago, Grace Davie popularized the notion that religion
in Britain involves 'believing without belonging'.[31] She identified
that, while church membership and attendance figures had continued to fall, levels of belief remained stable. Across Europe since
then, if anything, the indices of belief seem to have *risen*. According
to the European Values Survey (EVS), between 1981 and 1999,
belief in God, heaven, hell and the afterlife have all remained stable
or risen.[32] However, this picture needs to be balanced against the
statistics for Britain alone, some of which seem to suggest a more
pessimistic outlook. Robin Gill and others have made use of exten-
sive surveys over a long time period in order to gauge the trajectory
of belief in Britain. They conclude that, 'these surveys show a significant erosion of belief in God'. Moreover, 'the most serious decline
occurred in specifically Christian beliefs including belief in a personal God and belief in Jesus as the Son of God as well as traditional
Christian teachings about the afterlife and the Bible.'[33] However,
this conclusion is based on a trajectory beginning in the 1940s, and
does not take into account the levelling of statistics from the 1970s
onwards. Furthermore, Gill's data does not take into account any
survey after 1995. Had he been able to include the British data from
the 1999 EVS survey, I suspect his conclusions may have been
rather different. There we find that between 1981 and 1999, the
percentage of those who believe in hell and in life after death rose
around a dozen points, the proportion believing in heaven remained
virtually the same, and the figure for overall belief in God dropped
by only four points.

---

[30] *(continued)* more recently, J.G. Gallup and D.M. Lindsay, *Surveying
the Religious Landscape* (Harrisburg, PA: Morehouse Publishing, 1999).

[31] G. Davie, *Religion in Britain since 1945: Believing without belonging*
(Oxford: Blackwell, 1994).

[32] Using the EVS data I worked out averages for Western Europe: between
1981 and 1999 the proportion of Europeans who believe in God remained
stable at 74 per cent; belief in heaven rose from 40 to 44 per cent; belief in
hell from 23 to 29 per cent; and belief in life after death from 43 to 52 per
cent. See my unpublished PhD Thesis, 'Precarious Visions: A Sociological
Critique of European. Scenarios of Desecularization' (King's College,
London University, 2003).

[33] R. Gill, K. Hadaway et al., 'Is Religious Belief Declining?', *Journal for
the Scientific Study of Religion* 37 (1998), 514.

A more pessimistic view is achieved if we compare a British Gallup survey from 1981 with the BBC 'Soul of Britain' questionnaire from 2000 (both questioning a random sample of a thousand respondents). Here we find that belief in a personal God fell from 41 to 26 per cent over that period.[34] Furthermore, in the 1981 survey, the only other affirmative option was 'there is some sort of spirit or life force', and 37 per cent opted for this. However, the 2000 survey offered an additional possibility; respondents were given the option to affirm merely that 'there is something there.' With this option on the table, the proportion of those affirming 'some sort of spirit or life force' fell to 21 per cent, with a further 23 per cent affirming 'there is something there'. It seems, then, according to this survey at least, that in the last two decades of the twentieth century the proportion of British people believing in a personal God has shrunk by over a third. At the same time, it is evident that, although 70 per cent of British people believe that there is at least 'something there', for most of these people that 'something' is not personal, and many are unable even to affirm it as a spirit or life force. It is just 'something'. Consequently, Steve Bruce suggests that believers in Britain are tending to become 'Buddhist by default'.[35] Without realising it, he suggests, we are slipping into a set of religious beliefs in which God plays little, if any, part. Clearly, these figures conflict with the findings of the EVS and with Gill's statistics. Therein lies the problem of survey data and this should remind us to maintain a healthy scepticism towards it. However, two points are in favour of the Gill/EVS figures, against the 'Soul of Britain' survey. First, the 'Soul of Britain' survey is only one survey, whereas Gill's figures are derived from composite surveys. Secondly, for belief in a personal God, Gill's figures and the EVS figures agree. It seems, then, that by opting for the Gill/EVS figures we are on firmer ground.

A second indicator concerns religious identity. Once again, at the European level, the pattern seems to be one of stability. This conclusion may be drawn from the indicators of so-called 'religious disposition' supplied by the EVS data, which are somewhat arbitrary, but nevertheless afford a loose picture of what may be termed a 'religious disposition'. Four indicators make up the idea of a religious disposition: believing in a personal God; defining oneself as religious; gaining comfort and strength from religion; and taking time for prayer or meditation. Since 1981, the trend has been for these indicators to remain stable, except for belief in a personal God, which rose from 32, to 36, then to 40 per cent of Western

---

[34] BBC, '*Soul of Britain*' Questionnaire (Opinion Research Business, 2000).
[35] Bruce, *God is Dead*, 137.

Europeans over the three surveys to date. Among the stable indicators, self-definition as 'religious' fell three points in the 1980s but remained stable in the 1990s at 59 per cent. The proportion of those who gain comfort from religion also fell three points in the 1980s, but recovered five in the 1990s to 50 per cent. Those who pray or meditate have remained a stable proportion of the population at around 58 per cent.

Two conclusions can be drawn from these figures. One is the point already made that average religious dispositions have remained remarkably stable over two decades. The other is that more than half of Western Europeans may be classed as religious in these terms. A related point to notice is that these averages are themselves below the average figures for the whole of Europe. Eastern Europe is even more disposed to be religious than the West.

Once again, however, the 1999 EVS figures for Britain alone are lower than the European average. 31 per cent believe in a personal God (five points higher than the 'Soul of Britain' figure); 42 per cent define themselves as religious; 37 per cent gain comfort and strength from religion; and 50 per cent take time for prayer or meditation. Yet, when we compare changes within Britain over time, we do not find universal decline. Looking back to 1981, the EVS results for the four indicators of religious disposition are, respectively, 31, 58, 46 and 50 per cent.[36] Clearly, then, fewer people in Britain define themselves as religious or say that they gain comfort and strength from religion than they did a generation ago. Yet, looking at the first and last of these indicators, it seems over that period there has been *no change* in the percentage believing in a personal God (31 per cent) and *no change* in the proportion who take time for prayer and meditation (50 per cent). This apparent stability in belief in a personal God seems to contradict the conclusion of Robin Gill and others, quoted above, that 'the most serious decline occurred in specifically Christian beliefs including belief in a personal God'. However, as we noted above, a closer look at Gill's figures reveals that decline from the 1940s had bottomed out by the 1970s, and thereafter, in the 1970s, 1980s and 1990s the proportion of British believing in a personal God remained virtually the same (32, 32 and 31 per cent, respectively). Moreover, Gill's figure of 31 per cent accords exactly with the EVS figure for the same period. At the very least, we may conclude from these figures that 'religious disposition' in Britain over the past generation has not

[36] D. Gerard, 'Religious Attitudes and Values' in M. Abrams, D. Gerard and N. Timms (eds.), *Values and Social Change in Britain* (London: Macmillan, 1985), 60.

been uniformly in decline. The same proportion of people believed in a personal God at the end of the 1990s as did twenty years before; and the same percentage took time for prayer and meditation. In absolute terms, nearly a *third* of British people believe in a personal God and *half* of them take time for prayer and meditation. These figures hardly describe a secular society. They reveal a remarkable picture of a large sector of the British population in the closing decades of the twentieth century finding time to pray or meditate in the presence of a personal God. For these indicators, at least, 'stable religion' seems a going concern in the environment of late modernity.

The third indicator of stability is the level of 'confidence in the church,' in particular, confidence to answer moral, family, spiritual and social problems. This is, perhaps, a surprising trend: how can a population that has increasingly distanced itself from the institutional churches simultaneously applaud their pronouncements? Yet, according to the EVS data, rising levels of confidence have been expressed in the churches' answers to all four kinds of problem. Between 1981 and 1999, the percentage of Europeans expressing confidence in the church to answer various problems rose right across the board: confidence to answer moral problems rose from 36 to 43 per cent, family problems from 34 to 35 per cent, and spiritual problems from 44 to 59 per cent. Confidence to answer social problems was not asked in the 1981 survey, but rose from 26 to 30 per cent in the 1990s. As with the other indicators, *British* confidence in the churches is below the European average. In 1999, the proportions of British people expressing confidence in the church to answer various problems were as follows: moral, 33 per cent; family, 30 per cent; spiritual, 58 per cent; and social, 27 per cent. What matters for the scenario of stable religion, however, is not how these figures compare with the European average, but how they have changed over time. When we compare them with the EVS figures for Britain for 1981, we find that in the final two decades of the twentieth century, confidence in the British churches to answer moral problems rose from 30 to 33 per cent; to answer family problems fell from 32 to 30 per cent, and to answer spiritual problems rose from 42 to 58 per cent.[37] Taken together, these figures hardly represent plummeting confidence in the churches. Rather, they portray a mutation of confidence in which the overarching trend may be described as stable or increasing.

In sum, contrary to sociological predictions of inexorable decline, it seems that the last two decades of the twentieth century

---

[37] Gerard, 'Religious Attitudes', 60.

have seen 'stable religion' across certain indicators, even in 'below average' Britain. Some beliefs have remained stable (God as personal, God as spirit or life force, heaven), while others have increased considerably (hell, life after death). Likewise, some indicators of religious disposition have not changed for a generation (again, God as personal, prayer and meditation). Similarly, on some issues an increasing proportion of the British express confidence in the church (moral problems, spiritual problems). It is easy to miss these stubborn outcrops of stable religion in amongst the prophecies of statistical doom that are frequently applied to other indicators, such as churchgoing. Yet there they are, and they belong to the picture of religion in Britain just as much as the other indicators. It is important that these stubborn outcrops of religion in modernity are acknowledged, otherwise, as I suggested above, the rumour of secular society becomes a self-fulfilling prophecy.

Resilient religion

Stable religion is relatively easy to measure, but its emphasis on quantifiable indices such as belief, disposition or confidence means that it tends to overlook the less easily quantified evidence of persisting religion, such as those forms of religion that are deeply embedded in European culture. Martyn Percy has developed the notion of religious *resilience* to describe the embeddedness of religion in culture: 'many core religious ideas, images, values and motifs have become part of the "cultural furniture" of society.'[38] For Percy, the positioning of religion in culture need not involve a choice between traditional strategies of *either* accommodation *or* resistance. Instead, religion adopts both of these strategies at different times. Moreover, he suggests, this is to the advantage of both religion and culture: embedded religion benefits from the momentum of culture, while culture benefits from the 'social nutrient' of religion, which acts like the fertilizer or 'salt' in Jesus' description of the church as 'the salt of the earth'. Typically, resilient religion refers to the legacy of Christianity, as the religion predominating in Europe since about the fourth century. However, it is important not to forget that there also exists in Europe the 'cultural furniture' of Judaism and Islam: European culture is indebted to all three Abrahamic faiths.

Resilient religion is embedded within European culture – or cultures – in a number of ways. Christian symbols, language, rituals, art, music, architecture, politics, and styles of thinking are all buried

---

[38] M. Percy, *The Salt of the Earth: Religious Resilience in a Secular Age* (Sheffield: Continuum, 2002), 345.

deep in its strata. These are often buried so deeply that we, as Europeans, fail to notice that many of the cultural landmarks we take for granted owe their origins to Christianity. One striking example of this cultural myopia occurred around the millennium celebrations in 2000. The 'Millennium Dome' in London's docklands paid scant attention to the fact that this was the anniversary of the birth of Jesus, providing what many regarded as an uninspiring 'Faith Zone' on the periphery of the exhibition. In stark contrast, the central motif in the dome was a giant human form, suggesting that humanity and human achievement was at the symbolic heart of the celebrations. At the same time, around the country, many churches felt the need to remind the public of the meaning of the anniversary, with posters outside the churches proclaiming 'Jesus 2000 – it's his millennium!' This inability to access the meaning of culturally embedded Christianity raises important questions concerning the missiological significance of resilient religion. Put simply, are people in touch with their Christian past? Or is the memory of Christianity in Europe a wasting asset? These are important questions to which we shall return after we have had a closer look at some examples of resilient religion.

One of these is the prevalence of Christian *symbols*. A tourist walking through Oxford, for example, will encounter Christian symbols at every turn. Everywhere she turns she will encounter 'dreaming spires' topped with crosses pointing heavenwards. Below the spires, churches are laid out in a cruciform shape, all pointing East towards Jerusalem. If she is very observant, she may encounter the remains of the once colossal Osney Abbey, or the Priory at Godstow. She may visit colleges which recall Christ himself: 'Jesus', 'Corpus Christi' and 'Christ Church'. Others she passes may be named after Christian saints, bishops and heroes, such as 'Magdalen', 'St John's', 'St Peter's', 'St Edmund Hall', or 'Wycliffe Hall.' Still other places will call her attention to the main protagonists of the anglo-Catholic revival: 'Keble College', 'the Newman Rooms' and 'Pusey House'. If she glances at the street names, she may discover she is walking down streets named after holy places and yet more saints: 'St Giles', 'St Aldates', 'St Ebbes' and 'Holywell'. Other street names – 'North Parade' and 'South Parade' – draw attention to the position of the armies of Cromwell and of King Charles 'the Martyr.' On Broad Street she will encounter a cross on the road marking the spot where the 'Oxford martyrs' – Cranmer, Latimer and Ridley – were burned at the stake. As she rounds the corner, she will be confronted by the 'Martyr's Memorial' (strangely, one of the very few instances in Oxford of statues in a public place). At times she may stop to read wall plaques commemorating Thomas Cranmer, John Wesley, C.S. Lewis, J.R.R. Tolkein and others. Entering the colleges she will find that most have a chapel and a chaplain. Many of the portraits of past principals will portray men in clerical garb. In whichever term she visits, she will discover that it is named after one of the first Christian festivals of the term: Michaelmas, Hilary, or Trinity. The list of symbolic allusions to Christianity seems endless. Taken together, these amount to a very high density of Christian symbols. If our tourist had just flown in from another continent, she could be forgiven for thinking that Britain is an exceedingly Christian country. Clearly, Oxford is atypical in the density of Christian symbols it supplies. Nevertheless, a similar – if more dilute – picture could be painted across Britain and Europe as a whole. In addition, as I indicated above, symbols from other faiths can also be found. If our tourist is even more observant, she may notice a plaque informing her that she is standing in what was once the medieval 'Jewish Quarter' of Oxford. Similarly, if she is to catch sight of students on their way to an exam, she will see them wearing on their heads a black, tasselled 'mortar board', a development of the 'fez' worn in the medieval universities of the Islamic world.

Religious symbols are just one dimension of resilient religion. Another is the *language* we use. Embedded in our language are forms of speech that derive from a long acquaintance with the King James Bible of 1611, and from successive editions of Cranmer's Prayer Book. Whether or not people realise the origins of their speech, they habitually use phrases derived from the Bible: these include, 'going the way of all the earth' (Josh. 13:14); 'out of the mouth of babes' (Ps. 8); 'spare the rod' (and spoil the child) (Prov. 13:24); 'eat and drink, for tomorrow we die' (Isa. 22:13); 'salt of the earth' (Mt. 5:13); 'pearls before swine' (Mt. 7:6); 'Physician, heal thyself' (Lk. 4:23); 'no respecter of persons' (Acts 10:34); 'a law unto themselves' (Rom. 1:14); 'present in spirit' (1 Cor. 5:3); 'all things to all men' (1 Cor. 9:22); 'suffer fools gladly' (2 Cor. 9:19); 'fallen from grace' (Gal. 5:4); 'the patience of Job' (Jas. 5:11); and so on. Similarly, many of our phrases derive from our Christian heritage. The 'crux' of a matter is its 'crucial' aspect: both words derive from the idea of the centrality of the Christian cross. Enthusiasts for anything may now be described as being 'born again', or 'evangelical', in their zeal. An idea accepted as trustworthy and true is 'taken as gospel'. These phases borrow an idea associated with the Christian meaning of the word and recycle it in a new context. In other cases, Christian language is used to the exclusion of its Christian connotations, and its meaning has been lost. For example, the great language of salvation has been recycled, so that it is page margins on a computer screen which are now 'justified' and supermarket coupons which are 'redeemed'. The soteriological meaning of these words, borrowed from the law courts and slave markets of the ancient world, is now largely opaque to most modern people.

The resilience of European Christianity is also seen in its *aesthetic* productions. Europe is crowded with paintings, buildings, music and so forth that deal with Christian themes. This cultural inheritance is enjoyed for its beauty and brilliance by very many people who have no connection to the historic churches. What the cathedrals, museums, art galleries and concert halls of Europe recall for the art lover is not only the Christian narrative, but also the centrality of the Christian faith in European history. It is difficult to stand in the great cathedrals of York, Chartres, or Koln and dismiss the faith of the builders as merely 'a local cult called Christianity'.[39] The great cathedrals are living sermons in stone, testifying to a faith that has profoundly shaped our present. One interviewee commented, 'Rock, brick – it's like a tape recorder, it echoes things from the past.'[40] Similarly, Antonie Wessels has commented that, for the illiterate people of medieval Europe, 'The cathedral was ... a kind of book.'[41]

It is clear that Christian architecture serves a mnemonic function, recalling the content and past prestige of the Christian faith. This is also true for other forms of art. In 2000 the National Gallery in London hosted the exhibition, *Seeing Salvation*, which explored images of Christ in Western art. This enabled an aesthetically literate public to re-engage with the Christian themes of salvation in, 'an atmosphere of serious curiosity'.[42] Given the prevalence of Christian themes in European art, Grace Davie concludes that, 'the aesthetic or cultural memory associated with the Christian tradition is still very largely intact'.[43]

Christianity is also embedded in the *political* and *legal* framework of European societies. In England, for example, there still remains an established church whose connection to the state exists on many levels. Establishment is not only a legal arrangement (bishops in the House of Lords; the Queen as Supreme Governor of the Church of England, etc.), but is also a cultural fact. Bishops are still invited to sit on important ethics committees, to chair partnerships for urban regeneration, or to give their opinions on current

---

[39] Thomas Hardy, *The Dynasts* Act I, Scene VI.
[40] Hunt, 'Spirituality', 165.
[41] A. Wessels, *Secularized Europe* (Geneva: WCC Publications, 1996), 22.
[42] D.A. Martin, *Christian Language and its Mutations* (Aldershot: Ashgate, 2002), 5.
[43] Davie, *Modern Europe*, 172.

affairs. Eighteen per cent of primary school children are educated in Church of England schools, and the Church of England remains the default provider for religious funerals. None of these aspects of cultural establishment are exclusive to the Church of England – unlike the legal aspects – but it is fair to say that through them the Church of England still holds a position of prominence. Christian faith has also left its mark on our legal system. For example, Britain retains a blasphemy law, clergy are exempt from the duty of disclosure if someone confesses to them a criminal act, and trading hours on the Sabbath remain restricted. In these and many other ways, Christianity retains resilience through its embeddedness in the political and legal frameworks of European nations.

One final dimension of the resilience of European Christianity deserves attention: the inheritance of ideas. Christianity has bequeathed a profound *ideational* legacy. Europeans typically think along certain lines. For example, we find it hard to live with contradiction in a way that the Hindu mind does not.[44] We tend to conceive of history in linear terms, which makes us susceptible to utopian and apocalyptic scenarios, including the narrative of progress. As we saw above, our language has been shaped and defined through the Christian tradition, not least through the translation of the Bible into the vernacular in Europe since the sixteenth century. Our perception of time is also governed by the Christian story, from the date of the current year (AD), to the shape of the year which determines school, university and public holidays. Christian thought has therefore created ideational grooves in the European mind, which mean that, to some extent, its worldview is easy to grasp. These grooves form a tacit argument for Christian faith which promote its plausibility.

In short, then, Christianity shows its resilience in the fact of its being embedded in culture: in symbols, language, art, politics, law and thinking. Together, this stock of Christian content may be termed the 'cultural capital' of Christianity in Europe. It is an open question as to the future of this deposit.

One the one hand, some see it as a 'wasting asset'.[45] Religious symbols suffer distortion when they are recycled by advertisers or the music industry.[46] Likewise, Danièlle Hervieu-Léger sees religious symbols being re-appropriated primarily in order to construct ethnic identities, in the absence of more traditional socializing influences. Ultimately, she suggests, this constant reconfiguring

---

[44] Newbigin, *Foolishness.*
[45] Bruce, *God is Dead*, 102.
[46] E.g. D. Smith, *Mission After Christendom* (London: Darton, Longman & Todd, 2003), 92.

of religious symbols will render all such symbols meaningless.[47] Furthermore, Antonie Wessells notes that surprisingly few people recognize the central Christian symbol:

> Recent [1995] evidence of this came in newspaper reports of research conducted among 7000 people in six countries showing that the most familiar international symbol is the five interlocking rings of the Olympic movement (recognized by 92 percent of those interviewed), followed by the trademarks of Shell Oil and McDonald's (88 percent). Only 54 percent of those interviewed recognized the Christian cross.[48]

Similarly, the recycling and forgetting of Christian language may prise it from its cultural bed. Steve Bruce is of the opinion that, in thirty years time, 'the general cultural capital of Christian language and ritual will be so attenuated that the vast majority of the population will be utterly ignorant of the beliefs and values that once shaped their world.'[49] Knowledge of the aesthetic heritage may also be under threat. Davie, for example, quotes the view of a French head teacher who believed that, 'even the most highly educated French student no longer had sufficient knowledge to appreciate, let alone, understand, those parts of the artistic or literary heritage which draw on the Judaeo-Christian narrative.'[50] This pessimism is supported by a BBC poll conducted in the Autumn of 2003 in which 55 per cent of the sample of (1,001) British adults could not name any of the four Gospels.[51] On the political front, it is clear that the close ties between church and state in England are being gradually relaxed: for example, proposals have been made to reduce the number of bishops in the Lords to make way for representatives of other faith groups. Finally, the ideational heritage of Christianity has always co-existed with rival assumptions about the world. Two aspects of the Christian claim, however, seem particularly implausible to the modern mind – the particularity of revelation (truth must be apprehended through one man located remotely in space and time) and the exclusivity of election (God chose to reveal himself through the Jewish people). Both these assumptions contradict modern, scientific expectations concerning the accessibility and universality of knowledge.[52] Such are the threats to the cultural capital of Christianity.

---

[47] Hervieu-Léger, *Chain of Memory*, 158f.

[48] Wessels, *Secularized Europe*, 2.

[49] Bruce, 'Demise', 61.

[50] Davie, *Modern Europe*, 172.

[51] Poll conducted for the BBC 1 programme, *The Heaven and Earth Show*.

[52] In contrast, C.S. Lewis argues in *Miracles*, 86–7, that the human aversion to religious particularity is part of the 'permanent, natural bent of the

On the other hand, others believe this capital can be 're-invested' as Europeans get in touch once more with their Christian heritage. The increasing popularity of cathedrals, ancient pilgrimage routes, festivals, exhibitions such as *Seeing Salvation*, and historical documentaries on television, all point to the re-investment of cultural capital. One vivid example of such re-investment is the development of 'Christian Heritage Tours' in Oxford and Cambridge. A development of existing 'walking tours', these invite tourists to accompany a guide on a tour of various sites of historic Christian significance, including the saints and heroes associated with these places. Afterwards, walkers are invited to share in a discussion of the themes that have arisen, in an open, café-style environment.

Where the memory has become inaccessible, there is another option. Danièlle Hervieu-Léger suggests that groups alienated from their historical and religious roots actually reinvent 'chains of memory' that provide an 'imagined continuity' with their past and supply them with meaning and significance.[53] In other words, in the absence of authoritative traditions, people just 'make it up'. The romantic reconstruction of 'Celtic Christianity' in recent years is one such example.[54] Another is the 'reinvention' of Wicca in the 1940s.[55] However, regardless of whether such 'chains of memory' are real or imagined, the cultural capital of Christianity (and other religions) is being reinvested in imaginative ways. Embedded religion is thereby resilient religion – another example of the rude persistence of religion in modernity.

---

[52] (*continued*) human mind', which finds its expression in the default religion of Pantheism. In this case, the so-called 'scandal of particularity' has always been a problem for revealed religions, and is not necessarily a consequence of scientific assumptions.

Annie Dillard, in *Pilgrim at Tinker Creek*, provides an interesting counter to this problem: 'Well, the "scandal of particularity" is the only world that I, in particular, know … I never saw a tree that was no tree in particular; I never met a man, not the greatest theologian, who filled infinity, or even whose hand, say, was undifferentiated, fingerless, like a griddle-cake, and not lobed and split just so with the incursions of time.' (New York, NY: HarperPerennial, 1998), 81.

[53] Hervieu-Léger, *Chain of Memory*, 130.

[54] See, for example, I. Bradley, *The Celtic Way* (London: Darton, Longman & Todd, 1993). In later publications, Bradley acknowledges the danger of romanticizing 'Celtic' Christianity, and pleads guilty. E.g. I. Bradley, *Colonies of Heaven: Celtic Models for Today's Church* (London: Darton, Longman & Todd, 2000).

[55] J. Pearson, '"Witchcraft will not soon Vanish from this Earth": Wicca in the 21st Century' in Davie et al. (eds.), *Predicting Religion*, 170–82.

Holistic religion

A further scenario of religion in modernity is really a collection of popular styles of being religious which have in common the search for 'spirituality', conceived as a way of integrating the disparate elements of body, mind, spirit, community, the ecosystem and so on, into a meaningful unity. For this reason, I have called it 'holistic religion'. Holistic religion, despite the name, is also highly individualistic. It tends to be more concerned with individual wholeness and fulfilment, than with the codes of obligation, self-restraint and compromise, that are the necessary burden of congregational or communitarian life. It also has a strong therapeutic emphasis. Although its beliefs may be quite diverse, it is agreed on the reality of a spiritual dimension, however defined. Holistic religion embraces such phenomena as New Age practices, self-help groups, and what Woodhead and Heelas term 'spiritualities of life',[56] as well as a more generalized spiritual questing.

The popularity of holistic emphases over traditional religions may be witnessed in the very different responses to the terms 'religious' and 'spiritual' often expressed by young people in Britain. Martyn Percy, for example, comments:

> When I teach the sociology of religion to final-year undergraduates, I normally begin the course by asking how many of them are religious. Normally, not more than 10 per cent respond. However, if I ask how many of them would describe themselves as 'spiritual', I seldom get a response rate of less than 80 per cent.[57]

Somehow, even among a group of students of the sociology of religion (whom, one would hope, might be less credulous towards such distinctions), the designation 'religious' seems to be considerably less popular than an identity as a 'spiritual' person. Perhaps 'religious' tends to be associated with moribund institutions, whereas 'spiritual' implies an attractive, self styled religiosity.

The 'spiritual' has also gained in popularity over the 'religious' across the Atlantic. In 1998, Gallup conducted a poll which found that the 'percentage of Americans who say they feel the need in their lives to experience spiritual growth has surged twenty-four points in just four years, from 58 per cent in 1994 to 82 per cent in 1998'. It also observes that, 'Much of this spirituality, however, appears to be free-floating and vague and does not necessarily have an impact upon traditional religious beliefs.'[58]

---

[56] L. Woodhead and P. Heelas (eds.), *Religion in Modern Times* (Oxford: Blackwell, 2000).
[57] Percy, *Salt*, 177 n. 26.
[58] Gallup and Lindsay, *Religious Landscape*.

This extraordinary surge of interest in spiritual growth in America in the 1990s heralds the expansion of a religious style that is largely disconnected from mainstream Christianity, although no doubt has parallels within the traditional churches. Paul Heelas suggests that this surge in the popularity of the spiritual rides on certain 'cultural momenta' which favour the development of 'self-spirituality'. He points to the New Age, in particular, as, 'showing us what "religion" looks like when it is organized in terms of what is taken to be the authority of the self'.[59] The cultural momenta upon which this turn to holistic self-spirituality rides is a confluence of various trends, which include: detraditionalization; increasing subjectivization and individualism; a rejection of modernist dichotomies; a rejection of transcendent authorities and metanarratives; and the expansion of therapy.

This emphasis may be on the increase but it is certainly not new, as a brief backward glance will show. James Hunter, for example, points to the similar emphases in the nineteenth-century Romantic protest against rationalism: examples include the mysticism of the Transcendentalist movement of Emerson and Thoreau; the Eastern mysticism advocated by the upper-class intellectuals of the Theosophical society; and the later Vedanta society.[60] Such emphases were then revisited in the counter-culture of the 1960s. What is new, however, is that the preoccupations of the 1960s – authenticity, immediacy, and experience – are no longer marginal, but have now been disseminated throughout mainstream culture.[61] In other words, while only a minority might claim to adhere to 'New Age' ideas, a much larger group tacitly accept the premises of holistic religion. This is amply illustrated in an interview with Paul Weller, the ex-punk musician, by the *Independent Magazine*. When asked about his interest in spirituality, Weller commented:

> It's something that I am always thinking about, in an everyday way: why are we here, where do we come from, what's beyond? But what I've got no time for is organized religion. I believe in the spirit of the world and the soul of the world and in gods of some kind. I don't know about heaven – I think heaven and hell are what you create on earth, or

---

[59] P. Heelas, *The New Age Movement* (Oxford: Blackwell, 1996), 221.
[60] J.D. Hunter, 'The New Religions: Demodernization and the Protest Against Modernity' in L. Dawson (ed.), *Cults in Context: A Reader in the Study of New Religious Movements* (Toronto: Canadian Scholars' Press, 1996), 108.
[61] P.L. Berger, 'Postscript' in L. Woodhead, P. Heelas, and D. Martin (eds.), *Peter Berger and the Study of Religion* (London: Routledge, 2001), 189–98.

are created for you sometimes – but I definitely believe in some kind of spiritual afterlife.[62]

Here we find expressed the holistic emphases of individual quest-ing, the rejection of organized religion, and the entertaining of vague and fluid beliefs, combined with a definite confidence that there is a spiritual dimension to life.

It has often been said that this openness to 'spirituality' presents challenges and opportunities for the church. It seems to challenge the church because it suggests that people have not left the church because they have become secular, but because the churches have failed to meet their spiritual needs. Far from being an oasis of the sacred in a barren secular culture, the growth in holistic emphases implies that the institutional churches are simply not spiritual enough. There may be some truth to this, although as a criticism it is too simple. There may be many other reasons why people find it easier to claim 'spirituality', than to be traditionally religious – not least the differing costs of commitment. More positively, the open-ness to spirituality creates an opportunity for the churches to show-case their resources for addressing the human quest for transcendence and ultimate meaning. If the church has nothing else to offer, at the very least she can claim two millennia of experience in bringing people into relationship with God.

Consumer religion

Consumer religion refers to forms of religion which adopt the values, methods and ethos of consumer culture in order to succeed. John Drane, for example, has adapted George Ritzer's McDonaldization thesis,[63] to show how some of the same values that have enabled McDonald's to become a global fast-food chain have been adopted by the church.[64] Pete Ward, likewise, has applied the same thesis more narrowly to illuminate the success of the glob-ally disseminated Alpha course, a ten-week introduction to the Christian faith.[65] Similarly, Grace Davie senses a shift from obliga-tion to consumption in European religion and the opening up of a

---

[62] I. Birrell, 'Feature', *Independent Magazine* (21 September 2002), 11–12.
[63] G. Ritzer, *The McDonaldization of Society* (Thousand Oaks, CA: Pine Forge Press, 1993); G. Ritzer, *The McDonaldization Thesis* (Thousand Oaks, CA: Pine Forge Press, 1998).
[64] J. Drane, *The McDonaldization of the Church: Spirituality, Creativity and the Future* (London: Darton, Longman & Todd, 2000).
[65] P. Ward, 'Alpha – the McDonaldization of Religion' *Anvil* 15.4 (1998), 279–86.

religious marketplace.[66] David Lyon has made imaginative use of Disneyland as a heuristic metaphor in interpreting consumer religion.[67] Reginald Bibby, also from a Canadian perspective, has also argued that the modern approach to religion is a consumer one.[68] Although Steve Bruce calls this 'an exaggeration',[69] there does seem to be an emerging consensus that even traditional religious institutions have not remained untouched by consumer culture, but must now compete in a 'spiritual marketplace',[70] increasingly embracing the ethos of a creeping managerialism in order to do so.[71]

Consumer religion demonstrates the ability of religion to adapt itself to current conditions in a consumer society. It would have come as a surprise to secularization theorists of the 1960s to discover that at the turn of the century a large Anglican church in Kensington, London, would be promoting historic Christianity through a global franchise, supported by advertising on billboards, buses, a dedicated newspaper, a television documentary and a publications catalogue that lists 169 different products, including books, videos, worship CDs, beer mats and car stickers.[72] Nevertheless, this is just what Holy Trinity Brompton (HTB) has achieved through the Alpha course. Such has been the success of their advertising that their research shows that 20 per cent of the British population recognize and understand the Alpha brand. Moreover, the uptake of the Alpha course itself is impressive. *Alpha News* lists the growth of registered Alpha courses year by year since 1992. From five in that year, the number of courses grew to 750 in 1994; 5,000 in 1996; 10,500 in 1998; 17,000 in 2000; and 24,400 by the end of 2002. The cumulative number of those who have attended an Alpha course in that decade is estimated at around 5 million globally. Nearly 1.5 million of those have attended in the UK alone.[73] The

---

[66] G. Davie, *Europe: the Exceptional Case* (London: Darton, Longman & Todd, 2002), 147f.

[67] D. Lyon, *Jesus in Disneyland: Religion in Postmodern Times* (Cambridge: Polity, 2000).

[68] R. Bibby, *Fragmented Gods* (Toronto: Irwin Publishing, 1987)

[69] S. Bruce, 'Religion and Rational Choice – A Critique of Economic Explanations of Religious Behaviour' in S. Bruce (ed.), *The Sociology of Religion* (Aldershot: Edward Elgar, 1995), 353; S. Bruce, *Choice and Religion: A Critique of Rational Choice* (Oxford: Oxford University Press, 1999), 128.

[70] W.C. Roof, *Spiritual Marketplace: Baby Boomers and the Remaking of American Religion* (Princeton, NJ: Princeton University Press, 1999).

[71] R.H. Roberts (ed.), *Religion and the Transformations of Capitalism* (London: Routledge, 1995).

[72] Booker and Ireland, *Evangelism*, 13.

[73] Alpha, 'The Number of Registered Courses Worldwide', *Alpha News* (November 2003 – February 2004), 2. A more recent publication, the

marketing machine behind these figures is equally impressive. Mark Ireland notes:

> HTB now employs about 140 paid staff, mostly full-time, and the Alpha offices cover an entire floor that has been specially added to the church hall. In addition, many others are employed by Alpha offices overseas. *Alpha News*, edited by a news editor recruited from Fleet Street, is published three times a year. This 36-page tabloid newspaper has a circulation in Britain alone of 250,000.[74]

Far from disappearing then, or even sliding to the margins of social significance, forms of consumer religion in Britain provide another scenario of the ongoing vitality of religion in modernity. In chapter seven we will return to this theme in more detail when we consider the potential for consumer religion to connect with contemporary people, as well as thinking about its inherent dangers. Consumer religion often comes under attack from theologians and church leaders, and these criticisms deserve to be taken seriously. For the moment, the simple point I am making is that, sociologically, consumer religion seems to 'work'. It is yet another dampener on the rumour of a secular society.

Public religion

My final scenario of religious persistence is the notion of public religion.[75] I have already quoted Bryan Wilson's classic definition of secularization in terms of, 'the process whereby religious thinking, practices and institutions lose social significance'. On this definition, *de*secularization would occur when religion starts to *regain* social significance. One way in which religion seems to be doing this is by increasingly forcing itself onto the public agenda. It is refusing

---

[73] *(continued) Alpha International Annual Review* (Autumn 2003) indicates that six million have completed Alpha worldwide and that a total of 27,000 courses are running. At the time of writing, the most recent *Alpha News* (March – June 2004) puts the figure at 28,000 courses worldwide to date. Alpha is still growing.

[74] Booker and Ireland, *Evangelism*, 28.

[75] The notion of the 'public sphere' is contested within social science. It is generally seen as too simple to divide all of social reality into 'public' and 'private'. At the very least, it is important to acknowledge an intermediate sphere, which is sometimes called the 'voluntary sphere' or the sphere of 'civil society'. This level is of increasing interest to those studying religious institutions and other sources of social capital. My use of 'public' and 'private' is therefore a simplification intended to avoid an overly technical discussion of social 'spheres'. A recent contribution to the debate which includes the religious dimension is Herbert, *Civil Society*.

to accept its relegation to a 'private' sphere of personal preference, subjectivity, leisure, family life, etc. Instead, religion is raising its head in public as a potent force in politics, education and culture.

One of the most influential studies of this phenomenon is José Casanova's *Public Religions in the Modern World*.[76] Casanova contends that secularization is a three-stranded cord, comprising processes of social *differentiation*, religious *decline* and religious *privatization*. He argues that only the first of these – social differentiation – is irreversible. The second and third aspects of secularization, however, he claims are not ineluctable processes. The second aspect, decline, is clearly not a necessary correlate of modernization – Japan, Korea and America demonstrate that. More significantly, neither is the third strand, religious *privatization*. This is the core of Casanova's thesis: religion in the modern world can be socially significant. He demonstrates this through a series of case studies in which religion seems to be playing an increasingly *public* role in the modern world – cases of *'deprivatization'*. These include the New Christian Right in America, the role of the Catholic Church in supporting revolutionary movements in Poland and Central America, and the Iranian Revolution of 1979. In all of these cases, religion has refused to be relegated to a merely private preference of the heart and the home, but has achieved significance through its engagement at the public and political level.

Other examples of deprivatization have been cited in the spheres of politics, education and culture. In the sphere of politics, speaking of America, George Moyser observes:

> At the level of the political culture, religious beliefs make a contribution; at the constitutional level, issues of Church and state still remain contentious. And within the arenas of pressure-group politics, electoral politics and policy-making, religion takes a substantial part. Roman Catholic bishops assert their views on nuclear weapons and the rights of the unborn; powerful Jewish groups lobby on behalf of Israel; born-again evangelicals turn 'liberal' into a term of political derision.[77]

Turning to Britain, Jenny Taylor has argued that a process of *dedifferentiation* has taken place between the religious and the political spheres: 'It seems clear that the British government turned to the church at the end of the 1980s, following the futile and almost

---

[76] J. Casanova, *Public Religions in the Modern World* (London: University of Chicago Press, 1994).

[77] G. Moyser, 'Politics and Religion in the Modern World: an Overview' in G. Moyser (ed.), *Politics and Religion in the Modern World* (London: Routledge, 1991), 23.

catastrophically expensive post-war period of inner-city secular social policy.'[78] Likewise, Richard Roberts has pointed to four contexts during the Thatcher era in which religion rose to new prominence: the spat between Robert Runcie and Margaret Thatcher over the content of the Falkland's War memorial service in 1982; in the controversy over the 'Marxist' leanings of the churches' *Faith in the City* report of 1985; in David Jenkins' famously publicized doubts concerning credal dogmas; and in Thatcher's infamous 'Sermon on the Mound' in Edinburgh in 1988. In all these contexts, Roberts argues, 'religion forced itself back onto the political and social agenda despite wide acceptance of the broad theses of secularization'.[79] At the very least, these examples provide some evidence of public religion. It is interesting to observe that these debates have not subsided. In the aftermath of the Iraq War of 2003, the Archbishop of Canterbury repeated Runcie's caution concerning the danger of triumphalism in holding a service of thanksgiving to mark the end of the war.[80]

The second sphere of influence under consideration is education. Sophie Gilliat-Ray observes, for example, that religion in higher education has gained in significance both at the public and political level (say, in universities adopting equal opportunities policies that take into account growing religious diversity), and at the internal and practical level (say, in universities' provision of specialized foods or sacred spaces for those from minority religions.) She concludes that, 'far from religion losing its significance or influence on the activities of universities, the reverse appears to be occurring as religious issues become more evident and contested'. Moreover, 'through their ability to influence institutional life, faith communities on campus are recovering a political territory previously lost through "secularization"'.[81] At secondary-school level, too, there is also evidence of religion gaining in public significance. In France, for example, in the late 1980s and early 1990s, a storm of controversy arose over the rights of Muslim girls to wear the *foulard*, the Islamic headscarf or 'hijab' in school. The argument was poised between the rights of a religious minority to observe their own religious practices and the rights of a secular state to enforce religious

---

[78] J. Taylor, 'After Secularism: British Government and the Inner Cities' in G. Davie et al. (eds.), *Predicting Religion*, 129.
[79] R.H. Roberts, *Religion, Theology and the Human Sciences* (Cambridge: Cambridge University Press, 2002), 51–2.
[80] J. Petre, 'Williams: No Thanks for Iraq Victory' *Daily Telegraph* (8 May 2003).
[81] S. Gilliat-Ray, *Religion in Higher Education* (Aldershot: Ashgate, 2000), 143, 145.

neutrality in the public sphere.[82] At the end of 2003 the debate was reignited, this time with the secular liberal side of the debate making an additional claim that the *foulard* is an instrument of oppression against Muslim women. *Le Monde* reported that 57 per cent of respondents in a French survey favoured a law forbidding the wearing of any religious symbols in school, while, at the same time, the Christian churches in France expressed serious concerns about the proposed legislation.[83] Such controversies demonstrate the continuing potential for religious issues to force themselves onto the public agenda.

The third sphere of deprivatization is that of culture. Steven Vertovec, for example, has drawn attention to the increasing role of British Muslims in the public sphere. In the early 1980s, issues were raised over the (lack of) provision of *halal* food in public institutions such as schools, hospitals, and prisons. In the mid-1980s a well publicized controversy arose between minority faith communities and the allegedly racist head teacher, Ray Honeyford, head of a predominantly Asian school in Bradford. If this represented a conflict between religious minority groups and a right-wing section of the indigenous white population of England, more notorious still was the clash between traditionalist Islam and the left-wing, liberal elite in British society over the Rushdie affair, which erupted in January 1989, after the public burning of copies of Rushdie's *The Satanic Verses*, also in Bradford. This action was supported by Ayatollah Khomeini's *fatwa* against the author, the following month. Vertovec concludes that, 'thus, by 1990, albeit in a largely undesirable manner, Muslims had gained a firm place on the national political agenda'.[84]

As I will argue in chapter seven, it is important for religion to retain a public profile – even if it is known only for its notoriety – because its ongoing relevance and plausibility depends upon it remaining visible. Earlier, we noted Edmund Burke's (1729–1797) opinion that, 'Nothing is so fatal to religion as indifference', and invisibility invites indifference. Or, to put it differently, in a world where religion is most often politely ignored, there is no such thing as bad publicity.

---

[82] Davie, *Modern Europe*, 130f.

[83] X. Ternisien, 'L'appel commun des Eglises chrétiennes contre une loi sur la voile', *Le Monde* (9 Décembre 2003), 10.

[84] S. Vertovec, 'Muslims, the State, and the Public Sphere in Britain' in G. Nonneman, T. Niblock, and B. Szajkowski (eds.), *Muslim Communities in the New Europe* (Reading: Ithaca, 1996), 183.

Secularization: RIP?

The point of this extended chapter has been to survey a range of scenarios in which religion in Europe seems to have bucked the trend of secularization. These rather surprising facts are of interest to sociologists who may see them as nails in the coffin of secularization theory. They are also of interest to missiologists. If our concern is to restore credibility to the church, we need to understand what I am calling the 'dynamics of credibility'. As a first step in this exploration, this chapter has sought to uncover the dynamics of 'religion in modernity', those stubborn outcrops of dynamic religion that survive in the modern world.

So far I have not developed any of these scenarios into full-blown missiological proposals, although I have tried to illustrate ways in which missiological lessons might be learnt from them. In chapter seven I will expand on some of them, when I come to consider the dynamics of church in society.

This has been a first step – surveying the empirical evidence for the success of religion in modernity. We have simply looked at what there is 'out there'. In the next chapter, and beyond, I will consider *why* some forms of religion succeed. We will continue to think about the dynamics of credibility, but moving away from the idea of dynamic *forms* of religion in modernity, to 'dynamics' in the sense of the *inner workings* of credibility. How is credibility constructed and maintained? And what leads to its loss? The specific focus of the next chapter will be on the dynamics of *Christianity in consciousness*. How do Christian beliefs and values become lodged in consciousness? And how do they lose their foothold? By understanding these hidden dynamics, we will be better placed to shape a missiology which is capable of restoring credibility to the church – and to the timeless message she embodies.

5

Help Thou Mine Unbelief: Christianity in Consciousness

We saw in the previous chapter that religion is far from disappearing in the modern world, and that modern people are far from secular. Religion seems to pop up all over the place; in Peter Berger's evocative phrase, the world is 'dripping with reactionary supernaturalism'.[1] At the same time, in our contemporary world, believing has become paradoxical: people want to believe, but they cannot – or at least, not in a way they find satisfying. Time and again in conversations I have heard the refrain, 'I wish I could believe, but I can't.' Those who say this seem to acknowledge the value of Christian faith, and are even sympathetic to its truth claims, but somehow, their brain just won't do it. They cannot find it within themselves to believe. Often, on further discussion, it turns out that they suppose belief to involve some kind of suicidal 'leap of faith' which, against all reason, they must take in order to enter the guild of believers: reluctant to step off this imaginary precipice (quite rightly, in my view) they pace around the cliff-tops hoping to find another way down. Like the father of the tormented boy in Mark's Gospel[2] they tinker at the ragged edges of belief: one moment they say, 'I believe!' and the very next, 'Help thou mine unbelief!'

This experience draws attention to the fact that the processes by which we come to faith are not as simple as we may commonly assume. It is easy to assume, for example, that most people arrive at their religious beliefs after a simple examination of the relevant evidence. Given the evidence for the empty tomb and the resurrection appearances, it is a short step to believing that Christ has been raised from the dead. This has often been the assumption of Christian apologists and evangelists: if only they can convey their knock-down arguments for the truth of Christianity, their audience will be convinced. No doubt this does happen from time to time, but it is

[1] Berger, 'Desecularization', 4.
[2] Mark 9:24.

not the primary means by which people come to believe. No wonder, then, that someone can sit with all the evidence before them and find that their brain still draws a blank. They would like to believe, but somehow it just will not happen.

My main contention in this chapter is that the difficulty so many experience in finding (or keeping) faith is a consequence, not of gaps in the evidence, but of adverse *social* conditions. People require certain social and psychological structures to be in place in order for their beliefs to remain plausible to them; modernity undermines such structures, with the result that belief is hard to come by. To this extent, modernity may be thought of as a virus or disease that infects belief and drains it of vitality. If we can understand the ways in which these social and psychological structures operate, we are in a better position to construct 'vaccines' that are able to resist the debilitating effects of modernity. Perhaps, then, the church can in some measure become better inoculated against the cognitive diseases of the contemporary world.

Those who say, rather wistfully, 'I would like to believe', are unable to do so, then, because they inhabit a social and psychological context which is unsupportive of Christian belief. More than that, these contexts also promote the plausibility of alternative belief-systems – worldviews that compete with Christianity. It is not that my acquaintances believe nothing: rather, they tend to absorb whatever is in the atmosphere at the time. It so happens that in the modern world the pollutants we absorb from the prevailing factories of knowledge production are carried on the smog of liberal humanism. Those who hope for spiritual fulfilment must do so against a backdrop which insists at every turn that their longings are really only minority pursuits for the socially deviant. And if this is how those who would like to believe are made to feel, think how much more alienated from Christianity are the vast majority who are indifferent to the Christian story in the first place.

If credibility is to be restored to the church and her story, it is crucial that we try to understand how it is constructed in the first place; we must understand its dynamics. How does plausibility (or credibility) come about? How is it maintained? And how is it lost? If we are to heal the contemporary split between the truth of the Christian claim (which I take as axiomatic) and its plausibility for the church and the world, these are urgent questions to ask.

Before we proceed, let me be clear that in asking these questions, I am discussing only what constructs the subjective plausibility of Christianity and not its objective truth. It is because I believe in its objective truth that it concerns me when its subjective plausibility is undermined. Christianity is far less credible today than its credentials deserve. Its worldview has not been disproven, only discredited. Today, in the absence of the plausibility that Christian faith deserves, Christians are forced, quite literally, to believe the unbelievable; and so it is that they possess, in both senses of the phrase, incredible faith.

The outcome of the questions I have asked above has two direct applications. First, it should help us to organize church life in ways that nurture the plausibility of Christian faith. Secondly, it should also enable a greater appreciation of what might need to be done to give Christian faith a fairer hearing in the 'marketplace of ideas' – the contemporary equivalent of the Areopagus.[3] In short, if we can understand the dynamics of credibility, we are then in a position to try to construct and maintain the conditions that will cultivate credibility for the church and her story. In what follows, I will explore three ways in particular in which beliefs achieve and maintain plausibility for groups of people. I have called these 'the reasons of the head', 'the reasons of the heart', and 'the reasons of the home'.

The Reasons of the Head

The first reason why plausibility comes about is the operation of reason: we think ourselves into faith. We carefully sift the evidence, judiciously weigh the arguments and only then do we come to conclusions. Those conclusions are held as subjectively plausible beliefs. Conversely, we tend to think that beliefs arrived at in any other way are simply not worth holding. If we want to discredit another's belief, we can suggest that they only believe it because it suits them, or is fashionable, or is what they have been led to believe. When Isobel Kuhn put up her hand in class to admit she believed the Christian story, her professor responded, 'Oh, you just believe that because your papa and your mama told you so.'[4] In these ways, we can suggest that a person's beliefs are not valid because they are biased in some way; only if they can 'think for themselves', we suppose, do they have a right to their beliefs. Only reasoned beliefs are valid. Simple. This, at any rate, is how we like to think our beliefs have been achieved.

On closer inspection, however, this is too simple. Reason is not as innocent a basis for finding beliefs plausible as we might at first suppose; at times, it is downright duplicitous. For example, people may come to find beliefs plausible regardless of whether or not the

---

[3] See Acts 17:16f.
[4] I. Kuhn, *By Searching* (London: Overseas Missionary Fellowship, 1957), 9.

argument supporting them is valid. What matters for the construction of plausibility is that individuals perceive there to be a certain rightness to the reasons presented to them, not that they are able to recognize the difference between an argument that is logically valid and one that is not. Indeed, plausibility may be constructed on the basis of quite primitive and fragmentary logic, which, if extended, would end in nonsense. Since, however, common reason is not typically subjected to such scrutiny, a large number of false beliefs can remain plausible because of the logic that appears to underlie them.

Not all beliefs are equally at the mercy of plausible, but erroneous arguments, however. This is because truth is more likely to generate plausibility than falsehood. Positively, many of our true beliefs are reinforced so frequently in experience that their plausibility goes unquestioned. I believe that if I let go of an apple I am holding it will fall to the floor. This belief is confirmed so often in my daily experience of dropping things that its plausibility needs no further support. This simply cannot happen for false beliefs, unless our false beliefs have little empirical relevance. In this way, the empirical world continually intrudes on our beliefs, reinforcing some and casting doubt on others. Negatively, too, false beliefs are likely to be under 'pressure from real events'.[5] In other words, 'Truth does not always win out, but it has a head start, as it were.'[6] Reason is no guarantor of the marriage of truth and plausibility, but truth does have a way of keeping her husband faithful.

Apologetics

At this point, it may be worth considering the implications of what has just been said for the missioner most affected by the duplicity of reason – the Christian apologist. We have already seen that the apologist is the missiological thinker who, more than any others, places confidence in the avenue of human reason to bring people to faith. Some apologists will aim to 'argue people into faith', while others will adopt the more modest task of 'clearing away obstacles to faith', so that rational objections will not hinder the progress of the heart and the will. Either way, the apologist places great confidence in human reason as a means by which people may come to faith. If this is the case, what implications arise from the observation that reason is no guarantor of the marriage of truth and plausibility?

---

[5] J.T. Borhek and R.F. Curtis, *A Sociology of Belief* (New York, NY: John Wiley and Sons, 1975), 112.

[6] K. Dixon, *The Sociology of Belief* (London: Routledge and Kegan Paul, 1980), 129.

On the one hand, the apologist may discover that people are willing to believe his (or her) worst arguments with the same fervour as his best. In these circumstances, the apologist faces the peril of *credulity*. On the other hand, the same people may be willing to believe almost anything else, providing it 'seems logical'. Here, the apologist is up against the peril of *infidelity*. Overall, this indicates that many people will settle for a semblance of rational justification, if they are already well disposed towards the beliefs. Few people, after all, are trained in logic. The Christian apologist may therefore have to reckon with the fact that he may be giving some people excuses to believe, rather than reasons. He may also have to concede that his best arguments may have considerably less persuasive power over others than is merited by his careful elaboration of them.

Believing is a social activity

Reason, then, is not the pure basis for plausibility we might like it to be. It is enough for reason to provide us with the mere semblance of justification in order for us to believe. If this is one reason why we should not privilege reason over alternative bases for belief, another is that those alternative bases enshrine a principle that is as true for reason as it is for themselves: all thinking takes place in community. The lone thinker is a myth. The admission that I am a Christian because I grew up in a Christian family does not invalidate the faith of my family and, by that token, does not invalidate my faith. Isobel Kuhn may well have believed the Christian story just because her papa and her mama told her so, but is that such a bad reason to believe? Just because thinking takes place in community does not mean that it is irrational. All thinking takes place within a tradition of thought and one person's reasoning begins from a vantage point on the shoulders of previous thinkers. Even academics, who pride themselves on their 'academic freedom' – the freedom to follow evidence to its conclusion – acknowledge that their thinking takes place within an 'academic community'. An academic author who published an academic book with no references to the work of his colleagues would most likely be thought a plagiarizing egotist. Only rarely do exceptional thinkers manage to fly the cage of their own intellectual tradition and alight on a virgin field of thought. For most of the time, however, we think along lines inherited from older and better thinkers than ourselves. This does not necessarily invalidate our thinking: it merely invites us to examine its pedigree.

If our thinking is conditioned by a tradition of thought, it is also the case that our beliefs are conditioned by others' beliefs. Our beliefs are inherently social products; there are all sorts of ties that bind us to the beliefs of our community and make it very difficult to change our beliefs, even when reason whispers that we should. Furthermore, quite often we hold beliefs that we simply could not do without: we need them, regardless of their truth. The vast majority of people do not operate with the level of cognitive independence that would enable them to ignore these factors and, in consequence, the 'reasons of the head' are usually only ever supporting reasons for belief. They may be necessary for belief, but they are not the sole reason for it.[7] The missiological implications of these observations will be unpacked in the next two sections, as we consider what I have called the 'reasons of the heart' and the 'reasons of the home'.

If we are looking to restore credibility to the church and her story, it should be clear by now that merely offering good reasons to believe is not the simple solution it may at first appear. It is not simple because, as I have suggested, there are other more significant factors behind the construction of plausibility – factors we shall examine next. It is also not simple because, contrary to first impressions, reason can beguile us into finding as plausible beliefs which have no basis in truth. What this means is that reason is no more legitimate as a basis for constructing plausibility than are the reasons of the 'heart' and the 'home', which tend to work pre-rationally. What we might conclude from this is that the attempt to 'construct' plausibility – from any dynamic – is wholly unjustified, since it is bound to result in some kind of social engineering, emotional manipulation, or rhetorical hysteria.

This is, of course, a problem for all knowledge, and not only for Christian beliefs. Social reality helps to mould and construct what passes for knowledge in the whole of society, so that all knowledge is to some extent bound within particular social worlds. All knowledge is 'situated'. Secondly, we are quite familiar with the attempts of politicians, advertisers and sales people to engineer and manipulate our social world in order to gain credence. Politicians bribe us with tax cuts, advertisers bombard us with messages in every conceivable medium, and sales people manipulate language in order to disguise. Far from being a neutral sphere of activity, then, social worlds are arenas of conflict, in which vested interests struggle to define what counts as knowledge in society. Most of the time, we simply accept this situation. This does not make it right – as Lesslie Newbigin reminds us, our 'manner of speaking the truth must not be aligned to the techniques of modern propaganda'[8] – but it does mean we have a duty to be as wise as serpents as we attempt to speak our wisdom.

---

[7] Borhek and Curtis, *Sociology*, 85, 121.
[8] Newbigin, *Gospel*, 229.

From a missiological point of view, then, to ignore all this is simply naïve. Churches are also interested in defining reality in a particular way. From an ethical point of view, they may wish to repudiate many of the techniques and strategies of the political and commercial sectors. They remain, however, in the arena. If their definition of reality is to gain any chance of a hearing, they have to take seriously the reality of power and competition in the market-place of meanings. This means that it is not enough to sharpen our apologetics and enter the arena wielding some clever intellectual tools. We have to try to understand the full range of reasons why people find this or that meaning plausible. As Peter Vardy comments, 'You do not get someone saying, "Well, I thought there was a 68 per cent chance that God exists but I've just read an article in *The Philosophers' Magazine* which has increased the probability to 71 per cent so I'm off to be a Jesuit."'[9] We have to look beyond the reasons of the head, to the social and psychological determinants of belief. In short, if we are to compete in the crowded marketplace of meanings, we have to learn two additional factors: the 'reasons of the heart' and the 'reasons of the home'.

The Reasons of the Heart

A second explanation for the plausibility of beliefs, then, concerns the 'reasons of the heart'. Sometimes beliefs, and the community that embody them, acquire plausibility because they are able to resolve the needs of an individual. For some, the need is not for the beliefs of the community as such; what matters are the benefits received from membership of the community.[10] For example, churches very often attract people who feel lonely or in need of support, for whom worship is merely a way to belong. For others, it is the beliefs themselves that meet the needs of an individual and group membership is merely a way of appropriating those beliefs. For example, a young person seeking to make sense of the world may join a political or religious group in order to find meaning. In both of these cases, it is their ability to resolve the needs of the individual that renders the community and its beliefs plausible.

Faith communities may be able to meet all kinds of need – and thereby derive plausibility – in this way. As we saw earlier, Nigel Scotland identifies seven reasons why adherents of sectarian forms of religion find them attractive: they offer a definite moral code,

---

[9] Quoted in *Third Way* 27.2 (2004), 5.
[10] M. Argyle and B. Beit-Hallahmi, *The Psychology of Behaviour, Belief and Belonging* (London: Routledge, 1997), 125.

identity, community, certainty, the immediacy of experience, char- ismatic authority and a sense of mission.[11] In what follows, I will examine just three such needs – for identity, community and meaning – to illustrate in more depth how the 'reasons of the heart' may supply strong plausibility to religious beliefs and institutions.

The need for identity

Who are you? The way we answer this question is likely to depend on who is asking us. I was once asked this question by a detective. I was visiting a hospital to accompany two students on their way to confirm the identity of a friend who had died in an accident. I answered, 'I am the College chaplain.' When the Registrar asked me the same question when I went to register the birth of my daughter, I replied differently: 'I am the father.' If I ask myself the question, I will hear a different answer again. Identities are complex and multi- faceted, but what seems clear is that we cannot do without them. For most people, it is profoundly unsettling if our sense of identity is disrupted – if we lose a job, a breast, a partner.

If the need for identity is perennial, our consciousness of it is a peculiar product of modernity. The idea that we can choose or change our identity is a relatively novel one.[12] Prior to the Reforma- tion in Europe, religious identities were ascribed to the individual through the processes of socialization and the options for a change of identity thereafter were extremely limited. The ongoing, unproblematic socialization of successive generations into religious commitment could be explained in terms of the general need for identity within a sacred society.

Modernity, by contrast, forces identity choices upon the emerg- ing adult.[13] While identities may be constructed and reconstructed over an entire lifetime, religious identities tend to be chosen fairly early on. It has often been observed, for example, that those who join New Religious Movements are young, frequently between the ages of sixteen and twenty-four. At this stage of adolescence and early adulthood, young people are typically building cognitive systems to make sense of the world, seeking security and, most of all, developing an individual adult identity.[14] For others, religious belief is not a solution to the developmental crises of adolescence, but to the *permanent* identity crisis inflicted by modernity. James Hunter interprets the plausibility of New Religious Movements in

[11] Scotland, *Sectarian Religion*, 292f.
[12] Argyle and Beit-Hallahmi, *Psychology*, 138.
[13] Berger, *Heretical Imperative*, 11.
[14] Argyle and Beit-Hallahmi, *Psychology*, 116.

this way: they represent an 'anthropological protest' against the dehumanizing tendencies of modernity.[15]

The need for identity definitions, whether during childhood socialization, during the adolescent search for identity, or during an adult's conversion experience, is one explanation why a faith community may appear to be a plausible option to the individual. It helps to define the individual and ascribe an identity to him or her.

The Christian churches have long supplied identity to their worshippers, ensuring ongoing commitment. The very divisions between Protestant and Catholic, establishment and dissent, have provided the categories by which different kinds of Christian have been able to identify themselves. The rise of denominations provided a similar set of categories for identity: Baptist, Methodist, Quaker, Anglican, Presbyterian, and so on. More recently, the tendency has been to identify along party lines. Worshippers may class their liturgical preferences in terms of 'low', 'central', or 'high', and their theology as 'Pentecostal/charismatic', 'evangelical', 'liberal', or 'catholic' – or combinations of these. These variables alone mean that a very large number of options are available to shade and colour the style of churches and the identities of their members.

Theorists of postmodernity claim that the contemporary self has become 'decentred', so that identity is no longer something essential and given at the core of a person.[16] Instead, identities are now self-consciously made and remade over the course of a lifetime.[17] People 'reinvent' themselves. This means that there is greater fluidity in the identities that individuals are willing to ascribe to themselves than previously. In terms of religious identities, it means that people will more easily move in and out of churches and shift allegiances between denominations than in the past. Perhaps there is no more allegiance to particular denominations today than there is to specific fast-food outlets or particular brands of supermarket.

Nevertheless, the decision to start or stop going to church is still an identity choice as well as being a change in practice. For many, the attraction of Christian commitment lies in the identity conferred by the choice: whether one chooses to be 'churchgoer', 'convert', 'Christian', 'member', 'adherent', or whatever. Churches offer their members identity, and this is part of their attraction: 'You are a chosen people, a royal priesthood, a holy nation, a people belonging

---

[15] Hunter, 'New Religions', 108.

[16] J.R. Middleton and B.J. Walsh, *Truth is Stranger than it Used to Be: Biblical Faith in a Postmodern Age* (London: SPCK, 1995).

[17] D. Lyon, *Postmodernity* (Buckingham: Open University Press, 1994), 60.

to God … Once you were not a people, but now you are the people of God.'[18]

The need for community

Allied to the need for identity is the need for community. Identity is formed in the mirror of others' definitions of who we are.[19] Only in the context of belonging within some social group can we come to an understanding of our own identity.

When an individual is deprived of a sense of belonging within a community, this unmet need may lead the person to seek belonging within a particular social group. The religious group may be particularly conducive to meeting this need, as it offers not just belonging, but a sense of purpose and even a whole universe of meaning within which the convert's new identity and purpose make sense. Radical political or activist groups may function similarly. Empirically, James Borhek and Richard Curtis have observed that groups which set out to recruit converts may appeal particularly to those who suffer social isolation or dissatisfaction with interpersonal relationships, since such people are especially receptive.[20] Similarly, Michael Argyle and Benjamin Beit-Hallahmi cite studies of Jewish converts in Israel, Hare Krishna converts in America, and US televangelists, all of which found a high incidence of loss or absence of parents and of some kind of crisis preceding conversion. They concluded that, 'Individuals who have few personal ties to others and a weak sense of identification with family and friends are more likely to develop salvation careers.'[21]

These studies are concerned only with converts, who may have suffered particular social isolation. The fact is, however, that virtually everyone needs to belong within some kind of community. There is a very big difference between being in prison and being in solitary confinement. The human quest for community runs very deep. The need for community means that many will be attracted to churches because they provide ready-made communities of welcome. For them, Christianity is not a plausible option because it is true, but because it works in their experience. They find that there really is a new community of love. These are not the reasons of the head, but the reasons of the heart.

In a world of increasing isolation, the churches' potential for meeting these needs should not be underestimated. In many

---

[18] 1 Peter. 2:9–10, NIV.
[19] Berger and Luckmann, *Construction*, 44.
[20] Borhek and Curtis, *Sociology*, 96.
[21] Argyle and Beit-Hallahmi, *Psychology*, 119.

communities, the church is the only significant association and certainly the largest voluntary body. While it is true that most church
denominations have shrunk in recent decades, in many instances
they have not shrunk as fast as other communal associations (political parties, for example) and for this reason they remain important.
Their importance is also underlined by the increasing atomization
of social life: people's lives are becoming more solitary. For
example, according to the Office for National Statistics, between
1971 and 2000 average household size fell from 2.91 to 2.30
persons. Over the same thirty-year period, the proportion of one-
person households almost doubled from 17 to 32 per cent. Within
the 16–59 age group, the proportion has more than trebled (5 to 16
per cent). Similarly, the proportion of families headed by a lone
mother rose from 7 to 23 per cent. Today, it has become a commonplace lament that you are more likely to get to know a stranger in an
internet chat-room in California than you are to meet your neigh-
bour two doors down. High levels of geographical mobility, and the
expansion of buy-to-let housing, mean that many localities experience a constant turnover of people which is corrosive of
community.

   None of this has eroded the basic human desire to belong. No
doubt people find ways to compensate. Community based on geographical locale has given way to 'networks'. As Richard Tiplady
puts it, 'geography is history'.[22] Whether free-floating networks of
relationship can provide the same satisfaction as a community
rooted in a common place is an open question – but personally, I
doubt it.

   We have already seen that churches offer higher than average
levels of 'social capital' (networks of supportive relationships). As
voluntary organizations they are uniquely placed in society as
potential communities of welcome, depending on how they choose
to operate. There are many examples of good practice.[23] Churches,
as communities, may therefore attract plausibility as options for
belonging in the atomized society of late modernity.

The need for meaning
Plausibility may also be generated for beliefs on account of the
human need for meaning. This should be distinguished from the

---

[22] R. Tiplady, *World of Difference: Global Mission at the Pic 'n' Mix Counter* (Carlisle: Paternoster, 2003), 5.
[23] See, for example, S. Chalke and T. Jackson, *Faithworks 2: Stories of Hope* (Eastbourne: Kingsway, 2001); J. Hinton, *Changing Churches: Building Bridges in Local Mission* (London: Churches Together in Britain and Ireland, 2002).

rational pursuit of truth discussed above. Although the search for meaning may involve the rational pursuit of knowledge, at root it is a psychological need, rather than an intellectual quest. Different personalities seem to feel this need to varying degrees. In their attempts to account for conversion, social psychologists have sometimes disregarded the human quest for meaning altogether. By contrast, others have insisted that converts do define themselves as seekers who are dissatisfied with the answers they have hitherto received. Roger Straus, for example, criticizes the 'passivist paradigm', and proposes an alternative which treats conversion as the accomplishment of an actively strategizing seeker.[24] Argyle and Beit-Hallahmi also recognize the element of 'cognitive quest' which lies behind some conversions and, as we have seen, they attribute this questing mainly to adolescents and certainly to those no older than about thirty.[25]

Some people, then, may cling to certain beliefs because they provide an island of meaning in a sea of chaos and confusion. These beliefs are credible to them – not because they are ripe for rational justification – but because they provide an immediate resolution to the threat of bewilderment. For some, the anxious need for meaning – any kind of meaning – may overwhelm the task of evaluating critically the truth of particular claims. Where cognitive security is the dominant concern, certainties may be bought at any price – often at the price of intellectual freedom. An immature, urgent and compulsive need for a total explanation for everything may drive some people to find particular belief-systems plausible, particularly those which seem to have tied up all the 'loose ends'. The quest for meaning then becomes a quest for certainty.

For others, however, the search for meaning need not take the form of a feverish search for cognitive security. These may be more content to live with unanswered questions, puzzles and mysteries; they are unwilling to generate 'pat' answers in the absence of ones they can honestly believe. Churches that are able to accompany and resource such seekers on their journey will hold considerable attraction. Their plausibility as options for belonging will be supported to the extent that they are able to meet this human need.

Those who are attracted to churches because they are able to resolve the need for identity, belonging or meaning are not there under false pretences. Theologically, the benefits of identity, belonging and meaning do not supplant the gospel as reasons to

---

[24] R.A. Straus, 'Religious Conversion as a Personal and Collective Accomplishment', *Sociological Analysis* 40.2 (1979), 158.
[25] Argyle and Beit-Hallahmi, *Psychology*, 115.

belong; instead, they are part of its intrinsic benefits. For this reason, we need not fear that the gospel is made plausible only by association with churches that really attract members for other reasons – the reasons of the heart. Instead, the reasons of both head and heart combine to present a comprehensive and credible case for the truth of Christianity. A religion of mere propositions and logic, devoid of the emotional and human dimension must, in the end, be spurious.

In sum, the reasons of head and heart combine in the construction of religious plausibility. We turn now to the third of our trio of reasons for the ongoing plausibility of Christian faith, which I have termed the 'reasons of the home'.

The Reasons of the Home

The 'reasons of the home' is tidy shorthand which fits alongside the 'head' and the 'heart'; but shorthand can be misleading. What the 'home' really represents is the full complement of social structures in society that help to generate plausibility for beliefs. The home is only one of them.

I began this chapter by drawing attention to the plight of those who would like to believe but feel unable to do so. I suggested that people require certain social and psychological structures to be in place in order for their beliefs to remain plausible to them. If those structures are not in place, however much they might like to believe, in practice it becomes very difficult for them to do so. Believing becomes rather like trying to learn a foreign language in the absence of anyone else who speaks it. I further suggested that modernity undermines such structures, so that in the modern situation, belief becomes inaccessible, or at the very least, debilitated by the 'virus' of modernity.

In the remainder of this chapter I will lay out an understanding of the way in which religious plausibility is more or less determined by social structure. It will become clear that I think this particular explanation for religious plausibility is more significant than either the 'reasons of the head' or the 'reasons of the heart' outlined above, although these secondary accounts do provide a necessary context to what follows.

In this account, I will be drawing upon the sociology of knowledge developed by Peter Berger and Thomas Luckmann in the 1960s,[26] and upon Berger's subsequent application of their theories to the specific question of religious knowing.[27] In the process, I will

---

[26] Berger and Luckmann, *Construction*.
[27] Berger, *Sacred Canopy*.

also modify and augment their insights using the cognitive sociology of Eviatar Zerubavel.[28]

The sacred canopy

Berger coined the term 'the sacred canopy' to describe the way in which, in pre-modern societies, religion provided an overarching explanation for the whole of social reality. In medieval Europe, for example, religion was not an 'interest' or a 'preference', but rather a framework for making everything meaningful. In Berger's words, 'religion is the audacious attempt to conceive of the entire universe as being humanly significant'.[29] Religion in medieval Europe was no more a 'private preference' than gravity or democracy is for us today.

According to Berger, modernity rent the sacred canopy asunder. Like the temple curtain in Jerusalem, or the curtain that hid the Wizard of Oz, the sacred canopy was parted to reveal a world that was, it seemed, far more mundane than had been imagined. The medieval world was a world enchanted with saints and angels and spirits; it pulsated with mystery, miracle and magic. The holy of holies lay deep in every well and high on every hill. The modern world, by contrast, is a world that has suffered disenchantment.[30] Nature has ceased to be full of numinous powers and has become explicable in terms of a closed, mechanistic system. Humans have ceased to think of themselves as being bound within the 'givenness' of their natural and social worlds, and subject to the disadvantages of both. Instead, they have developed an attitude towards nature and society of confidence in their own human ability to master, control, manipulate and determine the shape of the natural world and the society in which they live. The natural, political and social sciences have been bequeathed to us as the tools of this endeavour.

With the gradual collapse of the sacred canopy, religious 'worlds' were forced to shrink. No longer did religious institutions and symbols legitimate the social order in total, but became limited to the maintenance of their own specifically religious worlds: as the marquee of religious meaning collapsed, people were forced to huddle under umbrellas. At this point, Berger has two important observations to make. The first is that modernity signals the shift

---

[28] E. Zerubavel, *Social Mindscapes: An Invitation to Cognitive Sociology* (London: Harvard University Press, 1997).

[29] Berger, *Sacred Canopy*, 28.

[30] The theme of disenchantment, and the accompanying rationalization of social life, was developed by Max Weber. See, for example, Gerth and Wright Mills (eds.) *From Max Weber*.

from one, unified religious world, to many, competing ones. Religion in modernity is inescapably *plural*. The second is that the subjective reality of each of these competing religious worlds cannot be taken for granted, as the medieval religious world had been, but must be deliberately constructed and maintained – umbrellas need to be held. Religion in modernity is inescapably *precarious*. Religious worlds need to be created and maintained in an ongoing way, otherwise their reality will crumble and they will give way to competitors.

Berger contends that the maintenance of religious worlds (indeed, all 'social life-worlds') depends upon three factors in particular. The first of these is the presence of viable *plausibility structures*. As we saw in chapter three, a plausibility structure is the social base required for the maintenance of subjective reality. Examples include the communities of school, church, workplace, peer group, and home. In addition to such visible communities, Berger's notion may be extended to include the virtual, or imagined, communities of those who think along similar lines. Examples here include the 'mnemonic', 'optical' and 'visionary' communities of those who (respectively) remember, attend and imagine in similar ways. In other words, plausibility is generated not only within concrete groups of people who share the same reality definitions, but also among those whose thinking is streamlined in particular ways, whether or not such people ever meet.

The second factor in the maintenance of religious worlds is the efficacy of the *processes of world maintenance*. If worlds are to remain real, they have to be renewed from generation to generation, through the process of socialization. In addition, they must be sustained over time through a process Berger terms 'conversation'.

Finally, religious worlds require legitimation. Every reality definition (religious or not) has to be explicable in its own terms, as well as having sufficiently robust defences in order to withstand attacks from competing versions of reality. These are what *legitimations* provide. Legitimations represent the cognitive dimension of world maintenance that are circulated within plausibility structures.

These three factors now require elucidation if we are to understand more fully the ways in which social structure constructs plausibility for beliefs – the dynamics of credibility. By understanding these dynamics more fully, we are better placed to develop a missiology capable of restoring credibility to the church. Only once these dynamics have been unpacked can we turn to consider ways in which the churches can learn to respond to the social context of believing.

Plausibility structures

The principle that local contexts define what counts as knowledge has long been observed. The medieval Islamic scholar, Al Ghazzali (d. 1111), noticed that those born in Muslim countries grow up to be Muslim, while those born in Christian countries grow up to be Christian. Similarly, Blaise Pascal (1623–1662) observed (with some distaste) that the same proposition might represent, 'Truth on this side of the Pyrenees, error on that.'[31] In other words, the local context supplies plausibility to its beliefs. Likewise, Emile Durkheim (1858–1917) noted that, 'We are aware of how much force a belief or sentiment may acquire merely because they are experienced within a single community of people in contact with one another … identical states of consciousness, intermingling with one another, strengthen one another.'[32]

Although the observation that local contexts define what counts as knowledge is hardly new, Berger and Luckmann may be credited with giving those local contexts a name: 'plausibility structures'.[33] I have suggested above that plausibility structures may be physical communities, as Berger sees them, or they may take the form of 'virtual' or 'imagined' communities. I will begin, then, with Berger's concrete conception, and deal with imagined communities second.

Concrete structures: home, school, church, work

Two basic functions are performed by the plausibility structure: *cohesion* and *exclusion*. The structure forms, in a sense, the 'walls' around the faith community, which may physically contain the believers and their beliefs,[34] and also filter out or exclude threatening influences from beyond the structure.[35]

Cohesion can take a variety of forms. It may refer to social cohesion among members, in terms of the strength of their commitment to one another, or the presence of significant others with whom strong affective bonds are forged. It may also refer to the cohesion among beliefs, that is, the extent to which members share the same 'cognitive subculture',[36] or the extent to which their beliefs comprise a coherent whole. Undoubtedly, one may lead to the other.

---

[31] B. Pascal, *Pascal's Pensees* (London: Routledge and Kegan Paul, 1950), quoted in W. Stark, *The Sociology of Knowledge* (London: Routledge and Kegan Paul, 1958), 178.

[32] E. Durkheim, *The Division of Labor in Society* (New York, NY: Free Press, 1964), 55.

[33] Berger and Luckmann, *Construction*, 174; Berger, *Sacred Canopy*, 45.

[34] Berger, *Sacred Canopy*, 178.

[35] Borhek and Curtis, *Sociology*, 43.

[36] Zerubavel, *Mindscapes*, 12.

Borhek and Curtis, for example, have observed that cohesion among members may lead to cohesion among beliefs, since learning a belief-system within a plausibility structure is accompanied by the reward of approval and the punishment of disapproval. In this way, differences become ironed out.[37]

Cohesion may be promoted in other ways, too. At one extreme, cults have been known to promote regression among members as a way of creating cohesion through creating dependence upon significant others.[38] Others have observed the importance of 'intensive interaction' in facilitating conversion.[39] At the other end, in less socially deviant groups, cohesion may happen more by accident, as like-minded believers develop friendships and become committed to one another, and to one another's beliefs.

Cohesion of beliefs may also be achieved through legitimating practices such as apologetics, which seek to demonstrate the inner rationality of belief systems in the face of competition. Likewise, cohesion of both beliefs and relationships may be facilitated through living in community.[40] Indeed, community may perform a 'cognitive survival function' for socially deviant groups.[41]

The same structures which contain also exclude. Borhek and Curtis use the language of entanglement and encapsulation to describe these two processes. Entanglement promotes cohesion through increasing members' dependence on the structure, while encapsulation involves the exclusion of information or contacts from outside which might invalidate the beliefs of members.

Two strategies of exclusion (or encapsulation) involve isolation and insulation. Isolation may involve physical separation, social separation, or censorship. Religious communities that live apart from 'the world', have limited interaction with outside contacts, and lack access to the usual media of television or newspapers, are able to benefit (cognitively) from their isolation. Insulation, by contrast, does not rely on physical isolation, but rather on legitimations

---

[37] Borhek and Curtis, *Sociology*, 100; T. Robbins, *Cults, Converts and Charisma: the Sociology of New Religious Movements* (London: Sage, 1988), 47.

[38] D.A. Halperin, *Psychodynamic Perspectives on Religion, Sect and Cult* (Boston, MA: J. Wright, PSG Inc., 1983), 227f.

[39] A.L. Greil and D.R. Rudy, 'What have we Learned from Process Models of Conversion? An Examination of Ten Studies' *Sociological Focus*, 17.4 (1984), 306–23.

[40] J. Lofland and R. Stark, 'Becoming a World-Saver: A Theory of Conversion to Deviant Perspective' *American Sociological Review* 30 (1965), 862–75.

[41] Hunter, *New Religions: Demodernization*, 112.

which discredit hostile beliefs. For example, if group members are told that the world 'out there' is evil, and doomed to destruction, then its views need not be taken very seriously.[42] Both these strategies are intended to ensure that members and their beliefs are encapsulated within the structure, through the exclusion of threats from without.[43] The plausibility structure, therefore, not only promotes plausibility, but protects plausibility through strict boundary control.[44] Not all plausibility structures are equally efficient. Indeed, some are quite weak, lacking both cohesion, and the power of exclusion. Where insulation or isolation from the outside world breaks down, particularly among socially deviant groups, disillusionment can quickly occur.[45]

While plausibility structures offer a neat theoretical explanation for the persistence of belief, the situation of late modernity in practice has created an extremely complex situation in which we might search in vain for one single example of such a structure. In particular, the *plurality* of plausibility structures, the *fluidity of their boundaries*, and their *degree of overlap* threaten to undermine all such structures.

First, the plurality of plausibility structures increases competition between them. The greater the competition, the harder it is for any one plausibility structure to maintain a sense of reality taken-for-granted for its participants, since the availability of other options presents a continual challenge. In this way, pluralism issues in a 'crisis of credibility'.[46] Secondly, in practice the 'walls' of such structures are far more fluid than Berger and Luckmann's model suggests, which makes the task of cohesion and exclusion very difficult. Parents may lose control of their children's values to schools, schools to peer groups, peer groups to the mass media, and so on. As I suggested in chapter three, a more accurate term might be 'plausibility shelters' – derived from the image of the bus shelter, which has some walls and a makeshift roof, but is less than watertight! Thirdly, contemporary people inhabit a bewildering multiplicity of such shelters and move freely from one to another on a global scale. What seems plausible in the family, the workplace, or in the mass media, may vary widely between one context and another.

What this amounts to is the necessity of avoiding a simplistic account of plausibility structures. Clearly, they do contribute as

[42] Borhek and Curtis, *Sociology*, 71, 105.
[43] E. Barker, *New Religious Movements* (London: HMSO, 1989), 79–81.
[44] Robbins, *Cults*, 83.
[45] S.A. Wright, *Leaving Cults: The Dynamics of Defection* (Washington, DC: Society for the Scientific Study of Religion, 1987).
[46] Berger, *Sacred Canopy*, 126.

'shelters' to belief, enabling the limited construction of plausibility through their modest powers of cohesion and exclusion. However, in practice they are unlikely to exist in an undiluted form.

Virtual structures: communities of memory, attention and imagination

Berger and Luckmann's concrete conception of plausibility structures may be extended to embrace a range of virtual or 'imagined' communities[47] which are also able to construct plausibility for belief. These are found not only in the home, church, school, or workplace, but in less visible clusters of like minds, such as may be found among environmentalists, feminists, New Agers, or political party members. What unites these virtual communities are their common ways of thinking about, and seeing, the world. Eviatar Zerubavel has coined the term 'thought community' to describe them. Three thought communities in particular may be identified around the cognitive categories of *memory*, *attention* and *imagination*, which form a temporal sequence. A group of people united around a common memory Zerubavel terms a 'mnemonic community.' Similarly, he describes a group whose attention has been streamlined to focus in similar ways as an 'optical community'. He does not deal with the category of imagination as such; however, the imagination seems to be an important component in the construction of religious plausibility, and for that reason I include those who share a common imaginative scope under the heading of the 'visionary community'. Adherence to these imagined communities streamlines the ways in which we think. And the ways that we think – what we remember, how we focus attention and what we imagine – all influence what we find it plausible to believe.

1. Mnemonic communities

How then are our *memories* maintained as plausible? This occurs chiefly through the fact that we participate in various mnemonic communities which form the plausibility structure around our individual memories.[48] They help to influence both the content and the meaning of our memories. The content of our memory is influenced by the way in which our mnemonic community selects certain experiences to loom larger than others as we recollect the past. Many people can remember where they were on hearing the news of the death of John F. Kennedy, but are unable to remember where they

---

[47] For the origin of the term, see, B. Anderson, *Imagined Communities: Reflections on the Origin and Spread of Nationalism* (London: Verso, 1991).
[48] Zerubavel, *Mindscapes*, 19.

were last Tuesday. Likewise, the meaning of our memories is influenced by the interpretations placed on them by those whose mnemonic community we share. The fledgling Orangeman is taught that the seventeenth-century Battle of the Boyne was a providential victory for Protestantism; this 'memory' in turn gives plausibility to the claims of the Orange Order to continue to practise their marching rituals on the Lower Ormeau Road.

Such meanings may be communicated to us overtly or indirectly through the choice of language, symbol and ritual by which we 'learn' the memory, particularly when the memory in question predates our own biography.[49] As we participate in the living memories of those older than us, we learn to 'remember' the gunpowder plot, the trenches, or the first lunar landing. But we are taught to remember not only the fact of these events, but also their significance, since their significance becomes embedded in the ritual, symbol or language which is used to teach us. The rituals of Guy Fawkes' night were not originally intended to provide a lesson in mere historical fact, but to remind everyone of the legitimacy and power of the (Protestant) religious and political order. The symbol of the poppy on Remembrance Sunday does not only remind us of war, but of the costly horror of war. Neil Armstrong did not merely set foot on alien soil, but took a 'giant leap for mankind'. These mnemonic devices legitimate certain meanings ascribed to the events they signify.

Since these mediators of a common memory carry such significance, it is unsurprising that they are often contested, as conflicting mnemonic communities vie for attention. Language is a prime example of such a contested arena, since the choice of language and the constraints of its meanings often determine the significance of the memory which is being mediated. The adoption of 'African American' to designate the ethnic origins of some North American citizens is one example of the deliberate use of language in the contest for a particular interpretation of a common memory. Such a designation is intended to dignify the status of this ethnic group by reminding the hearer that these people have a noble history prior to their treatment as slaves and second-class citizens.

Where the significance of public memories is contested, winners and losers are likely to emerge. Those who win stand to gain not only the dominant interpretation of history, but also the benefits which flow from this. For example, the idea that Columbus *discovered* the New World is seen as nonsense to the Native American. As Native Americans have gradually advanced their case over a

---

[49] Zerubavel, *Mindscapes*, 7; Berger and Luckmann, *Construction*, 84.

European interpretation of American history, their claim to power, land and rights has been strengthened.

Those who lose this battle face the relegation of their story from the league table of memories which are part of the common stock of the 'history' of a society. One example of the apparent loss of such a memory is the conflict between the Christian story and the story of evolution in the latter half of the nineteenth century. Western history is no longer interpreted in terms of creation and providence, but in terms of evolution and the triumph of human reason over nature.

Andrew Walker describes the condition of the gradual forgetting of the Christian story in British culture in terms of 'gospel amnesia'.[50] Similarly, Danièlle Hervieu-Léger describes European countries as 'amnesiac societies'.[51] The creeping loss of Christian meanings from various sectors of society points to this growing amnesia. Where the language, the symbols and the ritual which mediated the Christian story have been forgotten, or ransacked, the story is eclipsed and loses plausibility. Christian meanings are gradually unwoven from the warp and weft of culture, such that the story is uprooted and forced into competition with rivals for a place in the corporate memory. This obfuscation of the Christian story denudes it of plausibility, since it becomes an increasingly alien interpretation of our common history.

2. Optical communities

Social memories, then, are carried by particular mnemonic communities which function as plausibility structures for the meanings ascribed to those memories. If the mnemonic community is one kind of plausibility structure rooted in human consciousness, a second kind of plausibility structure is the 'optical community', the community which influences the scope of our *attention*.[52] What we attend to helps to determine what we find it plausible to believe. Since our attention is limited in time and space, whatever wins our attention gains important access to our thinking and thereby gains an advantage over its excluded competitors. It wins the 'market share'. Various optical communities will socialize participants into different ways of focussing their attention. The Protestant sects who once insisted on strict Sabbath observance understood this well. The prohibitions on card games, theatre-going, reading novels, and so on, were probably not based on a belief in the intrinsic evil of such pastimes, but rather on the fact that all forms of entertainment

---

[50] A. Walker, *Telling the Story* (London: SPCK, 1996), 48.
[51] Hervieu-Léger, *Chain of Memory*.
[52] Zerubavel, *Mindscapes*, 32.

were a distraction from attending to the serious business of true religion. They were rivals for attention. Entertainment could not be allowed to take over, since a tacit message would be communicated that religion was no longer important or relevant. Furthermore, only by insisting that space was made in the week for attending to one's soul could the sense of the immediacy of God's presence and the centrality of his claim over the lives of worshippers be plausibly maintained.

By contrast, where a movement has lost the attention of its public, it begins to drop out of sight and lose plausibility. This is because the message implied in a movement's recession from view is that it is no longer relevant, important, or true. For example, the claims advanced by the temperance societies may be as relevant today as they were in the nineteenth century (alcohol abuse is on the rise), but the invisibility of this movement today makes these claims implausible.

Attention is an issue particularly for those within faith communities. These face the demands of the host culture, on the one hand, and those of the faith community, on the other. Both contexts demand attention and the competition is most acute where ideologies conflict. In order to maintain a plausible faith it is often necessary to take steps which ensure that the faith in question is appropriately attended to. The teaching of Arabic and the Qur'an to young Muslim boys out of school hours is one example of this kind of strategy.

Action may equally be taken to prevent undue attention being given to the host culture. Samuel Heilman, for example, observes among the Orthodox Jews of North America the deliberate diversion of attention from discrepant situations in the host culture.[53] He observes two strategies: one of *inattention*, where one is aware of what goes on outside the faith community but does not get involved, and another of *disattention*, which represents a more active withdrawal of attention from the grey zone outside one's own circle. Similarly, Stuart McFarland has pointed to strategies of 'selective exposure' and 'selective avoidance' as means by which believers may maintain their beliefs against challenges to faith, particularly from the mass media.[54]

---

[53] S.C. Heilman, 'Constructing Orthodoxy' in T. Robbins and D. Anthony (eds.), *In Gods We Trust: New Patterns of Religious Pluralism in America* (London: Transaction Books, 1981), 153.

[54] S. McFarland, 'Keeping the Faith: the Roles of Selective Exposure and Avoidance in Maintaining Religious Beliefs' in D.A. Stout and J.M. Buddenbaum (eds.), *Religion and Mass Media* (London: Sage, 1996), 173–82.

Mnemonic and optical communities, therefore, function as plausibility structures which give credence to the particular interpretations of reality which they promote. They influence the way in which their members interpret their collective and individual memories, and the way in which they focus their attention in the world. Dissent from these norms is not easy and can entail the risk of social exclusion or ostracism. Minority faith communities may have to work hard to ensure that the plausibility structures of their 'mnemonic' and 'optical' communities are sufficiently boundaried to maintain their interpretations of the past and the present.

3. Visionary communities

Finally, the way we *imagine* the future may also condition the plausibility of beliefs. The plausibility structure which underlies what we imagine as a plausible scenario is the 'visionary community', the community of like minds who envision the future, or some hidden realm, in similar ways. The visionary community may comprise the collectivity of those who adhere to one particular vision of the future, as in the various political utopias that emerged as plausible futures in Europe in the past two centuries. Equally, it may refer to a collectivity that shares an other-worldly vision of the future, or a particular vision of the super-empirical world.

Much of the social world that we take entirely for granted is not accessible to our senses, but must be grasped by our imagination. In this sense, we all possess to some degree what C. Wright Mills termed 'the sociological imagination'.[55] We cannot literally *see* interest rates rising. We cannot smell an act of parliament that has newly become law. Nor can we touch what is reported on the radio. We cannot taste the public sphere, nor hear the collapse of the sacred canopy. All of these social 'facts' have to be imagined.

The way we imagine them is crucial. Imagination is open to a far higher degree of interpretation than sensory experience. If I hear ringing and you do not, it may be that I am suffering tinnitus, or that you are going deaf. But with a simple piece of equipment, we can settle the matter. With imagination, things are different. One group of people may imagine that the world is populated by angels and spirits, acting on a whim; another group may imagine the world is part of a naturalistic universe entirely bound within the rules of causality. There is no simple piece of equipment that can settle the matter. What seems plausible within one 'visionary community'

_____

[55] C. Wright Mills, *The Sociological Imagination* (New York, NY: Oxford University Press, 1959).

seems entirely implausible within the other, and vice versa. The 'vice versa' is all important, because it is not the case that the group imagining a supernatural universe have all the work to do, while the naturalists merely have to look around them at what exists. Far from it, the naturalists have to *imagine* the world as a closed, uninterrupted 'machine' every bit as much as the supernaturalists imagine it to be populated by spiritual beings.

Viewed in this light, the collapse of the sacred canopy involves not only the loss of a particular style of thinking about the world: it also requires that the world is *re-imagined* as an autonomous, secular sphere. Secularism is not the default position when Christianity retreats, any more than paganism is – indeed, rather less so. The secular sphere had to be imagined before it could be realized, every bit as much as the theological realm had been imagined (not invented) in response to the foundational events of the Christian story.[56] It was but one step from imagining an autonomous, secular sphere, to the secularist claim that this sphere contains the whole of reality. The visionary community who imagines this sphere of all-embracing secularity constitutes one particular plausibility structure; the visionary community of the church comprises another, competing, structure. Participation in either will help to determine what we find it plausible to believe.

In sum, the ways we remember, focus our attention and imagine are influenced by the particular thought communities to which we belong; more specifically, these cognitive activities are influenced by the mnemonic, optical and visionary communities which provide a kind of ideational base for our thinking. These communities function as plausibility structures which help to prescribe and maintain the meanings within them, as well as rendering implausible alternative accounts. These 'virtual' structures complement the concretely social plausibility structures identified by Berger and Luckmann.

Keeping it real

Plausibility structures cannot function at all unless the meanings that circulate within them are maintained in an ongoing way. In other words, the plausibility of their worlds requires the activity of specific *maintenance processes*. Two processes in particular buttress the reality of religious 'worlds': *socialization* maintains beliefs from one generation to the next, while *conversation* ensures continuing plausibility over time.

---

[56] Milbank, *Theology*, 9.

Socialization

The socialization of children (or adult converts) into a belief system is crucial to the ongoing maintenance of belief. This is because the vast majority of religious people grew up in religious families. L.B. Brown observes, for example, that, 'recent investigators ... have shown that prior experience or knowledge of a religious tradition overwhelms most of the other effects on the data'.[57] Religious socialization takes place chiefly within the family, via primary relationships with significant others, and to a lesser extent through the influence of school. The family is more important than other factors in socialization, because parents are generally the child's most significant others and it is the significant others which have the most influence on the child. The family is also important because religious socialization cannot be disentangled from the process of identity formation and the family is the chief place where this identity takes shape. Religious beliefs tend to be acquired only after the child's sense of group affiliation and identity has become established. However, it is not enough for parents to communicate abstract norms. Successful religious socialization comes as a result of seeing beliefs embodied in traditional practices in the home, particularly in the mother, and through involving them in the rituals of church, temple, synagogue, and so on. The child comes to adopt the norms and beliefs of his or her parents through seeing these modelled and then identifying with them.[58] The religious family therefore operates as a primary plausibility structure within which the process of socialization can take place, facilitating the emerging religious identity and faith of the child.

In addition to relationships within the family, and with significant others, socialization also takes place within the religious school, although its influence on religious socialization is much weaker.[59] Religious schools often try to create a weak religious monopoly which ensures a degree of cohesion within, and exclusion without, the boundaries of the school community. Studies have shown that among Christian schools this approach has not been successful; Catholic schools seem to have produced a very slight positive influence on attitudes to Christianity, while Anglican controlled schools a slightly negative effect.[60] This might suggest that

---

[57] L.B. Brown, *The Psychology of Religious Belief* (London: Academic Press, 1987), 218.

[58] H. Carrier, *The Sociology of Religious Belonging* (London: Darton, Longman & Todd, 1966), 149; Argyle and Beit-Hallahmi, *Psychology*, ch. 6.

[59] Argyle and Beit-Hallahmi, *Psychology*, 103.

[60] Argyle and Beit-Hallahmi, *Psychology*, 109.

there is too much 'noise' from other factors to allow state-sector Christian schools to be significant guardians of religious plausibility, and also that schools tend to lack the relationships with significant others which is necessary for religious socialization. (Private Christian, Jewish, or Muslim schools may function better in this regard.) By contrast, institutions which focus solely on the task of religious socialization (as distinct from general education) seem to succeed better in constructing religious plausibility. Steve Bruce observes, for example, that, 'evangelicals are in the main produced by evangelical parents, Sunday schools, youth fellowships, seaside missions and camps, Christian Unions in universities and colleges, and membership of one or more of the many inter-denominational evangelical organizations.'[61] In this way, whether through family, significant others, school, or some other agency of socialization such as the peer group or mass media, religious meanings are passed on from one generation to the next through the socialization process.

Successful religious socialization, then, ensures the transmission of plausible beliefs and practices from one generation to another (or from insiders to outsiders). The other maintenance process, which ensures the ongoing plausibility of beliefs over time, is that of *conversation*.

Conversation
The plausibility of religious beliefs will be maintained as they are continually rehearsed in everyday conversation. Literal conversation keeps the religious world 'on the agenda' for those who participate in it. It helps to reinforce the sense of the immediacy and relevance – indeed, the reality – of the religious world. The young mothers who pray together; the students who 'talk theology'; the pastor who helps a man to see God at work in his life; each of these in his or her own way is engaging in 'world-constructing' conversation. In talking about their faith, they are not 'talking themselves into it', as if they were colluding together in an act of self-deception. They are simply maintaining the subjective reality of what they already agree to be objectively real. All world-constructing conversation works in this way, whether the 'worlds' in question are religious or not. The difference today is that the conversation required to maintain the reality of a religious sub-universe is inherently precarious. It resides in fragile Bible study groups, infrequent church services, chance meetings with fellow Christians in the

---

[61] S. Bruce, *Firm in the Faith: the Survival and Revival of Conservative Protestantism* (Aldershot: Gower, 1984), 402.

supermarket, or on the shelves of the local Christian bookshop. By contrast, the conversation in support of the dominant 'world' (of, say, secular humanism) happens almost automatically. Its language and assumptions pour from every mouthpiece of the mass media and re-echo in emptying beer glasses up and down the land.

This is not to say that such conversation is deliberate. Perhaps, say, for the Victorian family who read and discussed a portion of Scripture during every meal, the attempt to nurture world-constructing conversation was intentional. For most of the time, however, conversation just happens. The working-class men who discuss jobs, wives, football teams and cars over a pint of beer are not trying to construct a world that excludes religion. Still less are they likely to be canvassing for the Humanist Association. They are more likely to be reflecting their world simply as they see it, a world largely indifferent to the sacred, a world in which the sacred is excluded from those topics of conversation that are closest to home.

One way in particular that conversation maintains the reality of specific worlds is through the choice of language. Language conditions the way we see the world, and thereby helps to construct it. As Berger and Luckmann put it:

> This reality-generating potency of conversation is already given in the fact of linguistic objectification … In the establishment of this order language *realizes* a world, in the double sense of apprehending and producing it. Conversation is the actualizing of this realizing efficacy of language in the face-to-face situations of individual existence.[62]

A good example of this is the use of jargon. New Religious Movements (not to mention sociologists!) often use jargon in order to construct particular meanings that are unavailable in language used more generally.[63] Some streams of the New Churches, for example, will use the term 'anointed' to describe a person through whom the Holy Spirit seems particularly to work ('an anointed preacher/ prophet/worship leader'). This use of the term constructs a particular pneumatology around the biblical 'anointing' metaphor, so that 'the anointing' becomes for the worshippers an entity as real as the plastic chairs on which they sit. In this way, the word has creative power.

While literal conversation may be a chief means by which beliefs are ongoingly maintained as plausible, the notion of conversation also includes the non-verbal or symbolic reaffirmations of belief. The presence of a great cathedral in a small town, for example, may

---

[62] Berger and Luckmann, *Construction*, 173.
[63] Barker, *New Religious Movements*, 79.

continually affirm and 'speak' of the power and immediacy of the beliefs which it represents. Likewise, the rituals which take place within the cathedral form a kind of ongoing conversation which repeatedly makes present the realities which they are intended to signify.[64] Similarly, Kenneth Cragg points to the role of repeated conversation within the Muslim community, as a means of giving ultimacy to the community and its sacred law. These, 'have their efficacy in solidarity and habituation ... The five-times daily *Salat*, or prayer ritual, both habituates piety and transacts powerful solidarity.'[65]

At the same time, conversation, and the reality which it maintains, is profoundly precarious. The world remains subjectively plausible to the individual only so long as he or she can continue the conversation which realized that world in the first place. If conversation partners move away, or become unavailable, the world as apprehended by the individual may begin to crumble. 'In other words, the subjective reality of the world hangs on the thin thread of conversation.'[66]

In sum, the processes of socialization and conversation are crucial to the ongoing maintenance of subjective reality for the members of any plausibility structure. Socialization ensures the maintenance of particular realities as plausible over generations, while conversation ensures this over time.

Defending reality

In addition to these processes, the plausibility of a given world is also dependent on the cognitive defences that circulate within the plausibility structure: in other words, on its stock of *legitimations*. It is not enough for beliefs merely to attract commitment; they must also achieve subjective validity. While they may achieve commitment independently of their validity, at some point their validity will have to be addressed in order for this commitment to be maintained.[67] Legitimations may, therefore, function as *post hoc* rationalizations for beliefs which are already held. Equally, they may simply seek to deal with the discrepant experience which confronts every belief system in varying degrees.

Legitimations may take a variety of forms. They may be concealed simply in the language we use. For example, the widespread sympathy in Britain towards the monarchy is tacitly reaffirmed every time someone who has been well received is described as

[64] Berger, *Sacred Canopy*, 40; Borhek and Curtis, *Sociology*, 122.
[65] Cragg, *Secular Experience*, 48.
[66] Berger, *Sacred Canopy*, 17.
[67] Borhek and Curtis, *Sociology*, 85.

having been 'treated royally'. It is doubtful whether the phrase would translate for France or Russia. Likewise, legitimations may take the form of a deliberate and sophisticated body of knowledge. The field of Christian apologetics, for example, is studied by those who wish to demonstrate the coherence of the Christian claim. The most all-embracing legitimation is at the level of a whole worldview, or 'symbolic universe', which aims to integrate all aspects of the institutional order within its scope.[68]

The need for legitimation only comes to the fore when a clash with opposing meanings takes place and a question mark is raised over the existing meaning. In a predominantly plural and competitive environment, the need for legitimation becomes crucial and legitimations come to dominate the maintenance strategies of belief-groups. Religious faith communities, for example, are forced to develop sophisticated apologetic strategies to legitimate their claims in the face of the many counter-claims made by competing elements in the modern world. This may involve any of the above forms of legitimation, from the deliberate use of legitimating language, to the attempt to demonstrate the universal coherence of the religious worldview.

Two strategies in particular are employed in the act of legitimation. One is the offensive approach of 'nihilation', which involves the attempt to annihilate, or render powerless, the threat from hostile interpretations. The other is the constructive, 'hermeneutic' approach, where the belief-system seeks to interpret as much of the world as possible within its own terms, in order to advance its claim to be the true interpretation.

Nihilation
The strategy of nihilation may aim to discredit the carriers of competing belief systems by presenting them as 'mere laughable barbarians.'[69] Equally, it may involve the attempt of one reality definition to swallow up competing definitions of reality – rather like Joseph's dream of the fat and lean cows – by interpreting competitors within its own terms. How, for example, do we account for the anthropological characteristics of the biblical God? Is God made in man's image, or man in God's? Ludwig Feuerbach argued the former: God is a mere psychological projection.[70] By contrast, C.S. Lewis argued the latter: the human mind is a divine reflection.[71] Both are trying to account for the phenomenon of belief in God, but within mutually hostile terms of

---

[68] Berger and Luckmann, *Construction*, 110ff.
[69] Berger and Luckmann, *Construction*, 132.
[70] L. Feuerbach, *The Essence of Christianity* (London: Trubner, 1881).
[71] C.S. Lewis, 'Transposition' in W. Hooper (ed.), *Screwtape Proposes a Toast* (London: Fontana, 1965).

reference. Each, if true, would 'swallow up' the other, by domesticating its opponent's claims within its own frame of reference. This is the strategy of nihilation: reducing the competition to 'nothing'.

Hermeneutics
A second way in which legitimations function to buttress the validity of the meanings found within any plausibility structure is through their hermeneutic potential, their ability to explain. This can work in two ways.

First, religion has traditionally helped to legitimate the existing social order through interpreting the mundane realm in sacred terms, as reflecting the supernatural realm. Social worlds are seen as a reflection and continuation of the order of the external universe, and are therefore 'natural'.[72] The medieval idea of the 'chain of being' is one example of this continuity; the belief that a hierarchy runs from God, via the angels, to humans and down through the social strata ('the rich man in his castle; the poor man at his gate') and below to the sub-human species. In such ways religion has traditionally served to reify the social world, making the contingencies of social arrangements look as if they are immutable absolutes.[73] This is a process Berger calls 'cosmization'.[74] In a similar way, religion has been used to legitimate the exercise of worldly power: 'As the drums roll before battle there is always a moment of silence in which the impending carnage is commended to the supernatural powers ...'[75] Religion that is privileged with the role of legitimating social arrangements and worldly power receives, in turn, reflected glory from the social order it supports. In other words, religion and power can exist in a symbiotic relationship of mutual legitimation.

Secondly, religious belief-systems have sought to be self-legitimating. They have acted as interpretative schemas that aim to make sense of the world in their own terms. They offer a cognitive map within which new experiences of the world can be located.[76] The cognitive map may be drawn in a number of ways: through the practice of apologetics,[77] through catechesis,[78] or through existing schema such as the Bible.[79]

---

[72] Berger, *Sacred Canopy*, 25.
[73] Berger, *Precarious Vision*, 21.
[74] Berger, *Sacred Canopy*, 28.
[75] Berger, *Precarious Vision*, 109.
[76] Borhek and Curtis, *Sociology*, 9.
[77] Berger, *Precarious Vision*, 123; Berger and Luckmann, *Construction*, 133.
[78] Carrier, *Sociology*, 138ff.
[79] M.A. Arbib and M.B. Hesse, *The Construction of Reality* (Cambridge: Cambridge University Press, 1986), 222.

In sum, legitimations complement the maintenance processes which take place within plausibility structures by providing a coherent context of meaning within which beliefs can appear plausible. Together with plausibility structures, and the maintenance processes which operate from within them, legitimations help to construct the plausibility of religious worlds.

So What?

This chapter has continued to trace the dynamics of credibility. We have seen how the reasons of the head, heart and home help to construct plausibility for beliefs. We are now in a position to think through some of the implications of these insights for the mission of the Church. In the next chapter, then, we will take a breather from our pursuit of the dynamics of credibility, in order to consider five specific practical applications of the argument so far. It is time to 'take five'.

6

Take Five

What might be some of the implications for the church's mission of the dynamics of credibility we have reviewed so far? In this chapter we will consider five particular applications of the argument to date. These are not intended to be specific proposals that could be implemented by any one church, but are offered as compass bearings for churches to follow and translate within their own unique contexts. Still less are they offered as a complete blueprint for local mission; they are simply an attempt to answer the question at the heart of this book: what, in practice, will sustain the credibility of the church and her story?

One: Build Plausibility Shelters

If we are to restore credibility to the church we will need to pay closer attention to the cognitive defences our churches provide – we will need to build plausibility shelters. We saw in the previous chapter that plausibility structures are never watertight. There are too many competing structures to hope that their various versions of reality will not seep into one another. In any case, most people do not inhabit only one structure, but many. We suffer the culture shock of dual citizenship. Instead, I suggested that we think in terms of 'plausibility shelters', makeshift structures which provide a degree of protection for beliefs, while being realistic about the fact that competing definitions of reality will clash in our everyday experience.

Plausibility shelters, then, are never watertight, but provide only provisional defence against cognitive threat. This not necessarily a bad thing – it could, indeed, be a blessing in disguise. There is a dark side to successful plausibility structures on account of their potential for coercion and control. Some religious communities defend the reality of their worlds at a high price. On occasion, leadership is authoritarian and controlling; questioning is discouraged; theological dissent is met with suspicion and ostracism; financial freedom is curtailed; outside social contacts are regulated; information is censored; the host culture is 'demonized', and so on. These are the strategies adopted in a modern pluralist society, just as witch hunts, heresy trials, pogroms and other such methods characterized the strategies of world-maintenance of a previous era. Clearly, if plausibility shelters are going to use such strategies, we would be better off without them. Perhaps we should be suspicious of plausibility structures that are too successful.

Social rhetoric

Should we then rejoice when our churches supply about as much cognitive protection as a battered bus shelter whose corrugated roof has blown off and whose windows are broken in? Not at all. If abusive structures are one extreme to be avoided, the other extreme is the complete absence of cognitive shelter. Why? Because modern democratic societies rain down upon us what may be termed 'social rhetoric', the persuasive power of society – particularly the public sphere – in constructing and maintaining as plausible a broad consensus as to what constitutes shared public values and public knowledge. Typically, this consensus excludes the Christian claim – indeed, all religious claims. The social rhetoric of modern societies is therefore inherently antagonistic towards the gospel's claim to be 'public truth' as opposed to private preference. We must reckon with the fact that the cognitive arena is not an empty stage, but a theatre of conflict between different interests vying for power and influence over what counts as real. There is no simple, neutral space. If we ignore the need for cognitive shelter, we should not be surprised to discover one day that we, and most of our fellow believers, find the secular consensus considerably more plausible than the Creed. Perhaps this has already happened. This experience is not a little inconvenient when you also happen to think the Creed is true.

The shape of the shelter

If, then, we are to build plausibility shelters, what might they actually look like? I have already suggested that plausibility structures require a fair degree of cohesion, both of beliefs and relationships, in order to work. Furthermore, they must be able to exclude competitors, through censorship, reclusiveness, or inattention. While they may consist of physical communities, they may also involve virtual communities of like-minded people whose memory, attention and imagination has been streamlined in specific ways. They must also be able to pass on meanings from one generation to the next and keep their faith alive over time. Finally – to complete this summary – they must circulate legitimations that demonstrate the coherence of their world and explain why competing views are wrong.

In my view, the kind of structure that is most likely to support plausibility will come into the category of what might be termed 'benign sectarianism'. However much we may dislike sectarianism in its extreme forms, it has to be admitted that sects (in the sociological sense of the word) work extremely well as plausibility shelters. We may not wish to embrace every strategy of the sect: yet we cannot but admit that they embody many (nearly all?) of the requirements for strong plausibility structures described in the previous chapter. I say 'benign' sectarianism, recognizing the need to avoid the abuses already mentioned which tend to appear whenever sects are particularly strong. In what follows, I will discuss the above characteristics of plausibility structures in more practical terms, in order to illustrate what a plausibility shelter – or a benign sect – might look like in practice.

Nurture cohesive communities

First, relationships. In a sense these are the fundamental building blocks of church life, yet it is remarkable how often churches are driven by concerns which place the quality of relationships within the church far down the agenda. Churches can easily become preoccupied with money, buildings, preaching, liturgy; at the same time the congregation becomes little more than an audience. By contrast, strong plausibility requires that relationships are close and supportive, so that faith and life in all their moods and colours are shared. Shared 'conversation', shared memories and a shared focus of attention are all required for the maintenance of religious worlds. This points to the need to prioritize community over congregation, a point to which I will return in detail below.

Next, beliefs. These too need to cohere if the religious world is to be maintained as plausible. Beliefs need to fit together to form a coherent picture of the world. More important still, there needs to be sufficient agreement between church members as to the content of their beliefs. Typically, churches with a conservative theology are more able to provide this cohesion than are liberal churches. This is because of the more 'open epistemology' of the latter: liberal church members are unable to reinforce one another's beliefs in conversation to the same extent as conservatives because they do not share the same degree of consensus.[1] Sociologically, then, the liberal hope

---

[1] Bruce, 'Demise', 57; D.J. Hall, *The End of Christendom and the Future of Christianity* (Valley Forge, PA: Trinity Press International, 1997), 26.

of attracting the 'cultured despisers' of Christianity by conforming the content of Christian doctrine to contemporary assumptions does not work. Historically, too, we have witnessed the dissipation of religious energy within the liberal denominations. As Steve Bruce has argued, the strength of liberal Christianity is essentially parasitic on a more conservative past. What then? We can hardly expect more liberal churches to change their theology overnight simply in order to become better containers of plausibility.[2] Rather, the lesson here is for the more conservative churches: cultural and theological accommodation is a poor strategy for mission. If missiological expediency (rather than honest doubt) is all that is driving the dilution of a salty, distinctive Christianity, the strategy is ill-conceived. Children can learn to love anchovies, but not by starting them on a diet of fishy water.

Cope with competition

Cohesion is the mother of plausibility; what then of its counterpart, exclusion? Can Christians avoid secular television, secular holidays, secular charities, secular music, secular magazines, secular trades-people, or secular schools? Is it possible? Drastic as this sounds, Steve Bruce paints a picture, based on a synthesis of his own experiences, of how American fundamentalists he visited in the early 1980s encapsulated themselves in just this way: parents sent their children to Christian schools and universities; vacations were spent running Christian summer camps; spare time was given over to supporting one of any number of church social relief programmes; families watched Christian television, listened to Christian music and subscribed only to Christian magazines; goods and services were bought from other Christians; holidays were spent at a leisure complex run by fundamentalists.[3] Likewise, there is strong evidence that the burgeoning home-schooling movement in America is dominated by those committed to a very conservative form of Christianity: the children of fundamentalists are therefore more likely than other groups to be cocooned within the home.[4] In other words, in parts of America at least, effective insulation from the host culture is at least an option.

---

[2] Perhaps, however, liberal Christians could try being a little more dogmatic in their liberalism. Dogmatic liberalism may sound like a contradiction in terms, yet many liberals are passionate about their beliefs. Does liberal Christianity necessarily have to suffer from the ongoing dissipation of cognitive energy?

[3] Bruce, *God is Dead*, 226.

[4] M. Mayberry, J.G. Knowles et al., *Home Schooling: Parents as Educators* (Thousand Oaks, CA: Corwin Press, 1995), 7.

In Europe, by contrast, it is not. Europe is too tightly packed to allow space for subcultures such as Bruce describes to flourish. It currently lacks widespread provision of Christian television and radio, home schooling is less common and in most places culture is already too diverse for any one group to enjoy a monopoly. As a result, religious subcultures are far harder to maintain in Europe. What this points to is the need for churches to lay greater emphasis on the kinds of strategies that enable them to cope with competing views, rather than opting for a strategy of sub-cultural retreat – which, in any case, many might find theologically objectionable. If this is the case, then education will take priority over fortification. Again, I will explore what this may mean for the churches in more detail below.

Finally, if physical plausibility shelters can be strengthened in these ways, what about the virtual 'thought communities' which also provide shelter for religious plausibility: the mnemonic, optical and visionary communities? How can these be strengthened?

Rehearse the memory

Mnemonic communities are of particular interest to missiologists because the range of people who participate in the Christian mnemonic community is far wider than the social community of the church itself. All sorts of people who have no formal connection with a church 'remember' and take an interest in our Christian heritage. Furthermore, the evidence seems to point to there being a growing interest in this heritage, and not only for the purposes of aesthetic appreciation or tourism. Many people outside the churches are finding ways to tap into the memory of Christianity in order to rekindle a spirituality for themselves. This trend can be seen in a wide variety of ways. In the past four decades, many old pilgrimage routes across Europe have been reopened or revitalized – Santiago, Medjugorje, Lourdes, Knock, Walsingham, Glastonbury, Iona, to name only a few. Moreover, increasing numbers of people seem eager to tap into the spiritual inheritance bequeathed by the past: retreat centres have experienced renewed interest in recent years; interest has been revived in a range of 'spiritualities' including the Celtic and Benedictine traditions; cathedrals are enjoying renewed popularity; exhibitions of historic Christian art (such as 'Seeing Salvation' referred to earlier) have proved popular; and historical documentaries on television attract a high number of viewers. What this suggests is that the mnemonic community which 'remembers' our Christian past, and even draws spiritual nourishment from it, is considerably larger than the social community of churchgoers. The ongoing plausibility of Christian faith for those within the mnemonic community – whether churchgoer or not – will depend on the extent to which that memory can be shared and reinforced in 'conversation'. What if, say, the churches made more effort to reclaim sacred art for the purpose for which it was originally intended – for example, as a devotional focus in a three-hour Good Friday meditation? In this way, the shared memory of the Christian story could be strengthened for churchgoer and art lover alike, as they engaged, together with a long-dead painter, in a silent conversation of world-creating power.

Pay more attention

In a similar way, the construction of plausibility shelters will involve the buttressing of optical communities, the community of those who share a particular way of 'seeing' the world. Jesus described the eye as the 'lamp of the body'.[5] What we take in determines who we are and what we are likely to believe. Churches are made up of people who (in theory) pay attention to the same thing for about an hour a week. In addition, their Christian commitment makes it more likely that they will attend to certain things during the week (say, Bible reading) than those outside the church. In reality, however, many churches create only very weak optical communities. A person employed in secular work outside the home may attend to their work (with its implicit assumptions, norms and values) for about forty hours a week, and may watch television for up to twenty hours; it is not surprising, therefore, if just one hour of attention directed to worship on a Sunday morning struggles to compete for 'optical socialization'. No wonder then if the plausibility of a secular outlook reigns supreme over the plausibility of the Christian story as it is viewed within the struggling optical community of the church. Christians simply do not have the opportunity to pay their faith enough attention. The scope of the optical community is extended a little where, say, Christians meet to say the daily office, where 'quiet times' are kept, or where workers meet for lunch-time prayer meetings. On the whole, however, in a society with a secular ethos, it is not difficult to ignore God between Sundays. What this points to is an urgent need for the re-enchantment of everyday life, for the re-integration of work and worship, and for a spirituality that will illuminate and sacralize our everyday experiences. Again, I will return to this below.

Share the vision

The third thought community is the 'visionary community', comprised of those who share a common way of imagining the future

[5] Matthew 6:22, NIV.

and the unseen world around them. The plausibility of the Christian story will depend to a large degree on the extent to which people are able to share a common vision. For example, much of Jesus' message has to be imagined before it can be grasped. This is the case most particularly for his central metaphor of the 'kingdom of God'. The many 'parables of the kingdom' show the care taken by Jesus to communicate this highly abstract, dynamic and, yet, universal reality. The kingdom is now and not yet; it is everywhere but it is also within you; it is a realm but it is also a reign. Hearing Jesus' parables of the kingdom we get the sense that he is straining to describe the ineffable. Our attempt to grasp this reality requires a feat of the imagination. The kingdom only becomes a reality for us, however, when our vision of the world infused with the coming reign of God is shared with others – when we participate in the visionary community. Seeing *together* is believing. Once again, I will return to this theme to unpack it further below.

Two: Prioritize Community over Congregation

In almost every Christian denomination in Britain, church attendance is declining. Clearly, some of this has to do with loss of faith,[6] and the broader context of secularization outlined in chapters two and three. Yet for many, ceasing to attend church is not accompanied by a rejection of Christian faith. Many people remain Christians yet do not attend church on a regular basis. Anecdotally, the many people I have come across in this position speak of being unable to 'hack it', of feeling that they can no longer simply 'go through the motions', or of being unable to find a church that was meaningful for them.

This phenomenon of homeless believers is frankly puzzling. One way to understand this trend towards 'believing without belonging' is to set it within the wider sociological context of the decline in associational activity in society more generally. When compared to the loss of membership from the Trades Unions or the mainstream political parties in Britain, church membership seems to have held up rather well. However, this observation only shifts the problem onto a different basis: the question becomes, 'Why have voluntary associations such as these experienced such drastic decline in recent decades?'

---

[6] In one study, those who gave 'loss of faith' as the precipitating reason for leaving church amounted to less than one fifth of the sample. See, Richter and Francis, *Gone*, 137.

The loss of collective obligation

One answer to this question lies in the loss of what may be termed 'collective obligation'. Prior to – let us say – the 1960s, commitment to associations was much stronger because most people had a firm sense of obligation towards one another, particularly towards the group as a whole. Parents could discipline not only their own children, but others' children as well. Community loyalties were tied in to locality, rather than simply belonging to dispersed networks of friendship. There was a far stronger sense of duty and obligation to the good of the whole society (however defined) than there is today. In such a context, churchgoing is supported by an ethic of duty (I go to support the church, even if I dislike or disagree with its emphases), and by a collectivistic spirit (this is our parish and our identity; this is where we belong). In contrast, collective obligation has now given way to an ethos of individual consumption. Attendance at church is now a question of 'Does it work for *me*?' 'What do *I* get out of it?' 'Does it feel good?' The twin emphases of consumer values and an individualistic mentality make up this attitude. In part, too, the rejection of collective obligation is seen as an emancipatory move: the so-called 'baby-buster' generation (born post–1965) believe that their parents and grandparents were being inauthentic and hypocritical in their slavish commitment to duty: hence, the contemporary malaise with institutional church life that is perceived to be merely 'going through the motions'.

How can this malaise be addressed, without shutting down every church service? Perhaps the first thing to say is that the malaise is far from universal. Despite Bruce's predictions (chapter one), the churches are not empty yet! More positively, the loss of collective obligation points to the urgency for *prioritizing community over congregation*. Those who dislike 'going through the motions', or those who 'can't hack it' any longer, have few problems when church life comes down to genuine community. Community is the yearning of the post-1960s generation. This points to the paradox of contemporary individualism: people only *seem* to prefer to act as individuals. Individualism only goes so far; we should not be beguiled by its claims. This can be vividly observed in, say, the case of fashion. The ostensible message of fashion advertising is an invitation to individual self-expression. 'Be someone who stands out', it seems to say. 'Be unique'. 'Shape a new image'. 'Carve an identity'. The practical reality of fashion items is, however, very different. These are typically mass-produced and targeted at particular social groups who subsequently appear together dressed almost identically. Designer clothing turns out to be little different from the school uniform; self-expression is unmasked as mere self-assignment to a particular group. The point of this observation is simply to illustrate the fact that beneath the rhetoric of individualism lies a strong collective mentality, a thirst to belong. We may be unable to 'hack it' with church services but we long for community.

Prioritizing community over congregation strengthens religious plausibility because it means that, in addition to the advantages afforded by the plausibility structure of the church congregation (the reasons of the home), it also answers more fully the need for community (the reasons of the heart). Added to this, community represents an intensification of the 'reasons of the home' because it affords greater relational cohesion than does the more diffuse congregation. It is salutary to observe that congregation can exist without community, and community without congregation. The two forms are quite distinct, although clearly they can overlap. I can sneak into the back of a cathedral service and join the congregation in worship. But I can also sneak out again and avoid all contact with people; so I avoid the community. Conversely, I can be part of a worshipping community, say, on pilgrimage, without there being any congregation in sight. In both cases, my faith may be uplifted by the plausibility structure of the group; however, the intensity of relationship on the pilgrimage is likely to build up my faith more than my anonymous cathedral experience. Community will satisfy my need for belonging, authenticity and relationship; it will also provide the closeness of relationships that enables world-constructing conversation to flourish. All in all, Christian community represents a better bet than congregation alone for the promotion of plausibility.

Rethink church: missiology is ecclesiology

If we are looking to prioritize community over congregation, what might this mean in practice? At its most basic, it means that we rethink what it means to 'be church'. Until fairly recently, many churches thought specialist agencies should be responsible for mission and evangelism. 'Mission' was to be conducted through dedicated missionary societies whose focus was overseas; likewise, 'evangelism' was the task of professional evangelists and their teams or 'associations', whose focus was at 'home'. Although evangelistic campaigns did involve local churches, the role of the local church tended to be with 'follow up' on interested parties, and 'discipleship' of new converts, rather than the regular worshipping congregations of the churches being at the centre of mission.

All this has changed. Missiologists are increasingly agreed that the traditional form of the overseas missionary society is looking very tired indeed. Richard Tiplady observes:

The mission agency as we know it today is the hybrid offspring of the marriage of two social models: the voluntary society and the joint-stock company or business corporation' and concludes that 'these models are not working quite as well as they should be'.[7]

More seriously still, David Smith has argued that European mission agencies grew alongside the expanding colonialism of the nineteenth century and benefited from its impetus. In so doing, however, they imbibed and exported a modernist mindset and a 'Christendom' mentality directed towards replicating Western models of church throughout the world. In a postmodern, globalized world, some of these agencies now look like dinosaurs[8] – although others are creatively adapting.[9] Further, if specialized agencies of overseas mission are in need of a rethink, so too are the evangelistic agencies which predominate at 'home'. Mike Booker observes:

> the [Anglican] Decade of Evangelism was also a decade in which a number of evangelists went out of business. The focus of thinking during the Decade moved from missions (as separate, one-off events) to mission (as an ongoing focus of church life).[10]

Missiologists tend to agree that too much emphasis has been placed on agencies of evangelism: instead, a consensus has emerged that it is the local congregation that should be seen as the primary unit of mission.[11] Hence, the local congregation has come to be seen as the crucial locus of mission at the very same time as it has come to be seen as deeply problematic. It is hardly surprising, therefore, that there is a groundswell of opinion that we need to rethink how we do church. Missiology has become ecclesiology.

Networks
What options are emerging, then, for new ways of being church? Richard Tiplady notes the growth of organizations based around

---

[7] Tiplady, *World of Difference*, 81, 86.
[8] Smith, *Mission After Christendom*.
[9] Tiplady, *World of Difference*, 151f. Richard Tiplady looks at three examples of mission agencies creatively adapting themselves to a world based around networks: Global Connections (previously the Evangelical Missionary Alliance); the Mennonite Mission Network; and SIM International.
[10] Booker and Ireland, *Evangelism*, 61.
[11] See, for example, Lesslie Newbigin's claim that, 'the only possible hermeneutic of the gospel is a congregation which believes it.' Newbigin, *Gospel*, 13.

'networks' of relationship in contrast to more traditional, bureaucratic institutions, and sees these as a model for the future. Their advantages include their ability to cope with contemporary variety and complexity; they can embrace a large number of stakeholders; they are flexible and adaptable.[12] Although his primary concern is with the future shape of mission agencies, the principle is frequently applied to the church. Church denominations are modern, bureaucratic institutions; hence, they lack the advantages of the network just listed. They represent what Pete Ward terms 'solid church': seeing 'congregation' as the only part of the life of the local church that really counts; being overly concerned with the size of plant and congregation; offering a 'one size fits all' package of worship; and involving many volunteers in a religious club which takes considerable effort to keep running. In contrast, Ward offers a vision of 'liquid church', in which, once again, the notion of networks comes to the fore. He offers a series of 'dreams' of how things could be different. In liquid church, congregation would be replaced by networks of communication; community would be based on fluid and continual communication, not just meetings; activity would be based around choice and interest, rather than preset programmes; leadership would be derived from grassroots recognition, not imposed from above; activities would harness to a much greater extent the power of the imagination; worship would become 'de-centred'.[13]

This is an engaging vision, but not without its problems. Ward wrestles to some degree with how a church can maintain a ministry of word and sacrament in the absence of a 'solid' congregation, but the exploratory nature of his thinking means that he is not pointing to an example: 'What I say here is an attempt to imagine rather than describe a different way of being church.'[14] A similar, unanswered, question is the location of power and authority in liquid church. Even if such a network of believers claims to have divested its ranks of all authority, power will continue to operate in groups of people regardless of whether or not it is invested in recognized and accredited individuals. Dodging the question of ecclesial authority (not only bureaucratic, but also ministerial and sacramental authority) does not get rid of the reality of power and authority but simply drives it underground. As Tiplady notes, even sprawling networks like the internet require facilitation and legislation; so do churches.[15] One further suspicion: networks can be rather cliquey.

---

[12] Tiplady, *World of Difference*, ch. 7.
[13] P. Ward, *Liquid Church* (Carlisle: Paternoster, 2002), chs. 1 and 10.
[14] Ward, *Liquid Church*, 1.
[15] Tiplady, *World of Difference*, 145f.

Because they transcend geographical communities and physical
spaces – such as the parish church – their points of contact tend to be
limited to one particular sphere of relationships. This makes it
much harder to get in on the network. As Ward himself notes, such
groups are 'self-selecting' and therefore in danger of being 'less
socially diverse' than regular churches.[16] Networks are a problem
for those who are poor at 'networking'. By contrast, one of the
glories of church congregations is their ability to embrace those
whose social skills are lacking. I can think of many churches which
provide much-needed social contact for people who are socially dis-
advantaged, or have special needs, but who have no access to the
mobile phone, text messaging, or email by which Ward imagines
that people will keep in touch. They can simply wander in at the
back of the service. As Mark Ireland observes, 'The long-term challenge is to see whether network churches can also work in areas of
social deprivation, where fewer people have their own transport
and where there is still a strong sense of local identity and
rootedness.'[17] Ward's notion of 'decentred' worship offers a better
chance for such people to be included – that is, if they ever get to
hear about it.

Keep it small

Another solution to prioritizing community over congregation is to
stick with 'solid' church, but to move towards seeing small communities within the church as primary and the congregation as secondary. This approach involves more than the creation of a few
midweek home groups for the keen, to supplement the Sunday diet.
Rather, it involves a move away from being a 'church *with* small
groups' to becoming a 'church *of* small groups'. The 'small Christian community' is therefore seen as the basic building block of the
local church and the primary agent for mission and action.

Jeanne Hinton and Peter Price speak of the value of 'small Christian communities' to the mission of the church. Hinton and Price
have worked together for a number of years under the umbrella of
'A New Way of Being Church' (or 'New Way'). This is 'a network of
people who seek to co-operate with Jesus Christ in the formation of
God's new order of justice, love and peace'.[18] Some within the
network see small Christian communities as a model for the church
at local level; others see them as places on the margins of the church,

---

[16] Ward, *Liquid Church*, 90.
[17] Booker and Ireland, *Evangelism*, 160.
[18] J. Hinton and P.B. Price, *Changing Communities: Church from the Grassroots* (London: Churches Together in Britain and Ireland, 2003), 88.

which can offer a prophetic edge and a haven for those who feel marginalized by the mainstream. Either way, the primary emphasis of such groups is not upon resourcing individuals through prayer and Bible study, as in a traditional home group, but rather seeing the group as an agent of change and transformation in society – a group that seeks first the kingdom of God. The emphasis here is also upon the beauty of smallness. Small groups or churches have advantages that larger churches do not. As Mike Booker states, 'Not only is the quality of relationships and the ability to spot and welcome newcomers higher, smaller churches are on average far more likely to grow than large ones.'[19]

A similar plea for prioritizing small communities over congregational gatherings comes from Steven Croft in his *Transforming Communities*:

> The concept of a transforming community is offered as a way of catching and articulating that dimension of the church's life which is caught by Jesus' travels with the disciples, by the early Christian house churches, by the monastic communities, by Methodist class meetings, by the house group movement of the twentieth century, and by the cell church and base ecclesial community movements of the world Church. It is my contention that the malaise of the church in the mainstream denominations is due at least in part to a neglect of that aspect of church life which can be expressed in these small communities: depth of friendship and relationship; discipleship within structures of mutual accountability; worship and prayer which arise from and are closely related to shared lives; and a common sense of purpose enabling one another to share in the mission of God. I would argue further that the renewal of the church will not come through the re-organization of ministry to serve existing structures but through the renewal of the whole Church in relationship and community.[20]

I quote from Croft at length because his summary makes three important points: prioritizing small groups has a long pedigree in church history; small groups embody community; small groups represent a viable structure for the renewal of the church, which many existing congregations do not.

Still greater priority is given to the small group within the expanding 'cell church' movement. Cell churches do not necessarily do away with the congregation altogether, but they see the 'cell' as the primary expression of the local church. In some parts of the world, cell churches have proved to be extremely effective in

---

[19] Booker and Ireland, *Evangelism*, 139.
[20] S. Croft, *Transforming Communities: Re-imagining the Church for the 21st Century* (London: Darton, Longman & Todd, 2002).

promoting growth. Commenting on this, Graham Tomlin observes such 'cells' are strong because they are invested with real responsibility and dignity; they promote intimacy, support and accountability among members; and they are focused outwards as well as in.[21] On this last point, small groups may take on a designated task which serves the wider community and becomes a group project. Similarly, the group is expected to invite people in – not in order to hear a presentation of the gospel, but simply to take part in the group and in its usual activities. This allows the group to act – in Newbigin's words – 'as hermeneutic of the gospel'.[22] Only in the context of the working, worshipping community does the gospel begin to make sense.

Other newer forms of church that give priority to community over congregation are identified in a report from a working group of the Church of England's Mission and Public Affairs Council, entitled *Mission-Shaped Church*.[23] In addition to the examples above, the working group identify 'alternative worship communities', 'base ecclesial communities', 'café church', and 'churches arising out of community initiatives'. Other examples they give place more emphasis on congregation, although these may also imply the existence of strong communities: 'multiple and midweek congregations', 'school-linked congregations', 'seeker church', 'traditional church plants', 'traditional forms of church inspiring new interest', and 'youth congregations'.[24]

In recent years, too, there has been much talk of 'emerging church'. The term is in danger of becoming meaningless if it becomes entrenched (a church cannot 'emerge' for ever), but for the moment it seems to be a good way both to capture the sense that established patterns of being church are increasingly moribund, and to give space for experimental patterns of church life to emerge

---

[21] G. Tomlin, *The Provocative Church* (London: SPCK, 2002), 150.

[22] Newbigin, *Gospel*, ch. 18.

[23] The Archbishop's Council, *Mission-Shaped Church* (London: Church House Publishing, 2004), 43ff.

[24] One further church-based approach to mission is the 'Natural Church Development' programme, developed in Germany, but little known in Britain. This aims to identify the 'quality characteristics' of growing churches. Mike Booker gives a very helpful introduction to it in, Booker and Ireland, *Evangelism*, 122–38. Booker and Ireland's book is an extremely helpful, realistic, and well-researched evaluation of a wide range of models and strategies for evangelism which deserves to be widely read. It complements the insights of *Mission-Shaped Church* (see previous note).

unhindered by premature definitions.[25] 'Networks', 'Cell Church', 'Liquid Church', 'Transforming Communities' and 'Small Christian Communities' are all ways of articulating what is emerging. These examples could be multiplied. What all of them seem to agree on, however, is that community must take priority over congregation if the church in Britain is to have a future. In one way, this sounds radical; in another, it seems obvious, as if we really knew it all along. Either way, this conclusion is supported by my observations concerning the dynamics of credibility outlined in the previous chapter. Small is beautiful.

Three: Re-enchant Your World

Earlier, I commented that contemporary society provides Christians with little opportunity to pay sufficient attention to their faith. It is not difficult to ignore God between Sundays. In consequence, it is harder to maintain faith as a plausible reality where it is routinely ignored. If church services sometimes seem a little unreal, it may be down to what does *not* take place during the week, rather than to what does take place on a Sunday morning. What does not take place during the week is the continual rehearsal of the reality of the religious world which characterized pre-Reformation society: whether through the cycle of a sacred calendar; the prayers and incantations that accompanied workaday activities; the belief in the power of local saints and sacred places; the continual sense of dependence on God for a plentiful harvest and deliverance from disease, and so on. Max Weber often used a phrase of Friedrich Schiller's to describe this loss of a sacred focus in everyday life: 'the disenchantment of the world'.[26] A world populated with monks, prophets, saints, angels, holy places, miracles and the awful facts of judgement and grace, gave way to a world of rational causes, the fixed laws of nature, technological advance, scientists and bureaucrats. In the modern world, the spell is broken: the enchanted world, like a floating, glistening, iridescent bubble, has now burst into a prosaic puddle of soapy water on the ground.

---

[25] Robert Warren offers a model for thinking about some of the differences there might be between church in 'inherited' mode, and emerging church. The structure of emerging church will be more flexible than fixed; its leadership will be more collaborative than clerical; its focus more whole-life than church-life; its form more community than organization; its pastoral goal more holy than happy; its expression more diverse than single; and its orientation more future than past. R. Warren, *Being Human, Being Church* (London: Marshall Pickering, 1995), 97.

[26] Gerth and Wright Mills (eds.), *From Max Weber*, 51.

If we are to restore the objects of faith as a vivid, plausible reality, our inner, subjective worlds need to become 're-enchanted'. Sunday must be welded to Monday; work and worship need to be seen as continuous; the sacred must be discerned in the everyday. At the end of every service in Iona Abbey, the worshippers are invited to leave – not to sit down again – still singing, or with the words of blessing ringing in their ears; this is to reflect the truth that worship is not confined to the Abbey, but is part of all we do. If we are to re-enchant the world of our subjective experience (and therefore, speaking theologically, walk more closely with God) we need to wrestle with three resources in particular: time, imagination and one another. I say 'wrestle', because the prevailing secular world as we typically experience it already streamlines these resources in particular ways. Habitually, most of us follow the route of least resistance: if normal employment demands a forty-hour week, we will work it; if the TV is on, we will watch it; if we see a friend, it is merely to relax and catch up. Yet, these resources of time, imagination and one another need to be wrested from the grip of conventional use if we are to have any chance of countering the drip-drip of social rhetoric which continually reinforces the reality of the consensus world. What might this look like in practice?

Redeem the hours
We have already seen that one of the major problems for the maintenance of religious worlds is the sheer inattention that they suffer in contemporary experience: an hour on a Sunday morning is small defence against the exposure to the consensus world we receive in the remaining 167 hours of the week. Part of the re-enchantment of the world in our experience will involve, crudely, putting in the extra hours. This is taken for granted in many evangelical student circles where it is expected that Christian students will observe a 'quiet time'; this is a period of time spent reading the Bible and praying. When I was at university, I knew of many fellow students who took great care not to stay up too late, so that they would be able to get up early and keep their appointed quiet time prior to lectures. Although the quiet time frequently became a focus for heroic acts of asceticism (longest, earliest, deepest, most journal pages written, etc.), and the attendant guilt for failure, nevertheless, it framed the day within a context of Bible study and prayer, intensifying the amount of attention given to the objects of faith. In my experience, however, when students graduate and enter the workplace – still more, if they have children – time for prayer seems hard to come by. No doubt some people do wrest back some time for prayer, but many, I suspect, limp through the week from Sunday to Sunday

until they eventually decide that even Sunday church is too much and they add themselves to the growing ranks of those 'believing without belonging'.

Others have found new ways to pray. A more structured approach to daily prayer can be found in the prayer books of many denominations. In Anglican circles, for example there is an expectation that priests and deacons will say morning and evening prayer daily; and many, in fact, do keep to some version of this commitment. Like the quiet time, the 'daily office' helps to direct attention to the sacred on an ongoing basis. It differs, however, in emphasizing a structured act of worship, rather than a period of Bible reading and reflection ending in prayer. The advantage of the 'daily office' form is that it can lead you into worship, whereas the quiet time requires considerable energy and impetus to maintain. Well-crafted liturgy can be quite forgiving to those who are still half asleep! Moreover, worship is more manageable if it is split between morning and evening into, say, two fifteen-minute periods. If we know in advance that we require only fifteen minutes, twice-daily worship starts to seem possible. There are a lot of resources available in bookshops for this purpose; Peter Millar's *An Iona Prayer Book*[27] is a good example of a simple resource of this kind, or you may wish to create your own. A still more frequent pattern is observed in the seven or eight monastic 'hours', which ensure that the entire day, whether at work or asleep, is punctuated with praise.

Clearly, most of us do not live in a monastery. If we are to maintain our faith as a vivid reality, we need to find ways of framing our time with world-enlarging worship. Whatever pattern we adopt should not ignore the rich inheritance of the past. In recent years there has been a renewed interest within the churches in the historic traditions of spirituality. If we are to avoid the danger of re-inventing an inferior wheel, these traditions demand our attention. Eugene Peterson reminds us, for example, that, 'The fundamental ascetic form – and this is the church's consensus for two thousand years – is the Psalms prayed daily in sequence each month.'[28] That is five psalms, every day, prayed through.

For still others, an annual cycle of retreat and prayer will be more realistic than a daily one. If finding time for worship during the day

---

[27] P. Millar, *An Iona Prayer Book* (Norwich: The Canterbury Press, 1998).

[28] E. Peterson, *Under the Unpredictable Plant: An Exploration in Vocation Holiness* (Grand Rapids, MI: Eerdmans, 1992), 105. I cannot recommend Peterson too highly as a tonic for pastors who feel their spiritual lives have been deadened by pastoral ministry. See, too, *The Contemplative Pastor*, *Working the Angles*, and *Five Smooth Stones for Pastoral Ministry*.

proves impossible, it may be that faith can be nurtured by going on a retreat or pilgrimage for a few days once or twice a year. Such experiences can act like slow-release tablets, whose benefits continue to operate long after they have been swallowed. It may also help to pray corporately. I know of two neighbours near where I live who (until one moved away) began each working day saying Morning Prayer together. Each held the other to the commitment. If this proves difficult, it may be that a local minister says Morning Prayer in your local church, or in a church you pass on the way to work. Imagine if our urban churches were packed for fifteen minutes every morning for a short act of vibrant worship as people criss-crossed through them on their journeys to work!

Redeem the moments

This is at least a beginning: reclaiming time for worship. We can go further, however, to think about significant moments in time, as well as sheer quantity. Time is not only *chronos* (sequential time), but *kairos* (opportunity, significant moment). How, then, can we re-enchant the moments of our days?

One way to do this is the setting of significant moments within a sacred framework through the use of prayers and blessings composed for this purpose. In the nineteenth century, Alexander Carmichael journeyed through the Outer Hebrides recording for posterity the oral tradition of 'Celtic' prayers and blessings held in the memories of the local people. His collection of these prayers was published in the six-volume *Carmina Gadelica*. What is striking about these prayers is the way in which they set the most mundane of activities (such as dressing, weaving, milking or lighting the fire) within a sacred context; at the same time, they bring up close the three persons of the Trinity. We read of the Father's 'fragrant clasp of love';[29] of 'Christ, King of tenderness';[30] of 'the bathing of the Spirit upon thee in every stream';[31] and of 'the kindly eye of the three'.[32] There are prayers for day and night, for journeying and resting, for farming and fishing, for ploughing and milking, for birth and death, for the hearth and the home. The sacred and the mundane are thus interfused. Esther de Waal paints a compelling picture of the enchanted lives of the communities who held these prayers in memory:

---

[29] E. de Waal, *The Celtic Vision: Prayers and Blessings from the Outer Hebrides* (London: Darton, Longman & Todd, 1988), 249.
[30] de Waal, *Celtic Vision*, 134.
[31] de Waal, *Celtic Vision*, 139.
[32] de Waal, *Celtic Vision*, 254.

> What they said and sung ... grew out of their sense of the presence of God as the most immediate reality in their lives. Religion permeated everything they did. They made no distinction between the secular and the sacred. They were unable to discern boundaries of where religion began and ended and thus found it natural to assume that God was lovingly concerned in everything they did. They felt totally at home with God.[33]

Today, such *kairos* prayers are less common, although we sometimes encounter them, say, where a family says grace before a meal, when a footballer crosses himself as he runs onto the pitch, or at the beginning of each parliamentary day. If we wish to imbibe the sacrament of the present, and ingest the sacred in the ordinary, we need *kairos* prayers. Many Christians do, of course, 'pray without ceasing', so that every corner turned each day is an occasion for conversational prayer. This ensures the inner conversation that is vital for the maintenance of religious worlds. However, it is less easy to pray such prayers corporately. *Ad hoc* prayers suggested at irregular intervals can catch participants off guard: for many it can feel awkward to be asked to pray out loud. Linette Martin recalls a time in her own experience when such requests were excruciating: 'I would have found it easier to take all my clothes off in a roomful of people than to pray aloud in front of them.'[34] Moreover, extempore prayers can sometimes be prosaic, flaccid and rambling; at worst, they can be dishonest in their attempt to seem spiritual. For these reasons, we should not neglect the vivid, robust poetry found in collections such as the *Carmina Gadelica*. Poetry has a way of standing up to frequent repetition that prosaic formulae do not. So, what if we were to colonize our days with familiar prayers, which made prayer ordinary and the ordinary prayerful? Waking up, getting dressed, eating meals, setting off, saying goodbye, greeting friends, starting work, facing pressure, coming home, giving thanks, going to sleep: any number of moments can be re-enchanted in this way.

A similar re-enchantment could be possible, in the longer term, through the recovery of the Christian calendar. Setting our whole conception of time within the framework of the Christian story is a powerful mnemonic experience, if we can stop long enough to tap into the latent meanings of Advent, Lent, Holy Week and Pentecost. Christians, of all people, have most reason to resist the consumer avalanche that buries us every Christmas. It is down to us to redirect our energies to make Christmas meaningful. Perhaps, too, it is time to re-engage with the 'pagan' festivals. One of the most moving

---

[33] de Waal, *Celtic Vision*, 4–5.
[34] L. Martin, *Practical Praying* (Cambridge: Eerdmans, 1997), viii.

celebrations in my experience is the May Morning celebration each year in Oxford. Many people stay up all night in the worship of 'Bacchus' – the God of wine – while others wear flowers, or dress as trees, to celebrate the fecundity of the earth and the rebirth of the year. The focal point of all this is the gathering of thousands at 6 a.m. at the foot of Magdalen Tower to hear choirboys sing from the top and Christian prayers of thanksgiving for creation. This gathering is reminiscent of the medieval church: a deep-rooted folk religion overlaid with Christian meanings; a passive but attentive crowd gathered to witness a remote, semi-audible liturgical act done on their behalf. As a chilly dawn breaks over Oxford, the crowd disperses for breakfast or cold beer, while troupes of burly Morris Men strike up their dances in the open air. For some it is a pagan celebration; for others it is a profound celebration of the vitality of God's creation. For both, it is rooted in the seasons, in tradition and in locality. In my experience, the May Morning celebration is deeply enchanted: the winter is past; the spring proclaims the Resurrection; the fecund God is oozing blessing; all is crisp, new, early, fresh. These roots tap into energies we would be foolish to ignore. In sum, then, instead of allowing the year to roll round in a meaningless sequence of weeks and months – time as a 'devouring beast'[35] – our time can be redeemed and set to work as a useful servant, as we re-enchant the moments of our days and the seasons of our years. In re-enchanting our world, then, time is of the essence.

Recapture the imagination

A second resource for re-enchantment is our imagination. Sometimes people claim that they are 'not very imaginative', by which they usually mean that they are not artistically gifted. Imagination is often seen as something that some people use in their spare time, say, to paint a picture or write a story. The assumption here is that the imagination is really an optional faculty that is to be used only if you want to, rather like a man might choose to use his fists for boxing.

In reality, however, we all live in our imagination much of the time. We continually imagine the future, for example: as we plan our day we imagine ourselves in the supermarket, or attending a meeting, or seeing a particular person. We also imagine things in abstract: nobody can 'see' an hour, a week, or a year, for example, but we all think in terms of them. We also imagine our fantasies: we may dream in our spare moments of a perfect partner, or a house in

---

[35] A.W. Tozer, *Gems from Tozer* (Camp Hill, PA: Christian Publications, 1979), 11.

the country, or an argument we are likely to have when we get home. Our thoughts may frequently be taken up with such hopes and fears. Further, we use our imagination every time we are creative, whether or not we think we are being 'artistic'. I can only put this sentence on the page by first conceiving of its meaning. There it is. A creative act that engaged my imagination and now engages yours.

Our spiritual lives, especially, depend upon our imagination. We walk by faith, not by sight. As soon as we try to talk about or describe spiritual realities, we are thrown back on using simile and metaphor. Daniel saw 'one *like* a son of man'; John saw someone whose 'eyes were *like* blazing fire'. Similarly, in order to help us come to grips with what God is like, the Bible gives us a range of metaphors: God is a king; God is a shepherd; God is a rock; God is a consuming fire; God is a loving father; God is an estranged mother. Even when we are trying to come to terms with our own experience of God, we cannot relay that experience directly, but must mediate our meaning through the filter of the imagination. When we say such things as 'God touched me', 'God showed me', 'God spoke to me', we usually mean that he did something that is aptly described by these metaphors. Far less commonly do we mean that we felt a physical touch, saw a vision, or heard a voice, although clearly all of these have been part of the Christian experience. Normally, we use metaphors, and metaphors require us to imagine. This suggests that it may be far more important than we often realise to pay close attention to our imaginative life and, recalling a theme from above, the kind of 'visionary community' to which we belong.

The visionary community of the local church develops its corporate imagination around its regular experience of worship. A church's worship space, music, liturgy, and use of Scripture may help or hinder the process of 'seeing' the sacred. For this reason, it is crucial that we think about the imaginative impact of these things, rather than opting for mere functional pragmatism. This is a huge area to consider. What follows is intended only to illustrate the kind of approach I have in mind.

Worship space is key. Any space used for worship will contain an implicit theology. Pointy gothic churches stress the transcendence of God; thirteenth-century chancels legitimate the power of the priesthood; café-churches emphasize feeding, informality, and community; warehouse churches stress numerical growth, and so on. What theology (or vision of God) do we wish our own worship space to communicate? It is not only architecture that informs this vision; the internal layout and décor of churches is also crucial. In the past, the church was the primary patron of the arts. Perhaps it is again time for the church to invest more freely in the arts and to invite Christian artists to assist church congregations to develop as coherent visionary communities. Similarly, music matters. The words that we sing virtually construct for us the objects of our worship right there in front of our inner eyes. Excessively subjective choruses coupled with trite tunes only deaden the religious imagination. Sacred song provides a unique opportunity to let rip the poetry of faith in an inferno of celebration; we should not settle for damp little ditties. The same could be said for liturgies. I am convinced that many are put off liturgy as a whole because their own experience of liturgy has been of something prosaic and lifeless, unimaginative. The discovery of vivid, poetic liturgies that connect with gritty experience can be a revelation. As Andrew Walker comments, 'Liturgy in postmodern culture *is* mission.'[36] Once again, where are our poets and why are we not paying them to write liturgies?

The point could be extended still further, to preaching. Every preacher knows well the 'glaze-over' moment in their sermons. It may happen after thirty minutes, or thirty seconds. What it signals is the fact that the preacher has lost his (or her) audience. After that point, until they wake up again, the content of the sermon is irrelevant – no one is listening. Preachers also know well the sudden wake-up they induce in their audience when they change tone and tempo, when they drop in a crystal-clear metaphor, or when they embark on a story. Instantly, people look up. It is said of George Whitefield that his preaching was so vivid that his hearers would cry out as if they were right there in his story. There is no point preaching to a dormitory. Sermons, like liturgies and songs, need to capture the imagination in vivid stories and images in order to feed the soul. People remember the pictures. It is partly down to the preacher, then, to gather the visionary community into a shared gallery of the imagination.

In all of these contexts, we can speak to every one of the five senses. Different churches will provide different experiences. In one, we may encounter the smell of incense and varnish, the taste of wine and wafers, the sight of a glittering reredos, the sound of exquisite music and the feel of hand-worn wood. In another it may be flowers and floor polish; coffee and croissants; murals and monitors; bass and bongos; paper and pebbles. Whether intentional or not, these experiences will form part of the total experience of worship, and play into our imaginations in one way or another. The

---

[36] Walker, *Telling*, 198. Looking again, after seven years, at Walker's 'Concluding Remarks: Indwelling the Story' I see how many themes I have unconsciously absorbed from his book – even if my articulation of them falls short of his poetic and prophetic prose.

antiseptic smell of a school hall may hinder worship every bit as much as cathedral music may help it; the aroma of coffee may welcome a newcomer as much as the sight of a bleeding statue may repel them.

Our imagination, then, requires feeding and guarding. In a British poll conducted around the turn of the millennium, John Lennon's *Imagine* was voted the favourite song of the century. It invites us to imagine that there is no heaven with the reassuring afterthought that it is easy if we try. And that is just the point. Nowadays, it is easy. What is less easy is for us to train our imagination to see a vision of the deeper reality of the unseen world. Humanly speaking, a fertile religious imagination will not pop up spontaneously; it will require creativity and work. But as we feed the collective imagination of the visionary community, we can expect the scope and plausibility of that vision to grow. In the words of A.W. Tozer:

> As we begin to focus upon God the things of the spirit will take shape before our inner eyes ... A new God-consciousness will seize upon us and we shall begin to taste and hear and inwardly feel the God who is our life and our all. God will become to us the great All, and His Presence the glory and wonder of our lives.[37]

Just imagine.

Spiritual direction for all

One further resource in the task of re-enchanting our everyday lives is the neglected treasure of one another. At its most basic, we need one another in order to form a plausibility shelter. As I indicated in the previous chapter, we find our faith subjectively plausible only because we perceive it to be an *inter*-subjective reality. Furthermore, I suggested that we have to talk about faith if it is to remain real – in Berger's words, 'the subjective reality of the world hangs on the thin thread of conversation'.[38]

The re-enchantment of our everyday lives demands, then, that we nurture faith-building conversation. If it does not happen in the normal course of our lives, then we need to make time for it. Once again, the following are only select examples intended to illustrate the kind of 'conversation' we might nurture. No doubt there are many more ways than these.

World-sustaining conversation can happen anywhere. I gave the example above of two neighbours who held each other to saying the

---

[37] Tozer, *Gems*, 8.
[38] Berger, *Sacred Canopy*, 17.

daily office together. Friends or neighbours can agree to hold one another accountable, and 'spur one another on towards love and good deeds'.[39] Increasingly, dispersed groups of people around the country are holding one another to a 'rule' of life, in what has been termed the 'new monasticism'.[40] Likewise, any small Christian community is likely to nurture such conversation. However, I want to think about one particular context in which this 'conversation' takes place and where we tap in to the resources of one another – in the case of spiritual direction.

Spiritual direction is a historic discipline in the church and yet it is made use of by only a minority of Christians. Even in those parts of the church where it is more common, considerable scepticism surrounds the term. Alan Jones tells of a monk who responded to a lecture he had given on spiritual direction by saying, 'What I want is some non-spiritual non-direction!'[41] What he was getting at is that good spiritual direction does not limit itself to some narrow 'spiritual' part of us; nor does it offer 'direction'. Instead, spiritual direction can provide a facilitating environment, in which a person may reflect on their everyday experiences, learn to discern the strategies of their own ego and discover the movements of the Spirit in amongst the ordinary. Jones goes on to warn that, 'For some, having a spiritual director is like having your own therapist or your own personal trainer at the gym. It gives one spiritual status. It promises a spiritual edge over others.' Spiritual direction may also imply that everything – even the spiritual life – is fixable, whereas, 'True spiritual direction is about the great unfixables in human life.'[42] These cautions are apposite. Nevertheless, there is no need to allow the trendiness that may have grown up around the practice to obscure its true value. If we are willing to give time and money to consultants, who will improve our finances, our homes, or our careers, is it so very strange that spiritual direction should be staple food for every Christian? Many denominations already have networks of spiritual directors to whom people can be referred, but those trained to offer direction remain proportionately few. There is some evidence, however, of expanding interest in the discipline,

---

[39] Hebrews 10:24, NIV.

[40] The report of the working group of the Church of England's Mission and Public Affairs Council, *Mission-Shaped Church,* lists a number of these (p. 74): the communities of Iona, Taize, Tertiary Franciscans, Northumbria, and the Order of Mission launched from St Thomas Crookes in Sheffield. The internet is also a forum for such groups to gather. See, for example, http://www.sanctus.org.uk.

[41] A. Jones, from the foreword to M. Guenther, *Holy Listening: the Art of Spiritual Direction* (London: Darton, Longman & Todd, 1992), vii.

[42] Jones, 'Foreword', viii.

even in evangelical circles where the term is foreign. (Perhaps it has long existed there too, but was simply called 'personal work'.) The November 2003 edition of *Christianity and Renewal* magazine, for example, has the term 'Spiritual Direction' splashed across its cover; inside, an interview with Selwyn Hughes explores a training course he offers in spiritual direction.

What if several wise heads in every church were to train as spiritual directors? These need not be clergy. Then the resources of one another could be released to facilitate growth and maturity in faith and life. World-building conversation, full of grace and seasoned with salt, could flourish in this environment. The subjective reality of the world need no longer dangle from a thread, but instead could be seated on a rich tapestry. For every person the weft of the Spirit could then be discerned within the fabric of everyday life – the very stuff of re-enchantment.

Four: Educate Adults

My remaining two points are briefer, but, I believe, still crucial. Earlier, I pointed out that we, as Europeans, are less able than North Americans to defend our faith using the strategy of sub-cultural retreat in the face of rampant pluralism. If we are to defend the subjective reality of our world, we must learn to cope with pluralism, rather than simply hide from it: education will take priority over fortification. Or, put differently, we will need to make use of the strategy of 'vaccination' instead of 'quarantine'.

It is an irony, therefore, that one of the chief ways we might 'vaccinate' the Christian community – through adult education – is widely practised in the USA, but almost completely ignored in Britain. Here, Sunday school ends when you reach adulthood. Or, if you first encounter Christian faith as an adult, you may take part in an Alpha course, but beyond that your Christian education is down to chance: piecing things together from sermons and snatches of conversation. Outside the Roman Catholic Church, there is very little by way of prolonged and systematic catechesis.[43] Notable

---

[43] It is interesting to note, for example, that the only mention of catechesis on the Alpha Course web site is in the section 'Alpha for Catholics'. This makes plain that 'Alpha is only the first step' and goes on to quote from the General Directory for Catechesis (para. 61), 'The functions of primary proclamation are to proclaim the Gospel and call to conversion. Catechesis, distinct from the primary proclamation, promotes and matures initial conversion, educates the convert in the faith and incorporates him into the Christian Community.' See, www.alphacourse.org/catholics/followup/index.htm.

exceptions are the Emmaus course and the three-year catechetical programme being developed by Andrew Walker for the Anglican Diocese of London.

Adult education implies more than simply getting to grips with the Bible – as home groups might – crucial as that is. It means acquainting the whole congregation with a framework for under- standing theology more widely conceived: it might include acquir- ing a basic grasp of biblical studies, church history, dogmatics, patristics, historical theology and ethics. This matters because the virtual absence of adult education has a number of serious consequences.

At its most basic, the paucity of adult discussion of Christian the- ology creates yet another silence that starves the Christian commu- nity of world-building conversation. More seriously still, it deprives people of the opportunity to develop the kind of apologetic skills that can place their faith on a firmer intellectual footing. Without these, the possibility for world-defending legitimations to circulate within the Christian community is more limited. Without, say, a framework for thinking about suffering (a theodicy), Christians suffering tragedy are more vulnerable to loss of faith in the face of it. More than this, the lack of widespread Christian adult education stunts the growth of maturing disciples. Christian maturity is multi- faceted: we can grow (or stagnate) in a number of dimensions – physical, spiritual, emotional, volitional and intellectual. The mere fact of developing physical or emotional maturity does not guaran- tee corresponding growth in spiritual or intellectual maturity. Even in churches composed of highly educated and (in their professional fields) competent individuals there can be an intellectual blind spot when it comes to issues of faith. This only contributes to the marginalization of faith in everyday life. I remember, as a curate, chatting to a man who had recently left our congregation for another, more liberal, church in the city. I asked him why he had left; he replied that there 'was nothing there' for him any more. Developmentally, he had hit a brick wall. By contrast, the more liberal church was giving him food for thought, evidenced by the fact that, when I spoke to him, he was already ploughing his way through Augustine's *City of God*. Mature thinking is important for restoring credibility to the church, because it acts like an anchor able to resist the pressure of winds and tides: the mature thinker is no longer 'blown about by every wind of doctrine', nor is she (or he) as vulnerable to the tides of social rhetoric dragging plausibility, now this way, now that.

In part, too, this anchor reaches deep down into memory. A person with a deep sense of the 'cloud of witnesses' who have held firm to the faith down the centuries will feel their faith to be more deeply grounded than the person whose sole acquaintance with Christianity has been ten weeks of Alpha. Put differently, credibility is safeguarded when we are rooted and grounded in tradition. The French sociologist Danièlle Hervieu-Léger has observed that we now live in what she calls 'amnesiac' societies; the 'chain of memory' reaching down like an anchor into the murky past has been broken. Yet people do not enjoy feeling cast adrift from their moorings; so, she suggests, in place of broken chains of memory, groups re-invent traditions by which they legitimate themselves. They create an 'imagined continuity' which connects them to an authoritative past. In this way, imagination and memory (the basis for two cognitive plausibility structures) work together to reconstitute religion. People invent substitute memories. No longer is the imagination harnessed to conceive a sacred canopy; it is employed to re-invent a chain of memory. In this way, modernity provokes the creation of new forms of tradition which provide stability and meaning.[44]

While this is true for certain re-invented traditions (say, Wicca, or Celtic Christianity), it is not the case for historic Christianity as a whole. Here, the chain of memory is perhaps a little rusty, but it is not broken. Instead, Grace Davie has argued that the memory of Christianity in Europe is merely mutating: it is undergoing mutation as change occurs in social attitudes ('vicarious memory'), education ('precarious memory'), the mass media ('mediated memory'), in patterns of religious immigration ('alternative memories'), and in culture ('aesthetic or symbolic memory'). Where Danièlle Hervieu-Léger speaks of the 'reconstruction' and 'substitution' of memory, Davie writes more optimistically of its 'handing on' and 'recovery'.[45] Whichever scenario is closer to the truth of what is taking place in Europe, it is clear that many people are looking to reconnect with authoritative traditions which give meaning and legitimacy to their faith in the present. Adult Christian education provides a crucial opportunity for people to do this.

True discipleship also demands that we pay attention to the renewing of our minds. There is a moral dimension to wilful ignorance. We cannot allow ourselves to become as culpable as serpents and as foolish as doves. In a complex world we cannot afford the luxury of a simple faith: it is part of Christian duty to wrestle with issues of global justice, politics, consumerism, bioethics and so forth. Only by engaging with these issues (as responsible citizens,

---

[44] Hervieu-Léger, *Chain of Memory*.
[45] Davie, *Modern Europe*.

apart from anything) can we avoid our faith being domesticated within the reigning structures of power in society – a house-bound status which proclaims only faith's irrelevance. The prophetic role of the church requires of us that we think. As we do this, a widening spectrum of our world will become intelligible in terms of Christian faith; every thought will be taken captive; every sight will be seen through the lens of the gospel. The renewing of our minds demands that we learn to wear our Christian spectacles, in order to be able to see the world aright.

Those for whom school was an experience they would rather forget may now be feeling rather agitated as they read this. 'Sunday school' for adults may sound less than appealing. So, if you can forgive the pun, some qualifications are in order. First, adult education is not about 'being brainy', or trying to turn everyone into an academic. It is merely about providing the opportunity for everyone to grow in their thinking to the best of their abilities. Secondly, there is sometimes a fear in church circles that if people are encouraged to 'think for themselves' they might think themselves out of faith altogether. Of course, this is a risk; and in fact, it is an important risk, because without it people tend to be credulous. However, in my experience it is only when people are taught irresponsibly (say, when the whole weight of nineteenth-century biblical scholarship is dropped, uncritically, perhaps by poor teachers, into the head of some defenceless Anglican reader-in-training) that they experience a crisis of faith. Furthermore, a related fear arises from the 'all-or-nothing' mentality of some Christians, particularly those from evangelical backgrounds. The fear goes that, if one part of my faith is allowed to be eroded by scholarship, the whole house of cards will collapse. This stifles independent thought and leads to the curse of some evangelical thinking – dishonesty. Ironically, most of the time this fear is wholly unnecessary: a little more thought will usually enable us to see how letting out some dirty theological bathwater here and there need not upset the baby one bit. Babies are tougher than we think: so is truth. Those who claim to love truth could perhaps relax a little when it comes to denouncing the intellect, and trust wisdom to speak for herself.

Five: Invest in Young People

My final practical imperative is that we should invest in young people. How often have you heard an older person proclaiming that young people matter because 'they are the church of tomorrow'? And how often have you heard frustrated youth and children's workers responding, 'No! They are the church of today!'

Sociologically speaking, of course, both are true. However, when we are thinking about the future of the churches in Britain, the former observation is particularly important. The fact is that most people in the church today were also in the church as children; it follows that most of the church of tomorrow will consist of the children of the church today. What this means is that any mission-minded church will want to place considerable emphasis on nurturing children and young people. I could go so far as to say that if a choice has to be made between employing a youth worker, and employing an evangelist or even (dare I say it) a priest, go for the youth worker. Gifted lay people can look after the adults: young people require dedicated attention. Such investment makes sound missiological sense.

For some, the point will seem obvious. Yet it is worth looking a little more closely at precisely why young people deserve such priority.

One way we can do this is to examine in more detail the statistical claim that most people in the church today were also there as children. In July and August 2001, as part of the Scottish Social Attitudes Survey, Steve Bruce and Tony Glendinning posed a number of questions to a sample of 1600 adults regarding their faith.[46] One set of questions asked respondents what religion they were brought up in and in what religion they are now. Five religious categories were used: 'Kirk' (the Scottish Presbyterian Church), 'No Religion', 'Roman Catholic', 'Other Christian' and 'Non Christian' religions. Four things stand out from the results: most people brought up in any one of these groups are still in the same category today;[47] hardly anyone changed allegiance from one Christian denomination to another; the only significant exiting from all religious groups was in the direction of 'No Religion'; and ten per cent of those who were raised 'No Religion' now claim a religious identity. This last point is quite heartening: people do become Christian in later life. In this snapshot, one in every ten of those raised outside the churches now see themselves as belonging within them. The evangelist (or was it the priest?) is not entirely redundant. More significant, however, is the first observation: if it is the case that most adults within the Christian denominations were also there as children, this suggests that the ongoing socialization of young people

---

[46] S. Bruce and T. Glendinning, 'Scotland is No Longer a Christian Country', *Life and Work* (June 2002), 14.

[47] Strictly speaking, only 47 per cent of those brought up in 'other Christian' denominations remained in that category, which is just short of 'most of'. The percentages for the other groups were: Kirk, 62; No Religion, 89; Roman Catholic, 75; Non-Christian, 93.

into the church is at least as important as evangelism for the mission of the church. Churches need to invest in young people. This is particularly so given the fact that, in the survey, the Christian denominations lost between one- and two-fifths of their young people to 'No Religion'. Bruce and Glendinning put it bluntly: 'Once gone, they are gone. With so few of the No Religions becoming religious, if a church cannot keep its children, it is doomed.'[48] As I suggested in chapter five, ongoing socialization is necessary for maintaining the reality of religious worlds from one generation to the next.

This survey provides some recent statistical grounding to the (perhaps rather obvious) claim that the church needs to invest in young people. Further, the dynamics of credibility we have so far examined suggest ways in which we might do this. At the risk of generalizing, young people are perhaps more susceptible than most to being influenced by the 'reasons of the heart'. Young people are forging identities, aligning themselves with this group or that and striving to make sense of things. More than other age groups, young people tend to be attracted to those groups which can most effectively resolve their needs for identity, community and meaning. In the church context, investing in young people will mean fostering solutions to this quest which form viable alternatives to those which a secular consumer society provides. A Christian identity, a Christian community and a Christian worldview can be attractive solutions to the typical core anxieties of young people. Exactly how we forge these resources is beyond my scope to consider, although my impression is that many churches could start by giving their young people considerably more power. If we cannot provide these solutions, we can be sure that some other locus of plausibility will.

Time Up

This concludes our five-point 'breather' taken from our exploration of the dynamics of credibility. The logic of chapter five suggested five imperatives for practical action for restoring credibility to the church: building plausibility shelters in order to protect beliefs from the hailstorm of social rhetoric; prioritizing community over congregation in church life; re-enchanting our worlds; educating adults; and investing in young people.

Time is now up. We need to return to the thread of the argument as we consider the third dimension of the dynamics of credibility: the location of church in society.

---

[48] Bruce, 'Scotland', 13.

7

Deep River: Church in Society

In this chapter we will explore the third dimension of the dynamics of credibility: the location of *church in society*. We saw in chapter four that outcrops of durable religion persist in the modern world – *religion in modernity* remains a dynamic force. Likewise, in chapter five, we observed that the configuration of *Christianity in consciousness* is a powerful determinant of religious plausibility. Here, the task is to consider how the different ways in which the church is positioned in society and culture influence the credibility of believing and belonging within her.

The classic work on the positioning of the church in society and culture is still Richard Niebuhr's *Christ and Culture*,[1] published over half a century ago. Niebuhr charts the 'double wrestle' of the believer as he (or she) tries to balance the demands of loyalty towards, on the one hand, Christ and, on the other, culture. He identifies five ways in which the church, historically, has positioned Christ in relation to culture, in order to apportion her split loyalties: Christ 'above', 'against', or 'of' culture; Christ the transformer of culture; and Christ and culture in paradox.

The categories I will use in this chapter are informed by Niebuhr, but they differ in some significant ways. Niebuhr's categories are essentially theological, whereas mine are sociological; he is concerned to chart the range of attitudes towards culture on the part of the church, whereas I am more concerned to identify options for the location of the church in society; his categories are derived from normative claims, mine from empirical observations. A further difference is that I have simplified the categories to only three. Each of these may be thought of as survival strategies. They may have been adopted consciously; or, more likely, they have simply evolved as the mechanism by which a particular church has succeeded to date. Each has something to recommend it. I am not going to argue for the superiority of one over another, even though the fault lines of many theological debates fall precisely between them.

---

[1] H.R. Niebuhr, *Christ and Culture* (London: Harper, 1952).

The three strategies I suggest that the church may adopt as she positions herself in society are the strategies of 'tension', 'momentum' and 'significance'. One way of illustrating the difference between these three strategies is to compare the church in society to a person wading through a river. The person represents the church; the river signifies the ever changing 'stream' of culture and society in which the church exists. There is no possibility of the person leaving the river: the social and cultural location of the church is an inescapable given. Nor will the river stop flowing: change is here to stay. What the person can do, however, is alter the way she responds to the river. One option is for the person to stand her ground against the current, to feel the pressure of water pulling at her legs and resist it. This is the tension strategy. A second strategy is for her to lie in the water, to float downstream in the midst of the current and simply go with the flow. This is the momentum strategy. The third option is for her to seek to redirect the motion of the current, to upset the direction of the water in some way and to make a splash. This is the significance strategy. These three strategies – to 'stand your ground', 'go with the flow', or 'make a splash' – represent three options for the positioning of church in society.

In what follows I will explore each of these strategies in turn; in each I will seek to identify the dynamics of credibility within them. What is it about these strategies that makes for success? I will then return to the various options open to the contemporary church in Britain, discussed in the previous chapter (cell, network, midweek churches, etc.), in order to see where they fit within each of these strategies. If we can begin to say why certain forms of church succeed, these forms will be better able to play to their strengths. In addition, this framework will identify strategies that are, to date, underused and therefore ripe for exploration.

The perceptive reader may have noticed that the scenarios of desecularization in chapter four were in fact grouped and presented according to the main strategy by which they succeed. In other words, these scenarios do not all succeed for the same reason: some succeed because they adopt a 'tension' strategy; others persist by 'momentum' and still others by 'significance'. Thus, the eleven scenarios described in chapter four adopt different strategies, as follows: 'sectarian', 'transitional' and 'defensive' religion all adopt a tension strategy; they may be thought of as 'tension scenarios'. 'Latent', 'vicarious', 'civic', 'stable', 'resilient' and 'holistic' religion are, by the same token, momentum scenarios. 'Consumer' and 'public' religion are significance scenarios.

Stand Your Ground: The Tension Strategy

The first of these survival strategies involves maintaining a high degree of tension between the religious group and its host culture. Like the wader in the stream, a tension scenario will aim to 'stand its ground' against the pressure to change and conform to the prevailing currents in culture and society. For this reason, tension scenarios are characterised by *distinctiveness*. They stand out as being different, uncompromising, strong. The logic of this mode of persistence is that nothing is to be gained by capitulating to culture. Hope for the future lies in maintaining the doctrinal (and often ethnic) purity of the group, against an apparently hostile, alien and even corrupt world.

Tension can exist at any number of points: belief, lifestyle, values, social circle, dress, jargon, interests and so forth. These can all conflict with what is considered 'normal' in the host culture. In chapter five we thought about the pressures placed upon plausibility structures by their host culture, and these pressure points are the very points of contact where the tension must be maintained. Tension scenarios must ensure that the beliefs, norms and values of contemporary 'secular' culture are not allowed to overrun the group so that it loses its distinctiveness. All the strategies of the successful plausibility structure – cohesion, exclusion, socialization, conversation, legitimation – must be energetically employed. These plausibility structures are not hard to spot. Defensive religions will gather a mnemonic community around a vision of religious nationalism, for example. Transitional religion has typically formed a 'ghetto'. Sectarian religion, too, makes excellent use of the plausibility structure inherent in the sect. As we have seen, the sect represents the embodiment of the plausibility structure *par excellence*; this explains why it has such strength

The previous chapter identified a range of options for the church today that may be thought of as tension scenarios: that is, they derive their strength – their credibility – from the tension they are able to sustain between themselves and their host culture. Most of these are forms of *sectarian* religion. Cell church, small Christian communities (or transforming communities) and traditional church plants all tend to succeed because they are able to perform the functions of successful plausibility structures: nurturing cohesive relationships; maintaining distinctive beliefs; excluding threatening competition; sharing a common memory, outlook and vision; ensuring ongoing socialization and 'conversation'; and circulating world-defending legitimations. (By contrast, one other tension scenario, the Latin American 'Base Ecclesial Community' is a form of defensive religion – the Catholic faith of members provides a rallying point for resistance to economic oppression.)

These tension scenarios succeed, then, because of their distinctiveness. Their disadvantage is that there is a high threshold to cross for those who wish to join. However, once inside, the new member is likely to offer a high degree of loyalty to the group. The problem is getting him (or her) in. Tension scenarios might be tempted to try to lower this threshold, in order to make it easier for people to join. This is, in effect, a lowering of tension between the group and its host culture. As I suggested in the previous chapter, this strategy is probably mistaken. Unless the group in question (be it a cell church, church plant, or whatever) is willing to shift wholesale to a momentum strategy (which we will explore in a moment), it may simply lose the advantages of distinctiveness, without gaining in any way. People can as easily walk out over a low threshold as walk in; watered-down sectarian religion pleases no one.

The paradox of sectarianism

What is the future for sectarian religion? Is it wise for the church to invest in such forms as cell church, small Christian communities, church plants, or even the suburban 'mega-churches' that are beginning to appear here in Britain? Perhaps. There are signs that these may remain viable; however, before we explore the signs, there is one caution. The caution arises from what I call the 'paradox of sectarianism'. This paradox arises from a basic conflict in sectarian churches between, on the one hand, the need to promote intensive interaction between members (in order to sustain world-creating conversation) and, on the other, the need for members to be 'in the world'. Put differently, sectarian churches must juggle the competing demands of discipleship and evangelism. This conflict is amply illustrated in my experience as a member of the Christian Union while at University. The ostensible purpose of the Christian Union was evangelistic; yet (at that time) its main 'teaching' meeting took place on a Saturday night; Christian students were thereby cut off from contact with non-Christian students on the most sociable night of the week. One of my friends even worked out that there were twenty-two Christian meetings of one sort or another he might be expected to attend in a week! Little wonder, then, that we had few friends outside our social circle with whom we could have shared our faith.

In other words, sectarian religion must insulate its members from competing definitions of reality; however, such insulation also cuts it off from the outside world. Sectarian religion may be strong, but, it seems, it will always be self-limiting. Sectarian religion, almost by definition, seems to be destined to remain a minority sport – unless, that is, something can be done about its competitive environment.

The American exception

What are the signs of hope, then? Is strong, subcultural Christianity eternally limited? Not necessarily. If we look to America, for example, we find sectarian religion flourishing within a competitive environment. This seems to go against all I have just argued. How can this be? Sociologists are divided over how to explain the happy co-existence of pluralism and religious vitality in America. As we saw in the previous chapter, Steve Bruce has argued that this co-existence is possible because religious groups in America are able to cocoon themselves within their own subcultures far more easily than in Europe. On a different tack, Bryan Wilson has argued that the strength of American religion lies in its ability to function 'as a surrogate for genuine community' in what is a highly mobile society.[2] In both of these explanations, the threat from pluralism is simply avoided. Other explanations play down the threat from pluralism. Rodney Stark and his associates (the 'Rational Choice' theorists) have argued that pluralism is actually good news for religion because it increases the number of options available, ensuring that there is something for everyone in a deregulated religious marketplace.[3] Again, Peter Berger has recently qualified his claims about the impact of pluralism on religion: he now suggests that pluralism does not affect the content of belief, but only its style.[4] We still believe, but our beliefs are no longer held with certainty, only with what he terms 'epistemological modesty'.[5] The historian John Coffey defuses the threat from pluralism in a still different way. He comments, 'we all know that pluralistic societies contain people with strong religious beliefs – if this were not the case they would not be pluralistic societies!'[6] In other words, the persistence of sectarian religious groups is part of the logic of pluralist societies.

---

[2] Wilson, 'New Images', 588.
[3] Stark and Bainbridge, *Theory of Religion*.
[4] P.L. Berger, 'Protestantism and the Quest of Certainty', *The Christian Century* (26 August 1998), 782–96.
[5] P.L. Berger, 'Epistemological Modesty: An interview with Peter Berger', *The Christian Century* (29 October 2000), 972–8.
[6] J. Coffey, 'Secularisation: Is it Inevitable?', *Cambridge Papers* 10.1 (2001), 3.

The emergence of co-operative pluralism

This is a complex debate and I am not going to attempt to arbitrate between these competing positions. There is one further option, however. The corrosive power of pluralism may have been lessened in recent years on account of the emergence of what may be termed 'co-operative pluralism'. The idea of co-operative pluralism fuses the Enlightenment stress on tolerance with postmodern agnosticism towards the possibility of arbitrating between competing positions. Thus, instead of pluralism undermining religious belief or certainty, the emergence of co-operative pluralism suggests that there is growing solidarity between people of faith. Against an individualistic, materialistic culture, religious people can find solace in shared impulses, even if they do not share the same religious contents. Moreover, co-operative pluralism indicates a growing tendency for the modernist impulse for conflict between rival views to be replaced with an attitude of mutual respect. This is quite different from a liberal, relativist position, or indeed from a comparative view that sees all religions as saying basically the same thing. Instead, co-operative pluralism affirms the certainties of particular faith communities, without feeling required (say, by some abstract ethic of rational enquiry) to account for the differences between them. In this way, the certainty of one's own position can be held alongside the integrity of another's different set of beliefs, without friction.

A good example of co-operative pluralism in action was the rhetoric of the 'two integrities' that was used to describe the rival sides in the debate over the ordination of women to the priesthood in the Church of England in 1992. In this instance, co-operative pluralism was very tangibly enshrined in the provision of 'flying bishops' to serve the needs of the losers in the debate. Similarly, websites such as 'beliefnet.com' provide a source of information, news and comment about religion, as well as a devotional dimension, that includes all the major religious traditions together on the same home page. More striking still, in Burnsville, Minnesota, local cinema advertising is used to attract viewers to a supermarket of beliefs operating out of Burnsville Elementary and Middle School every Sunday morning. Those who attend can expect to find around a dozen different groups offering worship from a range of religious traditions in adjacent classrooms on the same corridor. Visitors are invited simply to take their pick from the range of practices on offer. The attitude of co-operative pluralism is neatly summed up in the title of the 1998 Manic Street Preachers' album, *This is My Truth, Tell Me Yours*. The possibility of truth is admitted (unlike the relativist position), but there is no urgency to decide who has it.

What this amounts to, if this hunch is accurate, is a lessening of tension between tension scenarios and their surrounding context. This does not necessarily lower the threshold of entry to sectarian groups, but it does leave them more at peace with one another and with their host culture. Sectarian tension scenarios need not be viewed as the fossil remains of post-reformation dissenting and non-conformist groups. Small, intense, distinctive religious groups still have a future in the plural societies of the West. If anything, their time may have come. What matters is that sectarian forms of church understand why they succeed and continue to play to these strengths. Whatever one thinks of their theologies, it cannot be denied that they are structurally tough; they are survivors. Andrew Walker, in *Telling the Story*, concludes that if it is the case that the church is entering a new 'dark ages', it is the sectarian groups that will carry the candle through the night.[7] I agree. We should not underestimate them.

Go With the Flow: The Momentum Strategy

Tension is one strategy for positioning the church in society and culture. It involves standing your ground and being distinctive. A second option is the momentum strategy. The most obvious expression of this is what may be termed 'culture-Christianity'; that is, Christianity that is embedded in the values, norms and artefacts of a society and its culture. On this strategy, Christianity succeeds by going with the flow of cultural change and harnessing the power of the current. Momentum strategies view culture as an important 'carrier' of religious beliefs and practices. Examples include religious establishment, latent beliefs, civic religion and the whole cultural inheritance of Christianity described in chapter four under the heading of 'resilient religion'. This strategy acknowledges that Christianity is not only a counter-cultural movement, but (like all religion) a cultural artefact: religion is culture. Perhaps a better analogy for the momentum strategy is, instead of a *person* floating downstream, a sponge. The sponge is in the river; the river is in the sponge. Religion and culture interpenetrate, so that they are not easily separated. Christianity is carried *by* culture – by those tacit, unseen assumptions about the rightful place of religion in the world that have been built up over two millennia – but Christianity is also a carrier *of* culture. As we saw in chapter four, the Christian tradition in Europe has inspired the best musicians, artists and architects, as well as providing grounding for our legal, educational and welfare systems.

---

[7] Walker, *Telling*, 190.

Christendom: curse or blessing?

It is easy to assume that the future of religions in Europe lies with tension scenarios: religious sects, religious immigrants and religious nationalisms are highly visible against the contrasting backdrop of the prevailing culture, and for that reason seem to possess a kind of obstinacy and durability. By contrast, the rather amorphous, jelly-fish-like forms of momentum scenarios seem destined to be washed out with the receding tide of faith. In a hundred years' time, who will still marry in the Church of England? Who will have their children baptised? Who will still recognize the most basic of Christian symbols? It is easy to imagine that culture-Christianity is doomed to die.

Moreover, many missiological writers now see culture-Christianity as positively harmful. For them, it represents the legacy of a now defunct Christendom, which they blame for the decline of the church and its contemporary malaise. Theo Hobson, for example, has called the established Church of England, 'a mouldy piece of Christendom'.[8] Stuart Murray Williams has suggested that, 'there will be tremendous opportunities as the memory of Christendom fades – if we let go of our privileged but compromised past and false hopes of restoration and revival (both deeply flawed and backward-looking Christendom concepts)', and also claims that, 'the memory of Christendom is still strong enough in many parts of our society ... to frustrate our best efforts'.[9] Similarly, David Smith asks, 'has Christianity in the West been reduced to mere ideology, co-opted to serve the interests of movements largely at odds with the biblical vision of the world and its peoples?'[10] Likewise, Douglas John Hall has argued: 'Presumption upon the past power and glory of Christendom is perhaps the greatest deterrent to faith's real confession in our present historical context.'[11]

One of the main perceived abuses of Christendom, then, has been an unholy alliance between church and state, between temporal and ecclesial power. The reason Christianity succeeded in Europe from the fourth century was precisely because the temporal and ecclesial powers were in bed together. In many ways, these criticisms are valid. It cannot be denied that at times the cross and the sword have been indistinguishable. Eighth-century 'missionaries' destroyed the pagan symbols: Boniface, Apostle of Germany, cut down the Oak of Donar at Geismar, while Charlemagne fought the

---

[8] T. Hobson, 'Independence or Idolatry?', *Third Way* 26.8 (2003), 22.
[9] S. Murray Williams, 'The End of Christendom: Challenges and Opportunities', *Jesus Life* 65.1 (2004), 14.
[10] Smith, *Mission After Christendom*, 40.
[11] Hall, *End of Christendom*, 3.

Saxons and destroyed their central sanctuary, composed of trees that were conceived of as the pillars of the world.[12] The crusades of the high medieval period are the epitome of this collusion of power. Even where no blood was shed, other forms of power were harnessed for the mutual benefit of church and 'state'. In the thirteenth century it was common for men to be instituted as rectors of parish churches or prebendaries of cathedrals, but for them never to exercise their ministry; instead, they hired a poorly paid chaplain to discharge their duties, while they themselves took the income from their churches in order to support their careers as civil servants in Chancery or Exchequer.[13] In this way, the clergy were able to pursue their careers, and the civil authorities were able to take advantage of the large endowments of the church. Not everyone approved of these practices, of course: reformers such as Bishop Grosseteste of Lincoln fulminated against such abuses; yet, as late as the nineteenth century, many gentlemen clergy remained absent from their charges.

If this is Christendom, it is not difficult to see why commentators such as Stuart Murray Williams reject it. In truth, however, where do we see such unholy alliances today? Where privilege still exists, it is understood as the privilege of service, rather than the privilege of power. The few Anglican bishops who retain a foothold in the House of Lords, for example, hardly lord it over their constituents: they are usually extremely busy people who make time to serve the nation by bringing their own field of expertise to bear upon the concerns of the day. Today, in other words, the legacy of Christendom does not involve the church in an abuse of power. The political establishment of the church has all but vanished.

For others, however, the problem lies not in the political establishment of the church, but in her cultural establishment. Douglas John Hall comments:

> The establishment of the Christian religion in both Canada and the United States, particularly the latter, has been infinitely more subtle and profound than anything achieved in the European parental cultures. The reason for this is not very complicated. It is that whereas the old, European forms of Christian establishment were legal ones (*de jure*), ours have been cultural, ideational, social (*de facto*).[14]

---

[12] A. Wessels, 'The Inculturation of Christianity in Europe' in S. Barrow and G. Smith (eds.), *Christian Mission in Western Society* (London: Churches Together in Britain and Ireland, 2001), 31–49.

[13] C.H. Lawrence, *The Life of St Edmund by Matthew Paris* (Stroud: Allan Sutton, 1996), 19.

[14] Hall, *End of Christendom*, 29.

Hall argues that the church must seek to disestablish herself from culture if she is to recover her genuine vocation to mission in the world, instead of her identifying Christianity with the 'general social values and mores of the dominant classes'. He points out that the churches are being marginalized in any case, and he urges them to take control of their disestablishment, rather than falling into it by default. This will involve untangling the Christian message from the dominant assumptions of American society, so that the church can become 'salt, yeast and light'. 'To grasp this opportunity, however, we must relinquish our centuries-old ambition to be the official religion, the dominant religion, of the dominant culture.'[15]

I wonder: is this critique necessary? Is the establishment of the Church of England really to blame for its decline?[16] Does the memory of Christendom actually *frustrate* efforts at mission? Is Western Christianity mere ideology? And is there no place for the past power of the church in the contemporary world? The fact is that much of our religious life today relies on the cultural momentum accrued from the past, in whatever form: plant and endowments; older, more dutiful church members who continue to attend; the socialization of people who attended Sunday school as children; higher attendances at Christmas and Easter; support for the church among rural communities; the cultural embeddedness of Christian symbols; the expectation that people will turn to the church for rites of passage; the ongoing high levels of religious beliefs; the provision for religious broadcasting and religious education; the continuing role of senior church people in public life; Christian assumptions which undergird our ethical thinking; and so on. Simply to sweep all of this aside under the banner of a defunct Christendom and argue that now is the time for the church to focus exclusively upon radical, prophetic, intentional communities, seems to wash a 'crècheful' of babies out with the proverbial bathwater. It represents a root-and-branch philosophy that seems largely unnecessary.[17]

The fact is that there are some glacial energies involved in culture-Christianity: slow, yes, but with enormous power to scour and shape a cultural landscape. Christendom represents the successful inculturation of the gospel in the societies of Europe; today, it may be receding like a melting glacier, but it has by no means vanished. If these energies can be valued, and even harnessed, this may prove to be every bit as effective as a tension strategy. Graeme Smith

---

[15] Hall, *End of Christendom*, 49.
[16] For my response to Hobson, see D. MacLaren, 'God Serve the Queen?', *Third Way* 26.9 (2003), 16–18.
[17] Perhaps it is another example of the evangelical 'all-or-nothing' mentality I described in chapter six.

concludes his introduction to an important collection of missiological essays by pointing out that missiology need not involve, 'a lamentation of the failure of inculturation, but instead a critical exploration and celebration of successful inculturation, and how it may be developed'.[18] The dynamics of credibility could be found to be at work in momentum scenarios, too.

The dynamics of momentum

How then might they work? I have just indicated that the energy of momentum strategies (primarily, culture-Christianity) derives from its being 'carried' by culture. Culture-Christianity relies for its plausibility on assumptions already inherent in culture, on procedures and habits that have achieved an unstoppable momentum through force of repetition (imagine anyone trying to cancel Christmas), and on arrangements which tacitly confirm the social acceptability of Christianity in a variety of contexts. Consider, for example, the entrée Christian chaplains have into schools, universities, hospitals, prisons, shopping centres, airports, industry and the military. It is the unchallenged acceptability of the chaplain in these contexts that enables her (or his) ministry to operate. The chaplain has some responsibility not to exploit this privileged position, but also considerable freedom to represent Christ at the coalface of mission. (It is an irony that in some church circles chaplaincy is not considered to be 'real' ministerial experience!) Culture itself, then, supplies the plausibility structure for culture-Christianity. Likewise, it is the memory of Christianity carried within a whole culture which legitimates contemporary expressions of church. (Against this observation, Stuart Murray Williams' hope that the memory will soon fade seems astonishing – unless he means only the bad memories.) Similarly, it is culture itself that projects some social rhetoric in support of the plausibility of the momentum strategy – Western culture does part of the job of socializing people into a Christian worldview. This simply would not take place in, say, India or Japan. In all these ways, then, the momentum strategy of culture-Christianity is able to succeed.

Momentum today

Many of those who hope that the memory of Christendom will quickly recede so that we can get down to some real mission have, paradoxically, no problem with the idea of inculturating

[18] G. Smith, 'Introduction: Reviewing Mission in Western Society' in S. Barrow and G. Smith (eds.), *Christian Mission in Western Society* (London: Churches Together in Britain and Ireland, 2001), 11–28.

Christianity in the present. This is ironic: where Christianity has conformed itself to pre-modern or – still worse – modern culture, this is seen as 'compromise', 'ideology', 'presumption' or 'mouldy' faith; yet, where Christianity is creatively adapting to current circumstances, this is seen as 'bold', 'courageous', 'innovative' and 'cutting edge'. Seminars on the 'postmodern church' are all the rage: yet nobody seems to want to know how the church should relate to the modern and pre-modern cultures that are still with us. But why should we not remain sensitive to these cultures, too? In rural areas, the pre-modern parish principle is still strong; in suburbia, late-modernity is blossoming in large, conservative-evangelical congregations. It is tempting to look at yesterday's collusion with culture and despise the church's choices, like so much seventies' wallpaper. Yet, today, in the brushed-steel newness of our experiments in emerging church, we seem willing to bend over backwards to conform our expressions of church to contemporary culture. Why is it acceptable to seek relevance to contemporary postmodern culture, but not to the vestigial cultures of modernity and pre-modernity? Why is Christendom 'bad', but culturally-relevant emerging church 'good'? Are we not guilty of what C.S. Lewis termed 'chronological snobbery'?

Perhaps we make this distinction because it is easier, with hindsight, to see where our past attempts to be 'relevant' turned out to be little more than apostasy dressed as a whore. In the thrill of newness and experimentation, it is perhaps a little harder to see where today's flirtation with new forms of church will end up; so we give them the benefit of the doubt. What I want to suggest is that there is a place for harnessing the cultural momentum of both past and present, both of the 'downstream' momentum inherited from history and the 'upstream' momentum of contemporary cultural currents.

Downstream momentum

I am not advocating a return to Christendom: history is history. What interests me is the potential for harnessing the cultural momentum of the past. We considered some practical ways in which momentum scenarios might be made to work, in chapter four, under the headings of 'latent', 'stable', 'vicarious', 'civic', 'resilient' and 'holistic' religion. These examples were only intended to be illustrative; hopefully, practitioners on the ground will be able to see many more contexts in which the momentum of a Christian past may be harnessed. At this stage, I will simply add two more examples of the approach I have in mind, in order to flesh out this vision.

The first of these examples of a momentum strategy at work is the continuing provision, in many churches, of the Anglican liturgy for Holy Communion of 1662. Typically, this continues to be appreciated by worshippers at 8 a.m. on a Sunday morning, or sometimes midweek. Despite the fact that this service makes few concessions to 'accessibility', it continues to be appreciated by a variety of people: older people who have grown up with it; people with finely-tuned aesthetic sensibilities who value the language; and even some younger church-leavers. Anecdotally, I have come across a renewed hunger for this style of worship among younger people – the so-called 'Generation-X' – who may drop in to these traditional early services before going on to charismatic churches, or to Starbucks. A similar trend can be seen in the renewed interest taken in cathedral worship in recent years. Such attenders are not being offered accessible language, cosy community, or culturally congruent multi-media presentations: what they are finding is continuity with tradition which gives them rootedness and a space to explore.

The second example is the 'new monasticism' referred to in the previous chapter. This involves groups of people who may or may not be centred on a monastic 'house', but who hold one another to some kind of 'rule of life'. Instances include the associate communities of Iona, Northumbria, Taizé, the Tertiary Franciscans (and oblates of other monastic communities) and the Order of Mission launched from St Thomas Crookes in Sheffield.[19] The internet has also been used as a forum for networking, and gathering people together who are looking to frame their Christian journey within a structure of mutual encouragement and accountability. One such venture is the virtual community gathered under the auspices of www.sanctus.org.uk. What these ventures have in common is an attempt to draw upon a rich inheritance of spirituality in order to give structure and depth to lives of worship in today's world. Both these examples capitalize upon the forces inherent in 'resilient' religion, as I described it in chapter four.

Upstream momentum
If the energies of the past may be harnessed in mission, it is also true that *contemporary* cultural trends may be accommodated in order to lower the threshold of the church's doorway. Most of the proposals that have been put forward to increase access to the church make use of the energies of 'latent' religion; that is, they seek to tap in to the subterranean spirituality of contemporary people. They do this by inculturating a postmodern spirituality within social structures

---

[19] See n. 40 of the previous chapter.

that are familiar and easy for people to access. In other words, they make use of the cognitive momentum of latent religion, while at the same time harnessing the structural momentum of contemporary forms of social gathering. Churches based around networks, 'liq-uid' churches, 'alternative worship' communities, café churches, seeker-sensitive churches and youth congregations all make use of the momentum of existing social and cultural trends in order to lower the threshold of access. Clearly, this list of churches describes a diverse range of options: seeker churches, say, may be more theo-logically conservative than 'alt. worship' groups. However, what these churches share is an assumption that people are not basically antagonistic towards Christianity; they believe that most people have some interest and sympathy, but also need ways to belong that they can cope with. These options provide just that. Contemporary people are familiar with the café, the cinema and the internet as venues in which to meet. Churches that use these venues are capital-izing on the momentum of these cultural trends.[20]

Beyond latent religion, however, less attention has been given to the other momentum scenarios outlined in chapter four. Without repeating the examples I offered in that chapter, it is worth thinking of further ways in which the momentum of the other scenarios may also be harnessed. It may be that these ways will only become apparent as mission is worked out in messy, real-life contexts. What I am trying to offer here is simply a framework for thinking widely about the options that are available. News of stable religion might be important because it challenges the myth of a secular society, and helps to break the taboo on religion; civic religion could be affirmed and extended, widening the public plausibility structure for reli-gion-in-general; resilient religion is important for the reasons just given above in the discussion of downstream momentum; holistic religion might be important for lessons it can teach the church;[21] and vicarious religion may prove to be more enduring than we think.

Revisiting vicarious religion

This last point deserves special attention. Vicarious religion depends upon there being a large, passive majority of the

---

[20] A helpful exploration of potential approaches to latent spirituality can be found in Mark Ireland's chapter, 'Engaging with the search for spiritu-ality' in Booker and Ireland, *Evangelism*, 171–84.

[21] See, for example, J.W. Drane, *What is the New Age Saying to the Church?* (London: Marshall Pickering, 1991) and J.W. Drane, *What is the New Age Still Saying to the Church?* (London: Marshall Pickering, 1999).

population who do not attend church, but who do have some religious beliefs, and who do think of themselves as Christian (72 per cent at the last census). The question is, can we find alternative ways for these people to belong? In a recent interview on BBC Radio 4, Estelle Morris was asked how she thought the Labour Party could attract new members. She acknowledged that there are very many more supporters of the Labour Party than there are paid-up members (a good parallel with vicarious religion). She suggested that the Labour Party could look at other ways for people to belong, because, at the moment, the only option is full membership. Is this something the church could learn from? How could the church help the 72 per cent who call themselves Christian to feel a stronger sense of belonging?

One potential pattern can be found in those associations which have bucked the trend of declining involvement, such as the Royal Society for the Protection of Birds (RSPB) and The National Trust. The RSPB has over a million members, a network of 160 local groups and 130 youth groups, 176 nature reserves, over 8,800 volunteers and a staff of over 1,300. The National Trust has over three million members, over 200 historic houses, 38,000 volunteers contributing two million hours of their time, 4,000 seasonal staff and 4,000 regular staff. Interestingly, the fastest growing sector of annual membership is in the family group. Both organizations are a little over a hundred years old. There are several things to notice here: these organizations are growing their membership; they provide a variety of ways to belong; they offer degrees of commitment, from simple subscription, through to intensive volunteering; they have a small number of sites (relative to their membership); they have a high investment in paid staff; they are both geared to conservation; they are both charities. When we compare, say, the Church of England, with these organizations, we find many of the same attributes: a membership in millions (depending on your criteria); an army of volunteers; a high investment in paid staff; an interest in conservation; and a charitable status. Where the Church of England differs, however, is that it is not growing its membership, it provides few ways to belong and it has a very large number of sites to maintain. In some ways, these sites – over 16,000 churches and forty-two cathedrals – are a great attraction: around 31 million tourists visit them each year. The bill to maintain them, however, is more than £100 million per year – twice the entire annual income of the RSPB!

I am not suggesting we turn the Church of England into a heritage industry. I am wondering, however, whether there is scope for launching something like an ecumenical category of 'Associate

Member' of the Church. As with the conservation charities, associate members could belong by subscription, receive a magazine with information and inspirational content, be kept informed of courses the churches are running, and find ways of volunteering and committing themselves more fully. Associates could benefit from special access to historic Christian sites, or other services the churches offer. There could be various 'streams' of membership, including those whose interest is the conservation of historic buildings, music and forms of worship; or those who are looking for spiritual uplift; or those who want to support the church more broadly. It may be that associate members become interested in meeting others of a like mind in their local area – rather like the RSPB's local groups – perhaps even to worship together (perhaps to become church?). Associate membership would not necessarily constitute belonging within the covenant community in any theological sense: but nor does visible church membership. This, then, is not a theological vision of church, but simply an exploration of the sociological possibilities for a different way of belonging. Not every associate will take the route of repentance and faith and worship: but at least a new route would be open.

Make a Splash: The Significance Strategy

The two strategies of 'tension' and 'momentum' may be placed at opposite ends of a continuum that represents the degree of permeation between religion and culture. Put simply, tension scenarios persist in spite of culture, whereas momentum scenarios persist because of it. In terms of the historic Christian traditions, tension scenarios have generally been employed by the conservative Protestant sects, whereas momentum scenarios have been preferred by the mainstream denominations, and particularly by the established churches. This has tended to lead to a polarized view of the options for Christian mission among sociologists and historians. Beginning from the assumption that the Christian gospel is inimical to the values of the modern world (this in itself betrays sectarian assumptions) commentators have assumed that the only strategies for the churches to adopt in the shadow of modernity are either resistance, or accommodation. Either the churches live in tension with the world, or they change their message to make it more accommodating. Alan Gilbert, for example, writes, 'Accommodation is not the only possible response to the emergence of a post-Christian culture. But in the last resort there is but one alternative: the lonely sectarian road of resistance.'[22] Peter Berger, equally, has

---

[22] Gilbert, *Post-Christian Britain*, 133.

suggested that, 'the two basic options open to [religious institutions] are those of accommodation and resistance'.[23] David Lyon, too, uses similar terms: 'As we have seen, groups and individuals with clear religious identities engage in a continuing process of adaptation *and* resistance in respect to contemporary conditions.'[24]

What all these analyses lack is any sense of a middle option. Perhaps especially in Britain, with our history of living with the polarized options of either conformity or dissent in matters of religion, there has developed an imaginative blind spot in conceiving the relationship between religion and culture. Religion is either constituted in the human will, in decision, in conversion and in voluntarism; or it is constituted in culture, in tradition, in memory and in precedent. We can see no third way. What challenges this myopia are the empirical examples of voluntarism engaging with the sphere of the wider culture in order to shape it and change it. In chapter four, we looked at two forms of persisting religion that may be classed as significance strategies: 'consumer' and 'public' religion. We will look at these in more detail in a moment.

These kinds of religion refuse to be the religion of the prairies or the ghetto, just as they eschew the camouflage protection which makes them indistinguishable from culture. Instead – and this is the third way – they achieve *significance through engagement in the public sphere of* modern societies. This is the significance strategy: not stubbornly standing your ground in the stream of culture, nor passively going with the flow, but actively seeking to engage with culture – to make a splash. The word 'significance' is chosen deliberately, as an echo of Bryan Wilson's definition of secularization in terms of the declining social significance of religious beliefs, practices and institutions. The significance strategy creates plausibility for beliefs by *increasing* the public significance of religion. It does this in three ways.

The dynamics of significance

The first of these concerns the way in which significance strategies are able to engage with the public sphere of modern societies. Earlier, I suggested that, although there no longer exists a 'sacred canopy' over European societies, a sphere of shared values, norms, symbols and beliefs remains within contemporary European societies, which may be termed their 'public canopy'. This public canopy supplies modern societies with a normative consensus sufficient to avoid anarchy and to enable them to function. The public canopy

---

[23] Berger, *Sacred Canopy*, 155.
[24] Lyon, *Disneyland*, 139.

constitutes a culture-wide plausibility structure, against which smaller, competing structures in the private sphere struggle to construct their worlds. Part of the success of significance scenarios – 'public religion' and 'consumer religion' – is their ability to engage with and function within the public canopy. Because they form part of public 'conversation', their institutions share the same discourse as other social institutions and, as a result, their claims are treated as part of a legitimate debate. Conversely, they avoid the stigma associated with the apparently deviant conversation of religious groups in the private sphere. In short, significance scenarios enjoy a measure of plausibility gained by virtue of *participation* in the 'public canopy'.

Secondly, significance scenarios achieve success by harnessing the attention of one particular cognitive plausibility structure, the 'optical community'. Earlier, we saw how the other two cognitive plausibility structures, based on memory and imagination, were crucial ingredients in the construction of what Hervieu-Léger termed an 'imagined continuity', where chains of memory had been broken. Here it is the turn of 'attention' to come to the fore. As we have seen, Eviatar Zerubavel describes the range of people who have been socialized to see the world in a particular way as an 'optical community'. The optical community is constituted by those who turn their attention to the world in common ways. However, attention is never merely a passive consequence of socialization, but the way in which we attend is in perpetual flux as different agencies seek to compete for the limited resource of human attention, whether advertising agencies, political pressure groups, or religious institutions. These seek not only to grab attention, but also to streamline the ways in which we attend to, and 'disattend',[25] the world. To use a simple example, we may never have noticed a particular model of car before, but having been influenced by advertising to buy one, suddenly that model seems to be everywhere. Our attention has been awoken to it. Another example is the publicity stunt. Part of the success of significance scenarios lies in their ability to act as one of the agencies which streamline attention in their direction. 'Public religion' and 'consumer religion' both employ strategies which seek to create an optical community around their interests and, crucially, to draw attention to themselves from the pool of *public* attention. They do not, or do not only, seek to create a sub-cultural optical community. Rather they are inherently competitive as they engage in the battle for *attention* within the public sphere.

---

[25] Heilman, 'Constructing Orthodoxy', 144–57.

The third way in which significance scenarios succeed follows as a consequence of the previous two. If they manage to participate successfully within the public canopy, and win some of the competition for public attention, it follows that they will have achieved a high degree of public relevance, or what may termed 'social significance'. Relevance, in turn, functions to legitimate the claims of the group. Relevance is therefore a form of legitimation which lends plausibility to significance scenarios, on the basis that a set of beliefs and practices that appears to have social utility has more to recommend it than one that does not. If Christian faith inspired many church leaders in Eastern Europe to lead, or take part in, the revolutions of 1989, for example, that faith is clearly socially significant, and from that significance is derived a strong sense of its legitimacy. By contrast, the absence of relevance is a treatise for atheism. As Kenneth Cragg observes, 'The irrelevance [of religion] so readily concluded in the contemporary West spells [the] nonexistence [of God] so effectively that a rationally based case for atheism needs no making.'[26]

In sum, and taken together, significance strategies succeed for these three reasons. They are able to benefit from the plausibility conferred on them by virtue of their participation in the public canopy of modern societies. They achieve plausibility through their ability to influence public agendas and streamline attention in their direction. And their social significance supplies them with a legitimacy which confers additional plausibility on them.

It is now time to look at one significance scenario in more detail, in order to consider the viability of this strategy as form of mission. In chapter four, we considered 'public' and 'consumer' religion. Either of these would make interesting case studies. In the former case, religion is very much back on the public agenda since the Rushdie affair, the rise of the religious right in America, the role of the churches in ending Communism in Eastern Europe, '9/11', the pronouncements of the Catholic Church in relation to the AIDS epidemic, and the protracted debate on the wearing of religious symbols in French schools – to name only a few examples. As most of these examples show, however, public religion tends to win attention through its notoriety, which is perhaps not the best advert for it. A more fruitful line of exploration follows the other scenario, the emergence of consumer Christianity.

In chapter four, consumer religion was identified as a form of religion which adopts the values and methods of consumer culture in order to succeed. If we are to understand consumer religion,

---

[26] Cragg, *Secular Experience*, 4.

therefore, we need first to take a brief tour of some contemporary thinking about consumer culture. What is consumer culture?

Consumer culture

We begin with the sociological observation that social life is shaped not only by what we produce – by work and industry – but also by what we *consume*: 'consumption shapes social relations and social meanings in no less authentic a manner than does production.'[27] The parallel emphasis on 'consumerism' suggests that an ideology surrounds the act of consumption. Although the exact meaning of consumerism is contested, there are a number of characteristics which are identified as being more or less common to it. I have identified nine in all.

The first of these concerns the primacy of individual *choice*. Gabriel and Lang comment, 'Choice lies at the centre of the idea of consumerism, both as its emblem and as its core value.'[28] Only through choice may personal freedom be fully realized.[29]

Secondly, consumerism consists in the expectation of *novelty*. Since consumer needs are unlimited and insatiable[30] they are always calling forth new products. The expectation of novelty is further reinforced by the fact that innovation is a requirement of economic growth in a consumer society.

Thirdly, consumers believe in their natural right to *abundance*. In principle they can buy anything from the groaning shelves of our packed supermarkets. In Jean Baudrillard's words: 'Our markets, major shopping thoroughfares and superstores … mimic a new found nature of prodigious fecundity. These are our Valleys of Canaan where, in place of milk and honey, streams of neon flow down over ketchup and plastic.'[31]

Fourthly, consumer society accepts *obsolescence*. Baudrillard contrasts our attitude with that of previous civilizations:

> we live at the pace of objects, live to the rhythm of their ceaseless succession. Today, it is we who watch them as they are born, grow to maturity, and die, whereas in all previous civilizations it was timeless objects, instruments or monuments which outlived the generations of human beings.[32]

---

[27] G. Marshall (ed.), *Oxford Concise Dictionary of Sociology* (Oxford: Oxford University Press, 1994), 26.

[28] Y. Gabriel and T. Lang, *The Unmanageable Consumer* (London: Sage, 1995), 27.

[29] D. Slater, *Consumer Culture and Modernity* (Cambridge: Polity, 1997), 8.

[30] Slater, *Consumer Culture*, 28.

[31] J. Baudrillard, *The Consumer Society* (London: Sage, 1998), 26, 32.

[32] Baudrillard, *Consumer Society*, 25.

Fifthly, there is the duty to be *happy*.[33] Gabriel notes:

> Pleasure lies at the heart of consumerism. It finds in consumerism a
> unique champion which promises to liberate it both from its bondage
> to sin, duty and morality as well as from its ties to faith, spirituality, and
> redemption. Consumerism proclaims pleasure not merely as the right
> of every individual but also as every individual's obligation to him- or
> herself.[34]

'Objects exist no longer [to] serve *a purpose*; first and foremost they
serve *you* ... It is in the sun of this solicitude that modern consumers
bask.'[35] Pleasure is gained not only in the act of consumption, but
also in its anticipation. Aspiration is central to the generation of
consumer 'needs'. As Mike Featherstone suggests, 'consumer
culture uses images, signs and symbolic goods which summon up
dreams, desires and fantasies which suggest romantic authenticity
and emotional fulfilment in narcissistically pleasing oneself, instead
of others.'[36]

Sixthly, objects are not consumed primarily for their utility, but
for the *meanings* they communicate.[37] Indeed, Baudrillard goes so
far as to define consumption 'as the establishment of a generalized
code of differential values', by which he means that objects differentiate their consumers from one another in a status hierarchy according to the meanings that are being communicated.[38] Again,
'material objects express social differences as well as personal
meanings and feelings'.[39]

Seventhly, and following from the previous point, the meanings
communicated through consumption enable the construction of
identity:

> Consumption is not just a matter of satisfying material greed, of filling
> your stomach. It is a question of manipulating symbols for all sorts of
> purposes. On the level of the life-world, it is for the purpose of con-
> structing identity, constructing the self, and constructing relations with
> others ...[40]

---

[33] Baudrillard, *Consumer Society*, 49, 80.
[34] Gabriel and Lang, *Unmanageable Consumer*, 100.
[35] Baudrillard, *Consumer Society*, 159.
[36] M. Featherstone, *Consumer Culture and Postmodernism* (London: Sage, 1991), 27.
[37] Baudrillard, *Consumer Society*, 79.
[38] Baudrillard, *Consumer Society*, 94.
[39] Gabriel and Lang, *Unmanageable Consumer*, 47.
[40] Z. Bauman, *Intimations of Postmodernity* (London: Routledge, 1992), 223.

Paradoxically, consumers 'personalize' themselves through conformity to some prescribed model; yet, to the individual this is experienced as the formation of a unique identity.[41] Thus, consumer
culture is the privileged medium for negotiating identity and status
within a post-traditional society.[42]

The eighth characteristic is the framing of shopping as *leisure*.
Baudrillard points to the consumer mentality that conceives of
leisure as the sphere of freedom, and experiences leisure as the consumption of time. Shopping malls are not conceived of as merely
functional spaces facilitating exchange, but as leisure spaces.[43] In
place of the cathedrals of pre-modern societies, shopping malls now
function as the 'the signifying and celebrating edifice' of culture.[44]
This points to the possibility of there being a functional equivalence
between consumer norms and values and those of traditional religion; a point to be explored later.

The final major characteristic (and there are several others which
could have been included) is the possibility that consumer freedom
is illusory and that consumers are really victims of aggressive, but
tacit, forms of *social control*.[45] Advertising is one way in which the
'needs' of consumers may be streamlined, as Vance Packard argued
in *The Hidden Persuaders*.[46] And yet the plight of consumers seems
paradoxical. If they are enslaved to a system that exploits them,
they are, at the same time, the heroes of the system.[47] These nine
facets of the consumer mindset contrast with the assumptions of a
culture in which production is the predominant influence on
markets.

Consumer religion
Consumer religion picks up on these themes in a number of ways.
To begin with, religious institutions both 'produce' and 'consume'.
The institutions themselves produce the religious 'commodities'
that are on offer, while their members consume them. The impact of
consumerism on both producers and consumers can therefore be

---

[41] Baudrillard, *Consumer Society*, 88.
[42] Slater, *Consumer Culture*, 29.
[43] R. Shields (ed.), *Lifestyle Shopping: The Subject of Consumption*
(London: Routledge, 1997), 7.
[44] L. Langman, 'Neon Cages: Shopping for Subjectivity' in R. Shields (ed.),
Lifestyle Shopping: The Subject of Consumption (London: Routledge,
1997), 40–82.
[45] Bauman, *Postmodernity*, 17.
[46] Baudrillard, *Consumer Society*, 71.
[47] Slater, *Consumer Culture*, 33.

seen at work within religious institutions, and within the churches in particular. It is important, therefore, to consider the role of both consumers and producers in the construction of consumer religion.

Christians as consumers

On the side of consumption, it is clear that the move from 'obligation to consumption'[48] signals a carrying over of the 'cognitive style'[49] of consumerism from the marketplace of goods into the newly perceived religious marketplace – new, that is, since around the 1960s. As people come to view religious outlets not as objects of loyalty and commitment, but as service providers there to meet their spiritual needs and wants, they will tend to make the same ideological assumptions about such outlets as they make about the marketplace at large. This may have a number of consequences, following on from the list of characteristics of the consumer mentality above. In what follows, these consequences will be expanded upon in relation to the Christian churches.

First, the primacy of *choice* means that religious consumers will tend to choose their church according to what it can offer them, rather than according to any prior obligation to support one denomination or church locality over another. Consumer religion therefore supports voluntarist congregations over parochial churches.

Secondly, the expectation of *novelty* means that religious consumers will increasingly expect the church to continually innovate or entertain, as the price of their commitment. 'Behold, I am doing a new thing', is the familiar refrain of such contexts. The correlate to this assumption is that boredom is unacceptable. Consumer religion is therefore marked by a restless quest for stimulation, which is inimical to the rehearsal of traditional liturgies.

Thirdly, the assumed right to *abundance* may be translated into an expectation of continual ecstatic or therapeutic experience – 'life in abundance'. Consumer religion has no place for the 'dark night of the soul', unless, perhaps, this can be packaged as a novel ascetic experience.

Fourthly, the acceptance of *obsolescence* suggests that the religious 'commodities' that are consumed – the sermons, songs, choruses, liturgies, and prayers – are not expected to be used for very long, but have a 'shelf life', intended to make way for novelty. This

---

[48] Davie, *Europe: The Exceptional Case* (London: Darton, Longman & Todd, 2002).
[49] Berger et al., *Homeless*.

attitude favours the extempore over the written, the spontaneous over the planned and the creative over the given.

Fifthly, the duty to be *happy* may make it difficult for those adopting this cognitive style to identify with the darker side of human experience – to identify with a crucified God. Moreover, the form of happiness based on aspiration rather than present reality may encourage consumer-minded congregations to pin their hopes on idealistic promises of a 'deluxe version' of the Christian life which always seems to be just around the corner. Values of fortitude, patience and duty in the midst of present realities may suffer as a result.

Sixthly, the *sign-value* of commodities may be translated directly into church life on account of the merchandise that is bought through Christian shops, bookstalls, mail-order catalogues, or fairtrade outlets. Religious status may be communicated as much through these purchases as through any other – the proud owner of a prayer stool is evidently holier than thou.

Seventhly, since these purchases also construct *identity*, purchases of religious commodities enable the construction of religious identities, and different kinds of purchase help to differentiate and shade religious identities from one another. The buyer of an icon and the buyer of a 'WWJD' (What Would Jesus Do?) bracelet are clearly expressing very different religious identities.

Eighthly, the framing of shopping as *leisure* may have a counterpart in church attendance. Certainly, church attendance is widely conceived of as a leisure activity, since it takes place in the private realm of 'free time'. The expectation of entertainment supports this view. Rather than constituting a solemn obligation to worship, it is conceived as a form of recreation in which the worshipper comes primarily to receive rather than to give.

Finally, more contentious still are the implications of the theory that consumers are *victims* of tacit social control. Certainly, a consumer-minded congregation cedes considerable control over to the mediators of spiritual commodities. The potential for manipulation of needs is great among a credulous audience. Moreover, where physical commodities are interpreted as spiritual commodities, especially among the poor – as in the case of the 'prosperity gospel' – the scope for such control is considerable.[50]

These, then, are some of the ways in which the cognitive style of consumerism may translate into church life. Clearly, not all forms of church life exhibit these traits: many however, do.

---

[50] S. Bruce, *Pray TV: Televangelism in America* (London: Routledge, 1990), 159f.

Churches as producers

We can also consider the impact on the churches of the other side of
the equation, the side of production. Much attention has been given
to the possibility that some religious institutions, including the
churches themselves, have responded to this consumer-led situation
by absorbing the ethos of producers and service providers in the
secular marketplace. One of the most influential critiques in this
regard is the claim that church life has become 'McDonaldized',
after George Ritzer's McDonaldization thesis.[51] Put briefly,
McDonaldization is 'the process by which the principles of the fast-
food restaurant are coming to dominate more and more sectors of
American society as well as the rest of the world.'[52] These principles
are expressed in four core values. McDonald's 'offers consumers,
workers, and managers efficiency, calculability, predictability, and
control [through non-human technology]'.[53]

The McDonaldization thesis has been adopted by John Drane,
among others, in order to critique the production side of consumer
religion. He sees evidence of the principle of 'efficiency' in the way
that people are greeted – then moved on – at the church door, in the
sale of Christian 'how-to' books, in the specialization of Christian
ministries, in a programme-oriented focus and in the pre-packaging
of spiritual content. The second value, calculability, is carried over
into church life in the counting of heads as a measure of success,
often at the expense of personal and spiritual growth. The third
value of predictability Drane sees being reflected in church services,
in the conformity of opinions among some members, in expectations of the process of conversion and in attitudes towards the
action of God. The fourth value of control is mirrored in the traditional 'altar call' and subsequent processing of converts, in the
styling of lay ministry, and in the excessive control that may be exercised by those in authority.[54]

A more specific application of the McDonaldization thesis to
church life is Pete Ward's perspective on the Alpha course.[55] Ward
notes that, like McDonald's, Alpha operates on a global franchising
system. It has a recognizable 'product' with a strong brand label.
The central organization of Alpha retains fairly strict controls on
franchisees. It has global ambitions. Both McDonald's and Alpha
have spawned imitations. Beyond these superficial similarities,
Ward also notes the way in which the core values of McDonald's

---

[51] Ritzer, *McDonaldization of Society*; Ritzer, *McDonaldization Thesis*.
[52] Ritzer, *McDonaldization Thesis*, 1.
[53] Ritzer, *McDonaldization Thesis*, 12.
[54] Drane, *McDonaldization of the Church*.
[55] Ward, 'Alpha'.

are reflected in Alpha. Efficiency is present in the packaging of Alpha materials for easy use, and in the streamlining of the content of the course, enabling participants to get to the 'bare essentials' of the gospel quickly. Calculability is experienced in Alpha's 'predilection for numbers'. Predictability is translated into the guarantee of success if the Alpha formula is followed, and is woven into the timings of each evening and of the weekend away. Control is expressed through the Alpha material, which consists of talks on video, worship material, training manuals, a cookbook and various other resources. Control is also expressed through the tight copyright statement that seeks to preserve the integrity of the brand. Ward concludes that, 'This is a dynamic where power has shifted away from episcopal hierarchies and bureaucratic synodical government towards the market ... The movement to a market economy of religious life is a revolution of immense importance.'[56]

Ward's observation of the shift in power away from episcopal hierarchies does not mean that such hierarchies have themselves been immune to the temptation to imitate the market. Richard Roberts has pointed to the creeping managerialism that invaded so many institutions in Britain during (and after) the Thatcher era, including the Church of England.[57] He notes that George Carey, soon after his appointment as Archbishop of Canterbury in 1991, 'prominently advocated the implementation of managerial practices and schemes of appraisal that would enhance ministerial 'performance' and incidentally secure closer control of clerical ideology in what amounted to an ecclesiastical "neo-Fordism".'[58] In this quotation, Ritzer's themes of efficiency, calculability and control resurface quite explicitly. Even within the bureaucratic structures of the Church of England, therefore, it is possible to discern elements of consumer religion.

Consumer Christianity?
It should be clear by now that the Christian church in Britain has not escaped the tentacles of consumerism. Christians have imbibed a consumer mindset no less than anyone else: our thinking and, consequently our behaviour, is shaped by a consumer culture. The churches, likewise, are increasingly responding to consumer culture by styling themselves as flexible producers and service providers for whom the Christian consumer is sovereign.

---

[56] Ward, 'Alpha', 286.
[57] R.H. Roberts, 'Towards an Executive Church' in A. Walker and L. Osborn (eds.), *Harmful Religion*, (London: SPCK, 1997), 163–76.
[58] Roberts, *Religion*.

No doubt there is much that could be said, from a theological perspective, to caution against this situation. An uncritical capitulation to consumerism is likely to lead to the worship of the self and of mammon. However, my purpose here is not to develop a theological critique: the church has her prophets, and doubtless, we should listen to them. I simply want to ask, from a sociological perspective, to what extent is consumer religion a viable strategy for mission? Or, put differently, 'can we be "in" a consumer culture but not be bound by its underlying values?'[59]

As we saw earlier, consumer religion is a 'significance scenario'. In other words, it succeeds by 'making a splash' – forcing others to sit up and take notice. In particular, we saw that significance strategies gain plausibility by grabbing public attention, engaging in public conversation and demonstrating their public relevance.

One way in which consumer religion succeeds in gaining attention is in its ability to adopt the 'cognitive style' of consumerism. The point can be made by seeing how things have changed. Older forms of urban evangelism included preaching on street corners and knocking on front doors. Today, these methods rely upon an outmoded cognitive style – when was the last time you changed your beliefs on account of what was said to you on a street corner or on your doorstep? Instead, consumer religion recognizes that belief choices are part and parcel of whole lifestyle and identity choices. Consumer religion privileges choice (fear of Hell is no longer used as a motivator, for example); it leaves people time to browse; it uses humour and story;[60] it offers merchandise that enables consumers to commit themselves through the act of purchase;[61] it generates novelties (rather than recycling the old, old story), and so on. These are all examples of its adoption of a familiar cognitive style which, to some degree, we all now possess. Whereas the street preacher is anachronistic and, ultimately, fails to gain our attention, the billboard adverts, corporate logos, television exposure, press releases and national campaigns of consumer religion succeed in gaining

---

[59] Archbishop's Council, *Mission-Shaped Church*, xii.

[60] See, for example, the Churches' Advertising Network campaigns at http:/www.churchads.org.uk.

[61] See, for example, the Soul Survivor catalogue, offering books, CDs and videos. See also http://www.soulsurvivor.com. In a consumer culture, one of the primary ways in which identity is constructed is through the act of purchase. People can opt in to various sub-cultures according to what they buy (if they can afford to). Those who buy Volvo estate cars, green wellingtons, barbour-jackets, and golden labradors have constructed their identity in one particular way. Those who buy Vauxhall Novas, alloy wheels, baseball caps, and pythons, have constructed another.

some public attention. We instinctively understand their language. In this way, consumer religion is also able to enter into public conversation, both avoiding the stigma of sectarian religion, and demonstrating it has relevance for contemporary people.

Structurally, then, consumer religion has much to recommend it. But is it, in the end, hostile to the very nature of Christian discipleship? Does the medium eclipse the message? Can church really be church where the customer is always right? Jane Shilling offers us an important caution here:

> Spirituality, in short, is not a product, like laceless trainers or isotonic sports drinks, that we never knew we wanted. We want it, right enough. All the Church has to do is deliver. But it can't. And the reason is that, in its anxiety to chase the modern market, the Church no longer knows what it is. It has a brand name but no identity. People now – particularly, as it happens, young people – are intensely beguiled by authenticity and conviction, and quick to detect a lack of these. The plainchanting monks and nuns, the intensity and mystery of Orthodox Christian ritual, the leadership of the late Cardinal Hume seem to embody these qualities.[62]

This is one side of the argument. My purpose here, as I have said, is not to try to resolve it, but simply to raise the possibility that there may be another side to consider: perhaps the consumer mentality has important lessons to teach the church; perhaps it deserves careful attention, rather than hasty condemnation. One such lesson is offered by Pete Ward in his vision of 'liquid church'. Ward thinks that there is considerable mileage in privileging choice in worship over traditional set menus of congregational worship: articulating his 'dreams' he suggests that liquid church

> will challenge the assumption that what is offered in the morning service is good for you, even though it may be boring or unpalatable. It will present a responsive, flexible pattern of church life that seeks to deliver what individuals want and also draws on the depth and variety of the Christian tradition.[63]

'What individuals want' – well, why not, for a change?

Deep River

Our society is indeed a deep river for the churches to negotiate in today's world. There is no escape from society or culture. If the

[62] J. Shilling, *The Times* 2 (3 September 2001), 7.
[63] Ward, *Liquid Church*, 89.

churches are to avoid 'going under' they will need to make use of one or more of the strategies outlined in this chapter – strategies of resistance, accommodation and engagement. Corresponding to each of these strategies, they will seek to be distinctive, inculturated, and engaged.

Most expressions of church make use of only one of these strategies. However, these need not be mutually exclusive. Perhaps there are forms of church that are able to capitalize on all three? In the final chapter, I will reach back to one of the roots of Christianity in Britain to examine a little more closely a form of church that seems to have thrived on making use of all three of the above strategies – the Columban church of the sixth century.

Part 3

Credible Witness

8

Columban Mission: The Art of the Plausible

I began this book by claiming that much of the blame for the decline of the church in Britain is misplaced. I tried to show that the large-scale social and intellectual changes over the past 250 years provide a better explanation for church decline than finger-pointing and self-blame. Accepting this diagnosis, I then sought a cure within what I termed 'the dynamics of credibility'. This involved three tasks. First, I laid out a range of scenarios of desecularization in Europe – instances of religion persisting and even thriving against the backdrop of a so-called 'secular' society. Secondly, I explored the conditions required for religious worlds to remain plausible in contemporary consciousness. I then tried to root this theoretical discussion in five practical imperatives: build plausibility shelters; prioritize community over congregation; re-enchant your world; educate adults; invest in young people. Thirdly, I suggested three strategies for positioning the church in society and culture. These strategies capitalize on the inherent energies of maintaining tension with culture, riding the momentum of culture and achieving significance within culture. I have tried to root this discussion in concrete examples, some of which I hope will offer a way forward in mission.

So far, however, I have resisted the attempt to offer a blueprint for a 'successful' church derived from the foregoing sociological observations. Mainly, no attempt has been made because it seems clear that Western mission in the twenty-first century will not be uniform, but highly diverse. As the authors of *Mission-Shaped Church* contend, 'We need to recognize that a variety of integrated missionary approaches is required.'[1] The other problem with blueprints is that they are too easy to produce: the real world rarely conforms to our best laid plans. I have resisted creating a neat sociological model of church because such a thing would be unlikely ever to appear in the real world.

---

[1] Archbishop's Council, *Mission-Shaped Church*, xi.

A more interesting and fruitful way to pull together some of the sociological insights I have presented in these pages might be to look at one concrete historical example of Christianity thriving on account (it would seem) of the presence of many of the strategies we have been considering in this book. I have in mind the Columban church of the sixth century. We have already seen that one of the options identified by the authors of *Mission-Shaped Church* is a 'new monasticism'. This could mean a variety of things, from dispersed communities united by a common rule, to the restyling of cathedrals and minster churches as core communities serving a wide hinterland, or even the expansion of traditional monastic communities. If we are to consider a new monasticism, it will be worth taking a closer look at one expression of a very old monasticism that emerged in a pagan culture, grew rapidly and succeeded for at least six centuries. In our era of experimental (and ephemeral) churches, it is worth asking what sorts of communities we want to build for the next six hundred years.

The Columban church is also of relevance given that there has been a revival of interest in all things Celtic in the last few decades; this tradition has provided a distinctive resource for innovative forms of worship. If some churches have been heading in this direction already, where might their journey lead? At the same time, this revival has been much criticized for its romanticized view of history, which has allowed Christians to see in so-called 'Celtic Christianity' a mirror of their own concerns. In this way, the Celts have been championed as eco-warriors, radical feminists and democratic socialists. The darker, almost masochistic, side of these communities has, conversely, been overlooked. It is important to disentangle fact from fantasy in the tradition of Celtic Christianity. At the same time, however, perhaps it is too easy to dismiss the romantic: a tradition that is capable of inspiring romance is far from dead, even if its historical details require a closer look. The romantic elements at least imply a smoking gun.

For much of the thinking in this chapter I am indebted to Ian Bradley's work on the Columban church, most especially his two books, *Columba: Pilgrim and Penitent*[2] and *Colonies of Heaven: Celtic Models for Today's Church*.[3] Bradley prefers the term 'the Columban church' over 'Celtic Christianity' because,

> The notion of a Celtic Church, conceived of as a distinct ecclesiastical
> entity clearly distinguishable from, if not actually in opposition to the

---

[2] I. Bradley, *Columba: Pilgrim and Penitent* (Glasgow: Wild Goose Publications, 1996).

[3] Bradley, *Colonies*.

Roman Church, is profoundly misleading. It presupposes a degree of
uniformity among the highly diverse Celtic tribes and peoples of
Europe and a sense of self-conscious separatism which simply did not
exist.[4]

There is some debate as to whether Columba was a missionary at all
in the modern sense, or whether, rather, he was simply a founder of
monasteries which subsequently exercised a ministry of presence.
The twelfth-century Irish *Life of Columba* portrays him as an itiner-
ant missionary, but this seems like a later gloss. He has been credited with the evangelization of the Picts in the East; scholarly debate
has taken sides for or against this position with Ninian at Whithorn
as an earlier candidate for having Christianized the Picts and Aber-
nethy a third – possibly even earlier – locus of missionary activity.
What seems uncontroversial, however, is that he established
monastic communities. Adomnan describes him as 'the father and
founder of monasteries'.[5]

Even more relevant to contemporary missiology is the point at
which Columban Christianity emerged. By a strange, and rather
symbolic, coincidence, Columba died in the same year (597 AD) that
Augustine of Canterbury arrived in England with his commission
from the Pope in Rome to evangelize the Angles. These two rather
different strands of Christianity, the Celtic and the Roman, coin-
cided at this point. It was not until the Synod of Whitby in 664 that
they were formally to clash, over the date of Easter and a quarrel
about haircuts. 'Trivialities; but behind them lay a vast and many-
sided question – when such differences arise, who is to decide? Has
the Bishop of Rome in fact the last word?'[6] What the Roman form
of Christianity may be seen to represent is the arrival of the
Constantinian project – that historic expression of European Christianity in which the church is wedded to the structures of temporal
power in a relationship of mutual legitimation, somewhere between
the extremes of Erastianism and theocracy.

Living in the twilight of such arrangements, the time is now ripe
to reconsider a pattern of church life that existed before the spread
of Roman ecclesiastical organization and control – before the introduction of a comprehensive parish system governed by a non-
indigenous episcopal hierarchy.

---

[4] Bradley, *Columba*, 65.
[5] W. Reeves (ed.), *Life of St Columba, Founder of Hy (Iona), Written by
Adamnan Ninth Abbott of that Monastery* (Lampeter: Llanerch Enterprises, 1988), 34.
[6] S. Neill, *A History of Christian Missions* (Harmondsworth: Penguin,
1964), 71.

Wherein lay the dynamism of the Columban church? And of what relevance is it to the foregoing sociological discussion of the dynamics of credibility? We can begin to answer these questions with the observation that the Columban church succeeded in making use of all three strategies outlined in the previous chapter: it was distinctive (in tension with society), inculturated (carried by cultural momentum) and engaged (significant within the power structures of the day). How did it manage all this?

A Distinctive Community

The basic structure of the Columban church was the monastery. This could be large, comprising several thousand people, or small, consisting of a few hermits' huts. These were places of non-violence, where prayer, work, study, and artistic endeavour went on side by side.

The Celtic *monasterium* differed from what we think of today as the church in a number of important ways. Members followed a rule of discipline, lived together, observed a regular rhythm of worship, shared common work, pursued intellectual endeavour and were engaged in creative acts such as copying the psalms or creating illuminated manuscripts. The Celtic *monasterium* was also distinct from the Continental form in its severe bodily austerity (in food and vigils), in its combination of eremitical (solitary) and cenobitic (communal) living together, and in the fact that the single and the married lived side by side as well. It also differed in its zeal for studying local language and literature, as well as biblical and theological texts, and in the prominence of abbots over bishops as ecclesiastical rulers.

In other words, the Celtic *monasterium* formed a distinctive community, which embodied all the characteristics of a strong plausibility structure. The intensity and variety of its life, together with the strength of its boundaries, ensured a pattern that could be replicated for generations. It was both sociologically sectarian and theologically robust.

Ian Bradley has suggested that the *monasterium* provides a model for church life and mission from which we could learn. In a context where the Anglican parish system is increasingly creaking at the seams, he suggests it may be time to return to a pre-medieval pattern of monastic centres which service outlying satellite churches. Bradley does not think it necessary to establish actual communal living arrangements for the *monasterium* model to work: centres of a dispersed community could enable people to meet and pray together, to offer hospitality, to be developed as educational or resource centres, and to provide sacred space and the regular rhythm of prayer and worship. In this way, the monastery could remain distinctive and yet still disseminate its energies and resources to the churches it serves.

This sounds fine in theory, but when it comes to describing what this might look like in practice Bradley's vision appears to be very similar to what already exists. He points to the growth of lay ministry, team ministries, and deanery, diocesan and provincial synods as possible loci for a *monasterium* to take root, as well as cathedrals. What he does not go on to say is how an indistinct, spiritually diffuse institution (say, a deanery synod) can be transformed into anything like a Celtic *monasterium*. They are worlds apart. What seems to be missing here from his vision is the large element of charismatic personality, robust theology and uncompromising structure that enables the institutional dimension to flourish and resist routinization.

Perhaps Bradley has simply not gone far enough. The strength of the monastery is that it is a distinct entity or organism; approximations that leave the structure of genteel Anglicanism (or Presbyterianism, or whatever) basically intact are mere parodies of the original Columban communities. Structurally, the strength of the monastery is that it has strong boundaries which nevertheless allow traffic across them and provide hospitality and a range of other services to those around. Structures that are going to last for centuries need to be more robust than what exists at present. These days we rarely see communities where married and single, young and old, live together under a common rule. Perhaps the closest we come to this pattern is in groups such as the Jesus Army, or in our residential theological colleges. Ironically, the mainstream denominations have had a tendency to devalue both expressions of religious life: the Jesus Army is often viewed as a deviant group (despite their ability to reach those parts of society no other churches can reach), while the residential theological colleges of the Church of England seem perennially under threat from closure. Perhaps it is time for the churches to invest in a new round of monastery planting. If it is the case that some denominations in Britain have little more than a generation to go before the floodtide of decline sweeps over their heads, it could make excellent sense to build an ark. At the same time, we must be realistic about the fact that contemporary society is no longer organized along the lines of a Celtic *tuath*, or small kingdom. Today, a monastic community is certainly distinctive, but it can no longer claim to be a sensitive inculturation of the gospel. We must move on then to consider what an inculturated community might look like.

An Inculturated Community

The second strategy adopted by the Columban church was its ability to go with the cultural drift of Celtic society. It was not only distinctive, but inculturated. In order to examine this we need to look more closely at the location and shape of the Columban communities.

The story of the Columban foundation on Iona begins with Columba's journey from the north of Ireland to Iona. It is unclear whether this was a self-enforced exile – a penitential pilgrimage under-taken in response to his recklessness that led to the battle of Cul Drebne – or whether it was perhaps more a political manoeuvre. If the latter, it may have been that Columba intended to forge an alliance between the powerful northern Ui Neills of Ireland, the family from which Columba came, and the Scots of Dalriada, also of Irish descent, but living in the equivalent of modern Argyll. Whether penitential pil-grimage, or a political manoeuvre, what is clear is that Columba arrived in Iona in 563 and established a monastic settlement there. This grew to about 150 members by his death thirty-five years later, and established Iona as the centre of Christianity in (what is now) Scotland, for about 200 years, until the Viking invasions made Iona untenable as a monastic base.

Iona is often seen, somewhat romantically, as a remote outcrop of the Inner Hebrides, a periphery which enabled an intense reli-gious community to flourish, away from the strain and bustle of the city. Caught up in the myth of Celtic Christianity is a myth about the romantic, windswept remoteness of the Celtic churches on the periphery of Celtic society. In fact, something approaching the reverse of the myth is true. In the sixth century, Iona was far from being geographically or economically peripheral. The islands of the Inner Hebrides were on a major sea route for anyone travelling by sea along the west coast of Scotland. It was the land that was impassable, with few roads, high mountains and sea lochs reaching deep inland to thwart the progress of the traveller journeying north or south. Columba's journey to Iona from Ireland may be compared not to a person going to a remote place on retreat but to someone leaving London for Basingstoke down the M4 corridor. Iona was not so much a rural retreat as a sixth-century service station.

Planting monasteries was a canny ploy. Not only were they structurally tough, but they also blended into the contours of exist-ing power structures. For example, the rule of the abbot over his monastic *familia* was very similar to the rule of a king over his *tuath*. Abbots, like kings, tended to be authoritarian. They were also very often related to one another, in a kind of Celtic mafia. Certainly,

Columba promoted his relatives to lead the monasteries within his *familia*, just as he might have preferred them had he remained in Ireland and become a political ruler. Monasteries also developed some of the physical characteristics of the hill forts of their rulers, being protected by a boundary bank and ditch – the *vallum* – and by a wooden stockade. Columba ran his monasteries as though they were a kingdom, grouping them into a *familia*, or federation, bound together by kinship ties and establishing a dynasty to rule over them with himself as first high king. It is interesting to see in the eighth-century Irish poem, best known as the hymn 'Be Thou my Vision', that God is mentioned twice as the 'High king of heaven'. Kingship is seen as the ultimate form of rule. As Máire Herbert comments,

> The manner in which Colum Cille [Columba] organized the government of his monastic foundations would seem to have been based on established secular concepts of overlordship, kinship, and inheritance, so that the system had an in-built potential for survival and continuity in Irish society.[7]

The *monasterium* was a plausible institution for the members of Celtic society because its structures harmonized with the world that they knew. Undoubtedly this level of inculturation must have enabled the ministry of presence that the monasteries were able to perform. Today we do not typically live in community with one another. We balk at authoritarian leadership. We (in mainland Britain, at least) feel no need to live behind a defensive wall. Is it possible to retain the essential features of the *monasterium* today and still benefit from some measure of cultural momentum? Certainly, Bradley has identified the possibility that there are renewed currents of interest in a more demanding spirituality: 'Could it be that in the post-modern, pick-and-mix spiritual supermarket we now inhabit, people are actually craving commitment, discipline, and obedience?'[8] Perhaps, too, in a highly differentiated society there is an appetite for sites of dedifferentiation: places where activities and people come together in a complementary whole. Where people are able to work, worship and learn together there is the promise of community, which our mobile and fragmented society so desperately seeks. Perhaps, then, the monastery will once again become the shelter for lost souls, the dynamo of spiritual energy and the burial place of kings.

If there is a cultural current here, can it be harnessed? Can the postmodern quest for spirituality (identified in chapter four under

---

[7] Bradley, *Columba*, 43.
[8] Bradley, *Colonies*, 55.

'holistic religion') connect with the rise of social structures based around networks (discussed in chapter six)? One such experiment in creating a 'dispersed but intentional' community based around a common rule, to which I have already alluded, is the community centred on www.sanctus.org.uk. True to the structure of a network, this community is gathered around a virtual site on the internet. The site was initiated by a Baptist pastor, Simon Hall, in Leeds. Although the site quickly gathered enough subscribers to populate an average church, Hall thinks that it has not as yet provided a forum for community to develop. Soon after the site was launched, subscribers were invited to meet face-to-face to think about their future direction. This suggests that there is still a strong pull towards face-to-face community. In addition, Hall is already leading a church community (called Revive), many of whom are also subscribers. This means that there is considerable overlap between the concrete and the virtual community. What is not currently available is the opportunity for subscribers to meet in a virtual chat-room. If people can meet and fall in love over the internet, then surely it must be possible for a virtual community to thrive. It is too early to say how this particular experiment will develop, but it has the potential to foster a sustainable spirituality which – like the Columban church – is both distinctive and inculturated.

It is difficult for any religious community to remain both distinctive and inculturated, to be in the world but not of it. It is like trying to stand out from the crowd and blend in to it at the same time. This paradox is resolved if we make it our aim to be theologically distinctive but ecclesiologically inculturated – to be a church that costs nothing to enter but everything to belong.

An Engaged Community

There is another sense, too, in which we can be 'in the world but not of it', and that is to be both distinctive and *engaged*. In this case, being 'in' the world is not to do with blending in to cultural surroundings (the momentum strategy), but with engagement in the public life of communities and society (the significance strategy). This is the axis identified by Robert Warren in *Being Human, Being Church*.[9] Once again, there is a paradox here: it is hard for any church to manage both. 'Conservative or traditional churches find it easier to be distinctive than engaged, and liberal churches find it easier to be engaged than distinctive.'[10]

---

[9] Warren, *Being Human.*
[10] Warren, *Being Human*, 59.

Part of the attraction of the Columban church is that, yet again, it seems to have managed both. We have already seen that it was distinctive: how, then, did it engage?

Columba did not detach himself from politics when he left his native Ireland. He was an influential player in the politics of the time. He came from a royal family in Ireland, which ruled over one of the 150 or so *tuaths*, and there is a good chance that had he not left he would have become the leader of his *tuath*. There is a tradition that soon after arrival from Ireland he struck up a friendship with the king of Scots Dalriada, Conall mac Comgaill, who granted him Iona for his monastery. He was able to make use of his royal connections to further the cause of Christianity in what we now call Scotland.

Scotland in the sixth century was occupied by four distinct groups. Their rough location can be imagined by dividing Scotland into four quadrants, by a vertical division down the middle, and a horizontal one about level with the Forth. The Scoti, or Scots, occupied the north-west quadrant, Dalriada, with their royal seat at Dunadd. The north-east segment was occupied by the Picts, who were ruled from Inverness. The south-west sector was populated by the Strathclyde Britons, whose king was based in Dumbarton. Finally, the south-east segment was part of the Anglian kingdom of Bernicia and was ruled by the kings of Northumbria.

What is striking is that Columba seems to have had dealings with kings of all four of these regions. He was closest to the kings of Dalriada who were of Irish ancestry like himself, and in alliance with his own Ui Neill kinsmen. He was also on good terms with Roderc, king of the Strathclyde Britons, who seems to have been a Christian. There is no direct evidence of any contact with Bernicia, but twenty years after his death two Northumbrian princes fled to Iona for sanctuary, suggesting that some prior connection (no pun intended) may have existed. Columba also had dealings with Brude, the Pictish king. Bede suggests that Columba converted the pagan King eight years after he had become ruler of his people (i.e. in 566). Adomnan, his late seventh-century biographer, records an encounter near Inverness, but says that Columba only went to secure passage for a group of Monks who were living as hermits on Orkney, and does not mention any conversion. Columba also kept in touch with his royal relations back in Ireland. In 575 he presided over a convention between the northern Ui Neill and the rulers of Scots Dalriada which cemented the alliance between the two kingdoms.

Adomnan's life of Columba, written about a century after his death, seems to cast Columba in the role of the biblical Samuel, citing his king-making activities. It has been suggested that this was done in order to legitimate the ongoing role of the abbots of Iona in consecrating the kings of Dalriada. In this way, Columba may have provided Christian legitimation for the emerging institution of monarchy, as well as securing prayer and protection for the monarchs. In return, the Columban institutions would have enjoyed the patronage of royalty. Iona, we have noted, is the burial place of kings.

Columba, it seems, was not shy of worldly power, or of using it to advance his cause. His example – as royal heir, politician, diplomat, and king-maker – points to the missiological importance of charismatic figures who have the ear of political elites over against the merely institutional face of the church. Columba was no reclusive abbot – although he did spend considerable periods in solitary retreat: he was the leader of a distinctive community who was also able to engage in the politics of his day. Columban Christianity was neither geographically remote not politically inert; the community founded by Columba on Iona was a central institution in Celtic society; it was one of the busiest; it supported an ongoing ministry of hospitality and pastoral care at its heart; it fulfilled the role of school, library, hospital, guest house, arts centre and mission station. This was not a monastery withdrawn from the world, but one lying at the heart of its concerns. Columba succeeded in bridging the divide between the temporal and the religious, the mundane and the sacred.

In recent years, there has been renewed interest at the local church level in developing new ways of engaging with the voluntary and public spheres of contemporary society. Increasing recognition has been given to the potential for local church communities to make a difference in their locality, through developing properly researched, carefully planned community projects. In the 1990s, for example, the relief agency Tear Fund made use of its expertise in working with local churches in the developing world to assist churches in Britain to develop their own community initiatives. The 'Toolkit' developed by Tulo Raistrick was used to facilitate a process of local engagement for hundreds of churches. More recently, The Oasis Trust has developed the 'Faithworks' initiative to resource churches in a similar way.[11] These forms of engagement are not dissimilar to the hospitality, education and welfare offered in the Columban communities. It is worth remembering, too, that some parts of the church still have the ear of the ruling powers: the

---

[11] Stories of churches involved in transforming communities have been told in Chalke and Jackson, *Faithworks*, and in Hinton, *Changing Churches*.

current Archbishop of Canterbury is likely to act as kingmaker in the years to come; he has performed an important diplomatic function in facilitating dialogue between Christian and Muslim leaders in the Middle East; his opinion on issues such as the 2003 war in Iraq matters to those in power. And he is by no means the only Christian leader of influence. All these diverse examples show that there is plenty of scope for the churches to remain or become engaged in the public life of our society (the significance strategy). Like the Columban church, we can be both distinctive and engaged.

Three Dirty Words

In short, I am advocating that a missionary church community (whether monastic or otherwise) will be distinctive and inculturated and engaged. This sounds fine in theory until we confront the unpalatable counterparts to each of these strategies. The unpleasant fact is that each of these attributes carries with it a dark side that many of us prefer to avoid. This dark side may be summed up in three 'dirty' words sectarianism; nominalism; power. Unless we tackle head-on our negative reaction towards these seemingly perjorative terms, we are likely to shy away from all three strategies. The reason I want to look at them now is I think that all three words deserve a renewed sympathy.

For the Christian with an establishment cast of mind, *sectarianism* is anathema. However, as I have argued throughout this book, sectarian structures are the only social structures that are really capable of defending plausibility. We may dislike intensely the subculturalism and ghetto mentality associated with the sect, but if the church is a cognitive minority (as it now is) we have little choice but to regroup in communities whose cognitive and relational life is more intense than in the past. As Steve Bruce observes, 'sects are the greenhouse of faith'.[12] However, there is no necessary connection between sectarian structures and, say, fundamentalist faith, or cultural philistinism. We may lack empirical examples, but there is nothing to stop Christians building successful sectarian plausibility shelters which are also intellectually rigorous and culturally sublime.

The second dirty word is *nominalism*. Christians who prefer to drink their faith neat find the dilution that is nominal, culture-Christianity unpalatable. Rather than seeing how nominal faith may be developed, their tendency is to write it off as lukewarm faith – worse than if it were coldly hostile. Yet a different perspective on

---

[12] Bruce, *Modern Britain*, 70.

nominalism is also possible, as I have tried to argue in preceding chapters. Nominalism may be viewed as successfully inculturated Christianity. The reason such faith is 'nominal' is because it is so much part of the fabric of everyday life that people are able, simultaneously, to possess it and ignore it. As I pointed out earlier, it is an irony that much effort goes into making contemporary expressions of church life 'culturally relevant' (usually to the younger generation), while at the same time many expressions of nominal Christianity – which are already fully inculturated – are written off as bad faith. In previous chapters I have tried to indicate some ways in which the embers of nominal religion among the British might be fanned into flame: nominalism should be seen not as an obstacle to mission, but as a resource.

My final word is *power*. Why is so much contemporary missiology shy of it? It is true that 'God chooses the weak things of this world to shame the strong'; it is true that 'the meek shall inherit the earth'; it is true that 'he brings down rulers from their seats and exalts the humble and meek'; and it is true that 'his power is made perfect in weakness'. Does this mean that there is no place for power in the *Missio Dei*, the mission of God? A brief look at the New Testament suggests that worldly power, as well as divine power and human weakness, was crucial to the birth of the Church. Peter and John may have been 'unschooled, ordinary men',[13] but Luke and Paul – who together wrote half the New Testament – had been trained to think in their own fields of medicine and theology. We simply would not have the theological riches of the New Testament without the intellect and education of St Paul.[14] In Ephesus and Athens he takes on the philosophers, explaining and proving that Jesus is the Christ. Nor was Paul shy of using his connections: in Philippi and Jerusalem, Paul made use of his Roman citizenship in order to unsettle his enemies.[15] He was, 'a Jew, from Tarsus in Cilicia, a citizen of no ordinary city'.[16] His lists of 'boasts',[17] while underlining the fact that he places no confidence in his human advantages, are evidently meant to remind his hearers of his status: he is a zealous, circumcised, Israelite; a Hebrew of Hebrews; of the tribe of Benjamin; a descendant of Abraham; in regard to the law, a Pharisee. His pedigree and his *curriculum vitae* are second to none. This worldly status is clearly to his advantage: when he is placed on trial before Felix, Festus and Agrippa, he clearly impresses them; as

---

[13] Acts 4:13, NIV.
[14] Acts 22:3.
[15] Acts 16:37f.; Acts 22:25.
[16] Acts 22:39.
[17] See, for example, Philippians 3:4f.; 2 Corinthians 11:22f.

a prisoner on a storm-tossed ship he gains the trust of the captain and ends up devising the rescue plan. Whatever the situation, Paul seems to rise to the top. In part, then, his missionary activity succeeded because he was well educated, intelligent and privileged, with various ethnic and political advantages.

Those who view Christendom as a long, embarrassing chapter of church history are perhaps too hasty to wash their hands of worldly power. Power corrupts, it is true. But a genuinely incarnational church must be able to engage with worldly power, not only in the role of a prophet denouncing a king, but also in the role of adviser, ambassador and public servant. Just as Columba forged political alliances, crowned kings and ruled over his monastic *familia* like a tribal elder, so a missionary church may need to dirty her hands in the politics of the day. To retreat into Anabaptist seclusion is an abdication of responsibility; it is too easy to criticize from the sidelines. At times, the church will appear stained by the misuse of power – the tares will grow up with the wheat – but this is the price of a genuine encounter with the world. We may be accused of being a friend of sinners, a glutton, a drunkard, demon-possessed, out of our mind, keeping bad company – but these perceptions are no worse than Jesus suffered. If, sometimes, these criticisms are justified, then of course the church will need to reform; but at least she will not have evacuated the political sphere. She needs not only to 'speak truth to power', but to 'live truth alongside power'.

Mission Implausible?

The eclipse of the church in the West is just one chapter in a very long story. For Christians, that story begins 'in the beginning' with a world that is 'formless and void', and it ends in a new heaven and a new earth. Throughout the story of salvation history, Christians believe that God is at work, reconciling the world to himself. Against this cosmic picture, the steady decline of the church in Europe in the past four decades is little more than a footnote to history. Even now, across the globe, from Latin America to China, the church continues to grow. It is worth keeping this perspective in mind when we are tempted to believe that Christianity in the modern world is a spent force: far from it.

Yet we have seen that in our little corner of the world, in Europe, in just over a generation, the church has seen some dramatic changes. If these changes are thought of as unstoppable trajectories, then they do signal the disappearance of entire denominations a generation hence. From a missiological perspective, we are bound to ask whether that is the end of the story: is Europe heading for total secularity? Is the church now impotent to escape her sentence of death? In short, is mission implausible?

I have tried to argue in this book that total secularity is not the only possible outcome for European, and more specifically British, society. In particular, I have identified a range of scenarios in which religion is far from disappearing – scenarios of desecularization. I have also explored ways in which the implausibility of the Christian message in contemporary consciousness might be countered. And I have suggested that by paying attention to the ways in which the church is located in society – distinctive, inculturated and engaged – we can promote her plausibility. In all of these tasks I have been trying to expose the 'dynamics of credibility', the unseen forces and inner workings that decide the degree to which a belief-system and its carrier will seem plausible. I have sought out ways of restoring credibility to the church.

All this has been attempted, quite deliberately, within a sociological frame. Christians are social beings and churches are social institutions; therefore they can be studied, quite legitimately, with the tools of the social sciences. At the same time, it is important to remember that sociology offers only one perspective on the life of the churches – if you like, the human perspective. Sociology can say nothing of what God may or may not be up to in the life of the church. Sociology cannot prophesy; it can only predict. It can see the ebb and the flow, but not the tug of God upon the tides. That is the job of the prophet, the pastor and the theologian. This book is offered in the hope that those who are prophets, pastors and theologians may be able to take up these dry bones, and flesh out a missiological practice capable of restoring credibility to the church.

> As it was
> As it is,
> As it shall be
> Evermore,
> O Thou Triune
> Of grace!
> With the ebb,
> With the flow,
> O Thou Triune
> Of grace!
> With the ebb,
> With the flow.[18]

---

[18] de Waal, *Celtic Vision*, 257.

Bibliography

Acquaviva, S.S., *The Decline of the Sacred in Industrial Society* (Oxford: Blackwell, 1979)

Alpha, 'The Number of Registered Courses Worldwide', *Alpha News* (November 2003 – February 2004)

Anderson, B., *Imagined Communities: Reflections on the Origin and Spread of Nationalism* (London: Verso, 1991)

Arbib, M.A. and M.B. Hesse, *The Construction of Reality* (Cambridge: Cambridge University Press, 1986)

Archbishop's Council, *Mission-Shaped Church* (London: Church House Publishing, 2004)

Argyle, M. and B. Beit-Hallahmi, *The Psychology of Behaviour, Belief and Belonging* (London: Routledge, 1997)

BBC, *'Soul of Britain' Questionnaire* (Opinion Research Business, 2000)

Barker, E., *New Religious Movements* (London: HMSO, 1989)

Baudrillard, J., *The Consumer Society* (London: Sage, 1998)

Bauman, Z., *Intimations of Postmodernity* (London: Routledge, 1992)

Berger, P.L., *The Precarious Vision: A Sociologist Looks at Social Fictions and Christian Faith* (Garden City, NY: Doubleday, 1961)

—, *The Sacred Canopy: Elements of a Sociological Theory of Religion* (Garden City, NY: Doubleday, 1967)

—, *The Heretical Imperative: Contemporary Possibilities of Religious Affirmation* (Garden City, NY: Anchor Press, 1979)

—, 'Protestantism and the Quest of Certainty', *The Christian Century* (26 August 1998), 782–96

—, 'The Desecularization of the World: A Global Overview' in P.L. Berger (ed.), *The Desecularization of the World: Resurgent Religion and World Politics* (Grand Rapids: Eerdmans, 1999)

—, 'Epistemological Modesty: An interview with Peter Berger', *The Christian Century* (29 October 2000), 972–8

—, 'Postscript' in L. Woodhead, P. Heelas, and D. Martin (eds.), *Peter Berger and the Study of Religion* (London: Routledge, 2001), 189–98

Berger, P.L. and T. Luckmann, *The Social Construction of Reality* (Harmondsworth: Penguin, 1966)

Berger, P.L., B. Berger and H. Kellner, *The Homeless Mind: Modernization and Consciousness* (Harmondsworth: Penguin, 1974)

Bibby, R., *Fragmented Gods* (Toronto: Irwin Publishing, 1987)

Birrell, I., 'Feature', *Independent Magazine* (21 September 2002), 11–12

Booker, M. and M. Ireland, *Evangelism – Which Way Now?* (London: Church House Publishing, 2003)

Borhek, J.T. and R.F. Curtis, *A Sociology of Belief* (New York, NY: John Wiley and Sons, 1975)

Bosch, D.J., *Transforming Mission: Paradigm Shifts in Theology of Mission* (New York: Orbis, 1991)

—, *Believing in the Future: Toward a Missiology of Western Culture* (Harrisburg, PA: Trinity Press International, 1995)

Bradley, I., *The Celtic Way* (London: Darton, Longman & Todd, 1993)

—, *Columba: Pilgrim and Penitent* (Glasgow: Wild Goose Publications, 1996)

—, *Colonies of Heaven: Celtic Models for Today's Church* (London: Darton, Longman & Todd, 2000)

Brierley, P., *Religious Trends* (London: Christian Research, 1999)

Brinton, C., *The Shaping of the Modern Mind* (New York, NY: Mentor Books, 1953)

Brown, C.G., 'A Revisionist Approach to Social Change' in S. Bruce (ed.), *Religion and Modernization: Sociologists and Historians Debate the Secularization Thesis* (Oxford: Clarendon, 1992)

—, *The Death of Christian Britain* (London: Routledge, 2000)

Brown, L.B., *The Psychology of Religious Belief* (London: Academic Press, 1987)

Bruce, S., *Firm in the Faith: The Survival and Revival of Conservative Protestantism* (Aldershot: Gower, 1984)

—, *God Save Ulster: The Religion and Politics of Paisleyism* (Oxford: Clarendon Press, 1986)

—, *The Rise and Fall of the New Christian Right* (Oxford: Clarendon, 1988)

—, *Pray TV: Televangelism in America* (London: Routledge, 1990)

—, 'Fundamentalism, Ethnicity and Enclave' in M. Marty (ed.), *Fundamentalisms and the State – Remaking Polities, Economies, and Militance* (Chicago: University of Chicago Press, 1993)

—, *The Edge of the Union: the Ulster Loyalist Political Vision* (Oxford: Oxford University Press, 1994)

—, 'Religion and Rational Choice – A Critique of Economic Explanations of Religious Behaviour' in S. Bruce (ed.), *The Sociology of Religion* (Aldershot: Edward Elgar, 1995)

—, *Religion in Modern Britain* (Oxford: Oxford University Press, 1995)

—, *Religion in the Modern World* (Oxford: Oxford University Press, 1996)

—, *Choice and Religion: A Critique of Rational Choice* (Oxford: Oxford University Press, 1999)

—, *God is Dead: Secularization in the West* (Oxford: Blackwell, 2002)

—, 'The Demise of Christianity in Britain' in G. Davie, L. Woodhead and P. Heelas (eds.), *Predicting Religion: Christian, Secular and Alternative Futures* (Aldershot: Ashgate, 2003), 53–63

Bruce, S. and T. Glendinning, 'Scotland is No Longer a Christian Country', *Life and Work* (June 2002)

Budd, S., *Sociologists and Religion* (London: Collier-Macmillan, 1973)

Carrier, H., *The Sociology of Religious Belonging* (London: Darton, Longman & Todd, 1966)

Casanova, J., *Public Religions in the Modern World* (London: University of Chicago Press, 1994)

Chadwick, O., *The Secularization of the European Mind in the Nineteenth Century* (Cambridge: Cambridge University Press, 1974)

Chalke, S. and T. Jackson, *Faithworks 2: Stories of Hope* (Eastbourne: Kingsway, 2001)

Coffey, J., 'Secularisation: Is it Inevitable?', *Cambridge Papers* 10.1 (2001)

Combe, V., 'Church puts its faith in TV advert', *Daily Telegraph* (20 March 1997)

—, 'Catholics plead for Latin Mass', *Daily Telegraph* (22 July 1997)

Cragg, K., *The Secular Experience of God* (Leominster: Gracewing, 1998)

Croft, S., *Transforming Communities: Re-imagining the Church for the 21st Century* (London: Darton, Longman & Todd, 2002)

Davie, G., '"You'll Never Walk Alone": the Anfield Pilgrimage' in I. Reader and T. Walter (eds.), *Pilgrimage in Popular Culture* (London: Macmillan, 1993), 201–19

—, *Religion in Britain Since 1945: Believing without belonging* (Oxford: Blackwell, 1994)

—, *Religion in Modern Europe: A Memory Mutates* (Oxford: Oxford University Press, 2000)

—, *Europe: The Exceptional Case* (London: Darton, Longman & Todd, 2002)

Davie, G., P. Heelas and L. Woodhead (eds.), *Predicting Religion: Christian, Secular and Alternative Futures* (Aldershot: Ashgate, 2003)

Dillard, A., *Pilgrim at Tinker Creek* (New York, NY: HarperPerennial, 1998)

Dixon, K., *The Sociology of Belief* (London: Routledge and Kegan Paul, 1980)

Drane, J.W., *What is the New Age Saying to the Church?* (London: Marshall Pickering, 1991)

—, *What is the New Age Still Saying to the Church?* (London: Marshall Pickering, 1999)

—, *The McDonaldization of the Church: Spirituality, Creativity and the Future* (London: Darton, Longman & Todd, 2000)

Durkheim, E., *The Division of Labor in Society* (New York, NY: Free Press, 1964)

Edwards, D.L., *The Futures of Christianity* (London: Hodder & Stoughton, 1987)

Eliot, T.S., *The Idea of a Christian Society* (London: Faber and Faber, 1939)

Elmore, G., 'Insufficient Training for C of E Clergy.' *The Times* (17 January 2004)

Featherstone, M., *Consumer Culture and Postmodernism* (London: Sage, 1991)

Feuerbach, L., *The Essence of Christianity* (London: Trubner, 1881)

Gabriel, Y. and T. Lang, *The Unmanageable Consumer* (London: Sage, 1995)

Gallup, J.G. and D.M. Lindsay, *Surveying the Religious Landscape* (Harrisburg, PA: Morehouse Publishing, 1999)

Gellner, E., *Legitimation of Belief* (Cambridge: Cambridge University Press, 1974)

Gerard, D., 'Religious Attitudes and Values' in M. Abrams, D. Gerard and N. Timms (eds.), *Values and Social Change in Britain* (London: Macmillan, 1985), 50–92

Gerth, H.H. and C. Wright Mills (eds.), *From Max Weber: Essays in Sociology* (New York, NY: Oxford University Press, 1946)

Giddens, A., *The Consequences of Modernity* (Cambridge: Polity, 1990)

Gilbert, A.D., *The Making of Post-Christian Britain: A History of the Secularization of Modern Society* (London: Longman, 1980)

Gill, R., *The Myth of the Empty Church* (London: SPCK, 1993)

—, *Churchgoing and Christian Ethics* (Cambridge: Cambridge University Press, 1999)

—, *Changing Worlds: Can the Church Respond?* (Edinburgh: T&T Clark, 2002)

—, *The 'Empty' Church Revisited* (Aldershot: Ashgate, 2003)

Gill, R., K. Hadaway et al., 'Is Religious Belief Declining?', *Journal for the Scientific Study of Religion* 37 (1998), 507–16

Gilliat-Ray, S., 'Civic religion in England: Traditions and Transformations', *Journal of Contemporary Religion* 14.2 (1999), 233–44

—, *Religion in Higher Education* (Aldershot: Ashgate, 2000)

Gledhill, R., 'Bishop Warns Church that it May Disappear.' *The Times* (20 March 2004)

Greeley, A.M., *Religious Change in America* (Cambridge: Harvard University Press, 1989)

Greil, A.L. and D.R. Rudy, 'What have we Learned from Process Models of Conversion? An Examination of Ten Studies', *Sociological Focus* 17.4 (1984), 306–23

Guenther, M., *Holy Listening: The Art of Spiritual Direction* (London: Darton, Longman & Todd, 1992)

Gunton, C.E., *A Brief Theology of Revelation* (Edinburgh: T&T Clark, 1995)

Hall, D.J., *The End of Christendom and the Future of Christianity* (Valley Forge, PA: Trinity Press International, 1997)

Halman, L., *The European Values Survey: A Third Wave* (Tilburg: EVS, Tilburg University, 2001)

Halperin, D.A., *Psychodynamic Perspectives on Religion, Sect and Cult* (Boston, MA: J. Wright, PSG Inc., 1983)

Hay, D., 'Religious Experience Amongst a Group of Post-graduate Students: A Qualitative Study', *Journal for the Scientific Study of Religion* 18 (1979), 164–82

Hay, D. and A. Morisy, 'Secular Society, Religious Meanings: A Contemporary Paradox', *Review of Religious Research* 26 (1985), 213–27

Heelas, P., *The New Age Movement* (Oxford: Blackwell, 1996)

Heilman, S.C., 'Constructing Orthodoxy' in T. Robbins and D. Anthony (eds.), *In Gods We Trust: New Patterns of Religious Pluralism in America* (London: Transaction Books, 1981), 144–57

Herberg, W., *Protestant, Catholic, Jew* (Garden City, NY: Doubleday, 1960)

Herbert, D., *Religion and Civil Society* (Aldershot: Ashgate, 2003)

Hervieu-Léger, D., *Religion as a Chain of Memory* (Cambridge: Polity, 2000)

Hinton, J., *Changing Churches: Building Bridges in Local Mission* (London: Churches Together in Britain and Ireland, 2002)

Hinton, J. and P.B. Price, *Changing Communities: Church from the Grassroots* (London: Churches Together in Britain and Ireland, 2003)

Hobson, T., 'Independence or Idolatry?', *Third Way* 26.8 (2003), 22

Hunt, K., 'Understanding the Spirituality of People who Do Not Go to Church' in G. Davie, P. Heelas and L. Woodhead (eds.), *Predicting Religion: Christian, Secular and Alternative Futures* (Aldershot: Ashgate, 2003)

Hunter, J.D., *The New Religions: Demodernization and the Protest Against Modernity* (New York NY: Edwin Mellen, 1981)

—, 'What is Modernity?' in P. Sampson, V. Samuel, and C. Sugden (eds.), *Faith and Modernity* (Oxford: Regnum/Lynx, 1996), 12–20

—, 'The New Religions: Demodernization and the Protest Against Modernity' in L. Dawson (ed.), *Cults in Context: a Reader in the Study of New Religious Movements* (Toronto: Canadian Scholars' Press, 1996)

Ireland, M., 'Engaging with the search for spirituality' in M. Booker and M. Ireland, *Evangelism – Which Way Now?* (London: Church House Publishing, 2003), 171–84

Jones, A., 'Foreword', in Guenther, M., *Holy Listening: the Art of Spiritual Direction* (London: Darton, Longman & Todd, 1992)

Kreeft, P., *Between Heaven and Hell: A dialog somewhere beyond death with John F. Kennedy, C.S. Lewis and Aldous Huxley* (Downers Grove: InterVarsity, 1982)

Kuhn, I., *By Searching* (London: Overseas Missionary Fellowship, 1957)

Langman, L., 'Neon Cages: Shopping for Subjectivity' in R. Shields (ed.), *Lifestyle Shopping: the Subject of Consumption* (London: Routledge, 1997), 40–82

Lawrence, C.H., *The Life of St Edmund by Matthew Paris* (Stroud: Allan Sutton, 1996)

Leader, 'Raise the Rafters', *The Times* (20 March 2004)

Lewis, C.S., *Miracles* (London: Fount, 1947)

—, 'Transposition' in W. Hooper (ed.), *Screwtape Proposes a Toast* (London: Fontana, 1965), 75–93

Lofland, J. and R. Stark, 'Becoming a World-Saver: a Theory of Conversion to a Deviant Perspective', *American Sociological Review* 30 (1965), 862–75

Luckmann, T., *The Invisible Religion: the Problem of Religion in Modern Society* (New York, NY: Macmillan, 1967)

Lyon, D., *Postmodernity* (Buckingham: Open University Press, 1994)

—, *Jesus in Disneyland: Religion in Postmodern Times* (Cambridge: Polity, 2000)

MacIntyre, A., *Secularization and Moral Change* (Oxford: Oxford University Press, 1967)

MacLaren, D., *Precarious Visions: A Sociological Critique of European Scenarios of Desecularization* (Unpublished PhD Thesis, King's College, London University, 2003)

—, 'God Serve the Queen?', *Third Way* 26.9 (2003), 16–18

Marshall, G. (ed.), *Oxford Concise Dictionary of Sociology* (Oxford: Oxford University Press, 1994)

Martin, D.A., *The Religious and the Secular: Studies in Secularization* (London: Routledge and Kegan Paul, 1969)

—, 'The Secularization Issue: Prospect and Retrospect', *British Journal of Sociology* 42 (1991), 465–74

—, *A General Theory of Secularization* (Aldershot: Gregg Revivals, 1993)

—, 'Religion, Secularization, and Postmodernity: Lessons from the Latin American Case' in P. Repstadt (ed.), *Religion and Modernity: Models of Co-existence* (Oslo: Scandinavian University Press, 1996), 35–43

—, *Christian Language and its Mutations* (Aldershot: Ashgate, 2002)

—, *Pentecostalism: The World Their Parish* (Oxford: Blackwell, 2002)

Martin, L., *Practical Praying* (Cambridge: Eerdmans, 1997)

Mayberry, M., J.G. Knowles et al., *Home Schooling: Parents as Educators* (Thousand Oaks, CA: Corwin Press, 1995)

McFarland, S., 'Keeping the Faith: the Roles of Selective Exposure and Avoidance in Maintaining Religious Beliefs' in D.A. Stout and J.M. Buddenbaum (eds.), *Religion and Mass Media* (London: Sage, 1996), 173–82

Middleton, J.R. and B.J. Walsh, *Truth is Stranger than it Used to Be: Biblical Faith in a Postmodern Age* (London: SPCK, 1995)

Milbank, J., *Theology and Social Theory* (Oxford: Blackwell, 1990)

Millar, P., *An Iona Prayer Book* (Norwich: The Canterbury Press, 1998)

Mills, C.W., *The Sociological Imagination* (New York, NY: Oxford University Press, 1959)

Moyser, G., 'Politics and Religion in the Modern World: An Overview' in G. Moyser (ed.), *Politics and Religion in the Modern World* (London: Routledge, 1991), 1-27

Murray Williams, S., 'The End of Christendom: Challenges and Opportunities', *Jesus Life* 65.1 (2004), 12–14

Neill, S., *A History of Christian Missions* (Harmondsworth: Penguin, 1964)

Newbigin, L., *The Gospel in a Pluralist Society* (London: SPCK, 1989)

—, *Foolishness to the Greeks* (London: SPCK, 1986)

Niebuhr, H.R., *Christ and Culture* (London: Harper, 1952)

Paine, T., *The Age of Reason* (London: The Pioneer Press, 1937)

Pascal, B., *Pascal's Pensees* (London: Routledge and Kegan Paul, 1950)

Pearson, J., '"Witchcraft will not soon Vanish from this Earth": Wicca in the 21st Century' in G. Davie, P. Heelas and L. Woodhead (eds.), *Predicting Religion: Christian, Secular and Alternative Futures* (Aldershot: Ashgate, 2003), 170–82

Percy, M., *The Salt of the Earth: Religious Resilience in a Secular Age* (Sheffield: Continuum, 2002)

Peterson, E., *Under the Unpredictable Plant: An Exploration in Vocation Holiness* (Grand Rapids: Eerdmans, 1992)

Petre, J., 'Runcie lays into trendy clergymen', *Daily Telegraph* (9 February 1997)

—, 'Church "needs to read lesson from M & S"', *Daily Telegraph* (30 October 1997)

—, 'Bishops urged to resign over Church decline', *Daily Telegraph* (24 February 2003)

—, 'Williams: No Thanks for Iraq Victory', *Daily Telegraph* (8 May 2003)

Putnam, R., *Bowling Alone* (New York, NY: Simon and Schuster, 2000)

Reeves, W. (ed.), *Life of St Columba, Founder of Hy (Iona), Written by Adamnan Ninth Abbott of that Monastery* (Lampeter: Llanerch Enterprises, 1988)

Richter, P. and L.J. Francis, *Gone but not Forgotten: Church Leaving and Returning* (London: Darton, Longman & Todd, 1998)

Ritzer, G., *The McDonaldization of Society* (Thousand Oaks, CA: Pine Forge Press, 1993)

—, *The McDonaldization Thesis* (Thousand Oaks, CA: Pine Forge Press, 1998)

Robbins, T., *Cults, Converts and Charisma: the Sociology of New Religious Movements* (London: Sage, 1988)

Roberts, R.H. (ed.), *Religion and the Transformations of Capitalism* (London: Routledge, 1995)

Roberts, R.H., 'Towards an Executive Church' in A. Walker and L. Osborn (eds.), *Harmful Religion* (London: SPCK, 1997), 163–76

—, *Religion, Theology and the Human Sciences* (Cambridge: Cambridge University Press, 2002)

Robinson, J.A.T., *Honest to God* (London: SCM, 1963)

Robinson, M., *To Win the West* (Crowborough: Monarch, 1996)

Roof, W.C., 'Traditional Religion in Contemporary Society: A theory of local-cosmopolitan plausibility', *American Sociological Review* 41 (1976), 195–228

—, *Spiritual Marketplace: Baby Boomers and the Remaking of American Religion* (Princeton, NJ: Princeton University Press, 1999)

Roof, W.C. and W. McKinney, *American Mainline Religion* (New Brunswick, NJ: Rutgers University Press, 1987)

Schaeffer, F., *The God Who is There* (London: Hodder & Stoughton, 1968)

Scotland, N., *Sectarian Religion in Contemporary Britain* (Carlisle: Paternoster, 2000)

Shenk, W., *Write the Vision: the Church Renewed* (Leominster: Gracewing, 1995)

Shields, R. (ed.), *Lifestyle Shopping: The Subject of Consumption* (London: Routledge, 1997)

Shilling, J., *The Times 2* (3 September 2001)

Slater, D., *Consumer Culture and Modernity* (Cambridge: Polity, 1997)

Smith, D., *Mission After Christendom* (London: Darton, Longman & Todd, 2003)

Smith, G., 'Introduction: Reviewing Mission in Western Society', in Barrow, S. and G. Smith (eds.), *Christian Mission in Western Society* (London: Churches Together in Britain and Ireland, 2001), 11–28

Sorlin, P., *The Mass Media* (London: Routledge, 1994)

Stark, R. and W.S. Bainbridge, *A Theory of Religion* (New York, NY: Peter Lang, 1987)

—, 'Secularization, Revival, and Cult Formation' in L. Dawson (ed.), *Cults in Context: a Reader in the Study of New Religious Movements* (Toronto: Canadian Scholars' Press, 1996)

Stark, W., *The Sociology of Knowledge* (London: Routledge and Kegan Paul, 1958)

Straus, R.A., 'Religious Conversion as a Personal and Collective Accomplishment', *Sociological Analysis* 40.2 (1979)

Taylor, J., 'After Secularism: British Government and the Inner Cities' in G. Davie, P. Heelas and L. Woodhead (eds.), *Predicting Religion: Christian, Secular and Alternative Futures* (Aldershot: Ashgate, 2003), 120–32

Ternisien, X., 'L'appel commun des Eglises chrétiennes contre une loi sur la voile', *Le Monde* (9 Décembre 2003)

Tiplady, R., *World of Difference: Global Mission at the Pic 'n' Mix Counter* (Carlisle: Paternoster, 2003)

Tomlin, G., *The Provocative Church* (London: SPCK, 2002)

Tozer, A.W., *Gems from Tozer* (Camp Hill, PA: Christian Publications, 1979)

Troeltsch, E., *The Social Teaching of the Christian Churches* (London: Allen and Unwin, 1931)

Vertovec, S., 'Muslims, the State, and the Public Sphere in Britain' in G. Nonneman, T. Niblock, and B. Szajkowski (eds.), *Muslim Communities in the New Europe* (Reading: Ithaca, 1996), 169–86

de Waal, E., *The Celtic Vision: Prayers and Blessings from the Outer Hebrides* (London: Darton, Longman & Todd, 1988)

Wallis, R. and S. Bruce, 'Secularization: the Orthodox Model' in S. Bruce (ed.), *Religion and Modernization: Sociologists and Historians Debate the Secularization Thesis* (Oxford: Clarendon, 1992), 8–30

Walker, A., *Telling the Story* (London: SPCK, 1996)

Walter, T., 'War Graves Pilgrimage' in I. Reader and T. Walter (eds.), *Pilgrimage in Popular Culture* (London: Macmillan, 1993), 63–91

Ward, P., 'Alpha – the McDonaldization of Religion', *Anvil* 15.4 (1998), 279–86

—, *Liquid Church* (Carlisle: Paternoster, 2002)

Warren, R., *Being Human, Being Church* (London: Marshall Pickering, 1995)

Weber, M., 'Science as a Vocation' in H.H. Gerth and C. Wright Mills (eds.), *From Max Weber: Essays in Sociology* (London: Routledge, 1991), 129–56

Weimann, G., *Communicating Unreality: Modern Media and the Reconstruction of Reality* (London: Sage, 2000)

Wessels, A., *Secularized Europe* (Geneva: WCC Publications, 1996)

—, 'The Inculturation of Christianity in Europe', in Barrow, S. and G. Smith (eds.), *Christian Mission in Western Society* (London: Churches Together in Britain and Ireland, 2001), 31–49

Wilson, B.R., *Religion in Secular Society* (London: C.A. Watts & Co., 1966)

—, *Contemporary Transformations of Religion* (Oxford: Oxford University Press, 1976)

—, *Religion in Sociological Perspective* (Oxford: Oxford University Press, 1982)

—, 'Secularization: The inherited model' in P. Hammond (ed.), *The Sacred in a Secular Age* (Berkeley: University of California Press, 1985)

—, 'New Images of Christian Community' in J. McManners (ed.), *The Oxford History of Christianity* (Oxford: Oxford University Press, 1993), 587–617

Woodhead, L. and P. Heelas (eds.), *Religion in Modern Times* (Oxford: Blackwell, 2000)

Wright, S.A., *Leaving Cults: the Dynamics of Defection* (Washington, D.C.: Society for the Scientific Study of Religion, 1987)

Zerubavel, E., *Social Mindscapes: An Invitation to Cognitive Sociology* (London: Harvard University Press, 1997)

Index